how to

We invite you to make a sacred space in your day and spend ten minutes praying here and now, wherever you are, with the help of a prayer guide and scripture chosen specially for each day. Every place is a sacred space so you may wish to have this book in your desk at work or available to be picked up and read at any time of the day, whilst traveling or on your bedside table, a park bench ... Remember that God is everywhere, all around us, constantly reaching out to us, even in the most unlikely situations. When we know this, and with a bit of practice, we can pray anywhere.

The following pages will guide you through a session of prayer stages.

Something to think and pray about each day this week
The presence of God
Freedom
Consciousness
The Word (leads you to the daily scripture and provides help with the text)
Conversation
Conclusion

It is most important to come back to these pages each day of the week as they are an integral part of each day's prayer and lead to the scripture and inspiration points.

Although written in the first person the prayers are for "doing" rather than for reading out. Each stage is a kind of exercise or meditation aimed at helping you to get in touch with God and God's presence in your life.

We hope that you will join the many people around the world praying with us in our sacred space.

The Presence of God

As I sit here, the beating of my heart,
the ebb and flow of my breathing, the movements of my mind
are all signs of God's ongoing creation of me.
I pause for a moment, and become aware
of this presence of God within me.

SACRED SPACE

SACRED SPACE

the prayer book 2005
from the website www.sacredspace.ie

Jesuit Communication Centre, Ireland

VERITAS

acknowledgement

The publisher would like to thank Alan McGuckian SJ and Gerry Bourke SJ for their kind assistance in making this book possible. Gerry Bourke SJ can be contacted on feedback@jesuit.ie

Published 2004 by
Veritas Publications
7/8 Lower Abbey Street
Dublin 1
Ireland
Email: publications@veritas.ie
Website: www.veritas.ie

A catalogue record for this book is available from the British Library

First published by Michelle Anderson Publishing Pty Ltd, Melbourne, Australia

Design: Bernard Metcalfe, BizWrite Pty Ltd
Typesetting: Midland Typesetters Pty Ltd
Cover design: Deb Snibson Modern Art Production Group
Printed in Singapore by Kyodo Printing Co (S'pore) Pte Ltd
International Standard Serial Number ISSN 1449-048X
ISBN 1 85390 708 1

contents

november 28 – december 4

Something to think and pray about each day this week:

A time of preparation

Preparing for the arrival of a new baby, particularly if it's the first, is a time of fevered preparation. There is a room to be decorated, clothes, cot, bath and a hundred and one other things that a baby needs to be purchased. In the four weeks of Advent preceding the Christmas feast of the birth of Jesus in the stable at Bethlehem we can take a little time to prepare for this new born baby.

Ponder a little on that great gift of new life that surrounds you. It may be that there is a new baby in your extended family or circle of friends. You can look too at new life in the natural world of plants and animals.

What do you notice about this new life?

What is it about new born babies, or even baby animals that so fascinates people?

What can we learn by pondering the smallest new born creature?

If all new life has the power to move us deeply, what of the New Life that is coming at Christmas?

The Presence of God
I remind myself that, as I sit here now,
God is gazing on me with love and holding me in being.
I pause for a moment and think of this.

Freedom
I will ask God's help,
to be free from my own preoccupations,
to be open to God in this time of prayer,
to come to love and serve him more.

Consciousness
How do I find myself today?
Where am I with God? With others?
Do I have something to be grateful for? Then I give thanks.
Is there something I am sorry for? Then I ask forgiveness.

The Word
God speaks to each one of us individually. I need to listen
to what he is saying to me. (Please turn to your scripture
on the following pages. Inspiration points are there should
you need them. When you are ready, return here to
continue.)

Conversation
Remembering that I am still in God's presence,
I imagine Jesus himself standing or sitting beside me,
and say whatever is on my mind, whatever is in my heart,
speaking as one friend to another.

Conclusion
Glory be to the Father, and to the Son, and to the Holy Spirit,
As it was in the beginning, is now and ever shall be,
World without end. Amen

Sunday 28th November, First Sunday of Advent
Isaiah 2:1-5

The word that Isaiah son of Amoz saw concerning Judah and Jerusalem. In days to come the mountain of the Lord's house shall be established as the highest of the mountains, and shall be raised above the hills; all the nations shall stream to it. Many peoples shall come and say, "Come, let us go up to the mountain of the Lord, to the house of the God of Jacob; that he may teach us his ways and that we may walk in his paths." For out of Zion shall go forth instruction, and the word of the Lord from Jerusalem. He shall judge between the nations, and shall arbitrate for many peoples; they shall beat their swords into ploughshares, and their spears into pruning hooks; nation shall not lift up sword against nation, neither shall they learn war any more. O house of Jacob, come, let us walk in the light of the Lord!

- Christian faith says that these glorious days of peace and light have already come in Jesus.
- Can I see it? Or, do I just see war and threat and fear?
- Am I open to a gradual advent process of coming into "the light of the Lord"?

Monday 29th November
Matthew 8:5-11

When Jesus entered Capernaum, a centurion came to him, appealing to him and saying, "Lord, my servant is lying at home paralyzed, in terrible distress." And he said to him, "I will come and cure him." The centurion answered, "Lord, I am not worthy to have you come under my roof; but only speak the word, and my servant will be healed. For I also am a man under authority, with soldiers under me; and I say to one, 'Go,' and he goes, and to another, 'Come,' and he comes, and to my slave, 'Do this,' and the slave does it." When Jesus heard him, he was amazed and said to those who followed him, "Truly I tell you, in no one in Israel have I found such faith. I tell you, many will come from east and west and will eat with Abraham and Isaac and Jacob in the kingdom of heaven."

- I view the scene in my imagination. A confident, self-assured Roman, born to lead, turns to a simple Jewish rabbi with a problem that is beyond his power.
- What is going on here? How am I moved by what I see and hear?
- When I look at this scene, how am I moved to respond to Jesus?

Tuesday 30th November, St Andrew   Matthew 4:18-22

As he walked by the Sea of Galilee, he saw two brothers, Simon, who is called Peter, and Andrew his brother, casting a net into the sea—for they were fishermen. And he said to them, "Follow me, and I will make you fish for people." Immediately they left their nets and followed him. As he went from there, he saw two other brothers, James son of Zebedee and his brother John, in the boat with their father Zebedee, mending their nets, and he called them. Immediately they left the boat and their father, and followed him.

- In this passage, Peter, Andrew, James and John literally drop everything and respond to Jesus' invitation, without any questions. It sounds almost too simple.
- Imagine Jesus walking into your home or your workplace and making the same invitation to you. How do you react?
- Perhaps your reaction is not quite so straightforward. Perhaps you have questions. If so, bring those questions into conversation with the Lord.

4

Wednesday 1st December   Isaiah 25:6-9

On this mountain the LORD of hosts will make for all peoples a feast of rich food, a feast of well-aged wines, of rich food filled with marrow, of well-aged wines strained clear. And he will destroy on this mountain the shroud that is cast over all peoples, the sheet that is spread over all nations; he will swallow up death forever. Then the Lord GOD will wipe away the tears from all faces, and the disgrace of his people he will take away from all the earth, for the LORD has spoken. It will be said on that day, Lo, this is our God; we have waited for him, so that he might save us. This is the LORD for whom we have waited; let us be glad and rejoice in his salvation.

- Do I dare to hope for a great and glorious day in the future when all our tears will be wiped away, when all my short-comings and failings will count for nothing and I will rest, joyful, in God's loving presence?
- How does the Lord's promise resonate with me? Does it excite me and confirm my deepest hopes? Does it seem to go against the grain of my experience and leave me confused and unsure?
- Can I bring what is in my heart to the Lord, in this time of prayer?

Thursday 2nd December   Matthew 7:21, 24-27

Jesus said to his disciples, "Not everyone who says to me, 'Lord, Lord,' will enter the kingdom of heaven, but only the one who does the will of my Father in heaven ... Everyone then who hears these words of mine and acts on them will be like a wise man who built his house on rock. The rain fell, the floods came, and the winds blew and beat on that house, but it did not fall, because it had been founded on rock. And everyone who hears these words of mine and does not act on them will be like a foolish man who built his house on sand. The rain fell, and the floods came, and the winds blew and beat against that house, and it fell—and great was its fall!"

- It is not enough to hear the words of Jesus. They only have power when we act on them.
- What does "acting" on the words of Jesus mean in my life? Can I concretely see where my action issues from faith and prayer?
- Do Jesus' words challenge me about times of procrastination or lack of direction when I dodge the call?
- Can I be open, right now, to hearing the will of the Father, calling me, in ways small and great, into life?

Friday 3rd December, St Francis Xavier
Matthew 28:16-20

Now the eleven disciples went to Galilee, to the mountain to which Jesus had directed them. When they saw him, they worshipped him; but some doubted. And Jesus came and said to them, "All authority in heaven and on earth has been given to me. Go therefore and make disciples of all nations, baptizing them in the name of the Father and of the Son and of the Holy Spirit, and teaching them to obey everything that I have commanded you. And remember, I am with you always, to the end of the age."

- What do I do to make the love of God present and real to those I meet?
- Some of the disciples doubted. I may have doubts and fears too. Can I be open with the Lord about them?
- Listen to Jesus telling you, "Remember, I am with you always."

Saturday 4th December   Isaiah 30:19-21

Truly, O people in Zion, inhabitants of Jerusalem, you shall weep no more. He will surely be gracious to you at the sound of your cry; when he hears it, he will answer you. Though the Lord may give you the bread of adversity and the water of affliction, yet your Teacher will not hide himself any more, but your eyes shall see your Teacher. And when you turn to the right or when you turn to the left, your ears shall hear a word behind you, saying, "This is the way; walk in it."

- Does the promise that God will be gracious to me in my distress touch a chord with me?
- Do I feel I have been given the "bread of adversity" and the "water of affliction"? Or, do I feel for others in their affliction?
- As I listen to the Lord's promises, in what space do they find me? Buoyant and responsive? Weighed down and cynical? Vulnerable?
- Wherever I am today can I hear the Lord's words of consolation and offer of guidance?

Sacred Space

december 5–11

Something to think and pray about each day this week:

Preparing for Christmas
One way of preparing for Christmas is to take the first couple of chapters of the Gospel of St Luke, the part that talks of the events leading up to the birth of Jesus, and ponder a few verses of this each day. Imagine how people must have felt as these strange events unfolded. Put yourself in their place. Let this 2000 year old story interact with your own life and your own story.

The Presence of God

God is with me, but more,
God is within me, giving me existence.
Let me dwell for a moment on God's life-giving presence
in my body, my mind, my heart
and in the whole of my life.

Freedom

God is not foreign to my freedom.
Instead the Spirit breathes life into my most intimate desires,
gently nudging me towards all that is good.
I ask for the grace to let myself be enfolded by the Spirit.

Consciousness

In God's loving presence I unwind the past day,
starting from now and looking back, moment by moment.
I gather in all the goodness and light, in gratitude.
I attend to the shadows and what they say to me,
seeking healing, courage, forgiveness.

The Word

I read the Word of God slowly, a few times over, and I listen
to what God is saying to me. (Please turn to your scripture
on the following pages. Inspiration points are there should
you need them. When you are ready, return here to continue.)

Conversation

How has God's Word moved me? Has it left me cold?
Has it consoled me or moved me to act in a new way?
I imagine Jesus standing or sitting beside me,
I turn and share my feelings with him.

Conclusion

Glory be to the Father, and to the Son, and to the Holy Spirit,
As it was in the beginning, is now and ever shall be,
World without end. Amen

Sunday 5th December, Second Sunday of Advent
Matthew 3:1-6

In those days John the Baptist appeared in the wilderness of Judea, proclaiming, "Repent, for the kingdom of heaven has come near." This is the one of whom the prophet Isaiah spoke when he said, "The voice of one crying out in the wilderness: 'Prepare the way of the Lord, make his paths straight.'" Now John wore clothing of camel's hair with a leather belt around his waist, and his food was locusts and wild honey. Then the people of Jerusalem and all Judea were going out to him, and all the region along the Jordan, and they were baptized by him in the river Jordan, confessing their sins.

- The carpenter's son has not yet appeared: a wild-looking character is in the wilderness outside the city, declaring the Kingdom of God is near. It sounds unlikely.
- Many people are drawn to this. What is the attraction? Can I imagine myself going out to see and hear?
- "Repent, for the kingdom of heaven has come near."

Monday 6th December   Isaiah 35:1-4

The wilderness and the dry land shall be glad, the desert shall rejoice and blossom; like the crocus it shall blossom abundantly, and rejoice with joy and singing. The glory of Lebanon shall be given to it, the majesty of Carmel and Sharon. They shall see the glory of the LORD, the majesty of our God. Strengthen the weak hands, and make firm the feeble knees. Say to those who are of a fearful heart, "Be strong, do not fear! Here is your God. He will come with vengeance, with terrible recompense. He will come and save you."

- During Advent the Isaiah passages often bring us to the experiences of parched and lifeless wilderness. Can I bring to prayer a part of me that feels arid and withered?

- Can I let myself go with the promise of glory and majesty? Can I see the flowering of new life in my situation?

Tuesday 7th December · Isaiah 40:3-5

A voice cries out: "In the wilderness prepare the way of the LORD, make straight in the desert a highway for our God. Every valley shall be lifted up, and every mountain and hill be made low; the uneven ground shall become level, and the rough places a plain. Then the glory of the LORD shall be revealed, and all people shall see it together, for the mouth of the LORD has spoken."

- "Prepare the way of the Lord." This is the essence of this season of Advent. As Isaiah sees it, the earth-shaking preparations for revealing the Glory of God are themselves the gift of God.
- Can I apply this to myself and my own preparing to meet the Lord? Do the obstacles between me and new life—small or great—seem very immovable, beyond my efforts?
- If even the clearing of the obstacles is a gift of God, how can I open myself to the gift?

Wednesday 8th December, The Immaculate Conception of the Blessed Virgin Mary · Luke 1:26-38

In the sixth month the angel Gabriel was sent by God to a town in Galilee called Nazareth, to a virgin engaged to a man whose name was Joseph, of the house of David. The virgin's name was Mary. And he came to her and said, "Greetings, favored one! The Lord is with you." But she was much perplexed by his words and pondered what sort of greeting this might be. The angel said to her, "Do not be afraid, Mary, for you have found favor with God. And now, you will conceive in your womb and bear a son, and you will name him Jesus. He will be great, and will be called the Son of the Most High, and the Lord God will give to him the throne of his ancestor David. He will reign over the house of Jacob forever, and of his kingdom there will be no end." Mary said to the angel, "How can this be, since I am a virgin?" The angel said to her, "The Holy Spirit will come upon you, and the power of the Most High will overshadow you; therefore the child to be born will be holy; he will be called Son of God. And now, your relative Elizabeth in her old age has also conceived a son; and this is the sixth month for her who was said to be barren. For nothing will be impossible with God." Then Mary said, "Here am I, the servant of the Lord; let it be with me according to your word." Then the angel departed from her.

- By her "Yes," Mary first bore the Son of God in her heart, and then in her body.
- Can I watch the scene? A young woman, who could have had no idea of what was being asked or where it might lead, made a leap of trust.
- How does Mary's experience touch me? Am I called to "bear" God in my heart? What issues of surrender and trust arise in my case?
- Can I speak of these things to the Lord?

Thursday 9th December   Isaiah 41:17-20

When the poor and needy seek water, and there is none, and their tongue is parched with thirst, I the LORD will answer them, I the God of Israel will not forsake them. I will open rivers on the bare heights, and fountains in the midst of the valleys; I will make the wilderness a pool of water, and the dry land springs of water. I will put in the wilderness the cedar, the acacia, the myrtle, and the olive;

I will set in the desert the cypress, the plane and the pine together, so that all may see and know, all may consider and understand, that the hand of the LORD has done this, the Holy One of Israel has created it.

- Let's imagine the dramatic scene Isaiah paints: a desert, barren, parched and lifeless where God's people starve and thirst. By God's gift we follow its transformation.
- Where is my world barren or loveless? Where do I see people thirsting for life?
- Can I bring this situation to the Lord?

Friday 10th December   Matthew 11:16-19

Jesus spoke to the crowds, "But to what will I compare this generation? It is like children sitting in the marketplaces and calling to one another, 'We played the flute for you, and you did not dance; we wailed, and you did not mourn.' For John came neither eating nor drinking, and they say, 'He has a demon'; the Son of Man came eating and drinking, and they say, 'Look, a glutton and a drunkard, a friend of tax collectors and sinners!' Yet wisdom is vindicated by her deeds."

- Can I hear the frustration of Jesus in this scene? (Do I need to slow down and really listen to him?) It seems as if his life, which is meant to reveal the very essence of God, is being misunderstood and misrepresented.
- What about me? Do I misunderstand or misrepresent? Do I minimise or play down the significance of Jesus?
- Can I catch the frustration and urgency of God, desiring to be heard? By me.

Saturday 11th December   Matthew 17:10-13

And the disciples asked him, "Why, then, do the scribes say that Elijah must come first?" He replied, "Elijah is indeed coming and will restore all things; but I tell you that Elijah has already come, and they did not recognize him, but they did to him whatever they pleased. So also the Son of Man is about to suffer at their hands." Then the disciples understood that he was speaking to them about John the Baptist.

- God's messengers, whether it was Elijah, John the Baptist or even the Son of Man, tend to be rejected and even eliminated.
- This is a very bitter truth about our human condition in the midst of our Advent journey. Advent still calls us to a fulfilment promised and guaranteed by God. In my prayer can I hold together both the promise and the shadow?
- It is good to talk to the Lord about these things.

Sacred Space

december 12–18

Something to think and pray about each day this week:

"I thank you for the wonder of my being."

Psalm 139

Each year as we approach the great feast of Christmas we re-live the story of the birth of Jesus in a stable at Bethlehem. The events leading up to the birth of Jesus are foretold by prophets long before his birth. The birth of Samson and John the Baptist also point to the coming of the Jesus. Our readings of these days tell of so many strange events that we sense we are faced with a birth of great importance.

Your own birth may not have the same world shattering impact as that of Jesus Christ, but it was still a marvel. Just as Mary and Joseph were chosen to bring up Jesus, so your parents were chosen for you. The angels sang at your birth too.

In these final days of Advent as you ponder on the events leading up to the birth of Jesus, allow his story, his birth, to interact with your own story.

The Presence of God

To be present is to arrive as one is and open up to the other.
At this instant, as I arrive here, God is present waiting for me.
God always arrives before me, desiring to connect with me
even more than my most intimate friend.
I take a moment and greet my loving God.

Freedom

Everything has the potential to draw forth from me a fuller
love and life.
Yet my desires are often fixed, caught, on illusions of fulfillment.
I ask that God, through my freedom, may orchestrate
my desires in a vibrant loving melody rich in harmony.

Consciousness

How am I really feeling? Lighthearted? Heavy-hearted?
I may be very much at peace, happy to be here.
Equally, I may be frustrated, worried or angry.
I acknowledge how I really am. It is the real me that the
Lord loves.

The Word

I take my time to read the Word of God, slowly, a few times,
allowing myself to dwell on anything that strikes me. (Please
turn to your scripture on the following pages. Inspiration
points are there should you need them. When you are ready,
return here to continue.)

Conversation

What feelings are rising in me
as I pray and reflect on God's Word?
I imagine Jesus himself sitting or standing beside me,
and open my heart to him.

Conclusion

Glory be to the Father, and to the Son, and to the Holy Spirit,
As it was in the beginning, is now and ever shall be,
World without end. Amen

Sunday 12th December, Third Sunday of Advent
Matthew 11:2-11

When John heard in prison what the Messiah was doing, he sent word by his disciples and said to him, "Are you the one who is to come, or are we to wait for another?" Jesus answered them, "Go and tell John what you hear and see: the blind receive their sight, the lame walk, the lepers are cleansed, the deaf hear, the dead are raised, and the poor have good news brought to them. And blessed is anyone who takes no offense at me." As they went away, Jesus began to speak to the crowds about John: "What did you go out into the wilderness to look at? A reed shaken by the wind? What then did you go out to see? Someone dressed in soft robes? Look, those who wear soft robes are in royal palaces. What then did you go out to see? A prophet? Yes, I tell you, and more than a prophet. This is the one about whom it is written, 'See, I am sending my messenger ahead of you, who will prepare your way before you.' Truly I tell you, among those born of women no one has arisen greater than John the Baptist; yet the least in the kingdom of heaven is greater than he."

- "Go and tell what you hear and see: ... the blind receive their sight ... "! What do I see and hear? Do I see the signs of God's kingdom breaking through in the world around me? What does it look like?
- If I don't see any positive signs, why not? Do I need to look again, or look differently? Am I somehow looking for "soft robes" and "royal palaces" when God is offering me a prophet?
- When he says that the least in the kingdom of heaven is greater than John, is he including me?

Monday 13th December   **Matthew 21:23-27**

When Jesus entered the temple, the chief priests and the elders of the people came to him as he was teaching, and said, "By what authority are you doing these things, and who gave you this authority?" Jesus said to them, "I will also ask you one question; if you tell me the answer, then I will also tell you by what authority I do these things. Did the baptism of John come from heaven, or was it of human origin?" And they argued with one another, "If we say, 'From heaven,' he will say to us, 'Why then did you not believe him?' But if we say, 'Of human origin,' we are afraid of the crowd; for all regard John as a prophet." So they answered Jesus, "We do not know." And he said to them, "Neither will I tell you by what authority I am doing these things."

- In this exchange, Jesus might look as if he is playing a cheap trick on the chief priests and elders. But notice the differences between them.
- The chief priests and the elders are motivated by a desire to protect their own position and authority, and by fear—they are afraid of the crowds. Jesus, on the other hand, always speaks out fearlessly, regardless of how it might jeopardise his popularity.
- Do I let fear run my life? Do I make decisions on the basis of preserving my position and power? Can I talk to Jesus about this, and ask for the grace to be free, as he was?

Tuesday 14th December   **Matthew 21:28-32**

Jesus said, "What do you think? A man had two sons; he went to the first and said, 'Son, go and work in the vineyard today.' He answered, 'I will not'; but later he changed his mind and went. The father went to the second and said the same; and he answered, 'I go, sir'; but he did not go. Which of the two did the will of his father?" They said, "The first." Jesus said to them, "Truly I tell you, the tax collectors and the prostitutes are going into the kingdom of God ahead of you. For John came to you in the way of righteousness and you did not believe him, but the tax collectors and the prostitutes believed him; and even after you saw it, you did not change your minds and believe him."

- Well, which am I?

Wednesday 15th December   Luke 7:19-23

John summoned two of his disciples and sent them to the Lord to ask, "Are you the one who is to come, or are we to wait for another?" When the men had come to him, they said, "John the Baptist has sent us to you to ask, 'Are you the one who is to come, or are we to wait for another?'" Jesus had just then cured many people of diseases, plagues, and evil spirits, and had given sight to many who were blind. And he answered them, "Go and tell John what you have seen and heard: the blind receive their sight, the lame walk, the lepers are cleansed, the deaf hear, the dead are raised, the poor have good news brought to them. And blessed is anyone who takes no offense at me."

- Do I find that I need to ask the exact same question about Jesus: "Are you 'the one'?"
- John the Baptist didn't fear the question but sent disciples to ask Jesus straight.
- Can I ask Jesus straight to his face: "Are you the one?"
- What answer do I expect? What answer does he give me?

Thursday 16th December   Luke 7:24-30

When John's messengers had gone, Jesus began to speak to the crowds about John: "What did you go out into the wilderness to look at? A reed shaken by the wind? What then did you go out to see? Someone dressed in soft robes? Look, those who put on fine clothing and live in luxury are in royal palaces. What then did you go out to see? A prophet? Yes, I tell you, and more than a prophet. This is the one about whom it is written, 'See, I am sending my messenger ahead of you, who will prepare your way before you.' I tell you, among those born of women no one is greater than John; yet the least in the kingdom of God is greater than he." (And all the people who heard this, including the tax collectors, acknowledged the justice of God, because they had been baptized with John's baptism. But by refusing to be baptized by him, the Pharisees and the lawyers rejected God's purpose for themselves.)

- What made John so great—and what an affirmation Jesus gives him!—was his readiness to take second place and point people towards Jesus.
- Are there situations in my life where I am asked to take "second place"? (The person in "second place" is often necessary but not prominent.)
- Am I happy with "second place" like John the Baptist? Do I feel Jesus' affirmation of me?
- Do I hate "second place"? Is there something I need to talk to the Lord about?

Friday 17th December   Genesis 49:2, 8-10

Jacob called his sons, and said to them, "Assemble and hear, O sons of Jacob; listen to Israel your father. Judah, your brothers shall praise you; your hand shall be on the neck of your enemies; your father's sons shall bow down before you. Judah is a lion's whelp; from the prey, my son, you have gone up. He crouches down, he stretches out like a lion, like a lioness—who dares rouse him up? The scepter shall not depart from Judah, nor the ruler's staff from between his feet, until tribute comes to him; and the obedience of the peoples is his."

- As Jacob was dying he called his twelve sons around him to give his testament and tell them what lay in store for them.
- "The scepter shall not pass from Judah … until he come to whom it belongs." In the words of the old man we Christians hear the promise of the "one who is to come."
- Can I begin to let myself feel some of the hope and expectation of those who wait for a promised Messiah?

Saturday 18th December   Jeremiah 23:5-8

The days are surely coming, says the LORD, when I will raise up for David a righteous Branch, and he shall reign as king and deal wisely, and shall execute justice and righteousness in the land. In his days Judah will be saved and Israel will live in safety. And this is the name by which he will be called: "The LORD is our righteousness." Therefore, the days are surely coming, says the LORD, when it shall no longer be said, "As the LORD lives who brought the people of Israel up out of the land of Egypt," but "As the LORD lives who brought out and led the offspring of the house of Israel out of the land of the north and out of all the lands where he had driven them. Then they shall live in their own land.

- When God breaks in to human affairs it often catches us by surprise and upsets out expectations.
- "And he shall reign as king and deal wisely, and shall execute justice and righteousness in the land." How did Jeremiah understand this "king"? How do I understand Jesus as a king?

- Can I begin to feel that the coming of this king will bring great change to my world? What changes has it meant for me already? Do I sense that there is more change ahead? Does that make me uncomfortable or fill me with expectation?

december 19–25

Something to think and pray about each day this week:

Waiting and watching

Two great characters come to mind when we try to live in the spirit of Advent. Mary and John the Baptist. Each of them, in their own way, knew what it was to wait for the coming of Christ. They speak to us of two very different kinds of waiting.

Mary was called to place her whole trust in God and be radically open to the working out of God's plan. She said "Yes." And then, she waited. Her waiting was truly pregnant. Mary has the confidence of someone who believes that the promises made her by the Lord will be fulfilled.

John the Baptist doesn't so much inspire confidence. He announced the coming of the Son of God, with his winnowing fork in his hand, ready to sort the wheat from the chaff. John's approach is full of excitement and challenge and urgency. He too calls us to watch and wait. His waiting is repentant.

In my praying these days I may at times share in the patient confidence of Mary. Sometimes I might be disturbed by the fiery call of John. Advent graces come in different forms.

The Presence of God

What is present to me is what has a hold on my becoming.
I reflect on the presence of God always there in love,
amidst the many things that have a hold on me.
I pause and pray that I may let God
affect my becoming in this precise moment.

Freedom

There are very few people
who realize what God would make of them
if they abandoned themselves into his hands,
and let themselves be formed by his grace. (St Ignatius)
I ask for the grace to trust myself totally to God's love.

Consciousness

I exist in a web of relationships—links to nature, people, God.
I trace out these links, giving thanks for the life that flows
through them.
Some links are twisted or broken: I may feel regret, anger,
disappointment.
I pray for the gift of acceptance and forgiveness.

The Word

God speaks to each one of us individually. I need to listen
to hear what he is saying to me. Read the text a few times,
then listen. (Please turn to your scripture on the following
pages. Inspiration points are there should you need them.
When you are ready, return here to continue.)

Conversation

What is stirring in me as I pray?
Am I consoled, troubled, left cold?
I imagine Jesus himself standing or sitting at my side,
and share my feelings with him.

Conclusion

Glory be to the Father, and to the Son, and to the Holy Spirit,
As it was in the beginning, is now and ever shall be,
World without end. Amen

Sunday 19th December, Fourth Sunday of Advent
Matthew 1:18-24

Now the birth of Jesus the Messiah took place in this way. When his mother Mary had been engaged to Joseph, but before they lived together, she was found to be with child from the Holy Spirit. Her husband Joseph, being a righteous man and unwilling to expose her to public disgrace, planned to dismiss her quietly. But just when he had resolved to do this, an angel of the Lord appeared to him in a dream and said, "Joseph, son of David, do not be afraid to take Mary as your wife, for the child conceived in her is from the Holy Spirit. She will bear a son, and you are to name him Jesus, for he will save his people from their sins." All this took place to fulfill what had been spoken by the Lord through the prophet: "Look, the virgin shall conceive and bear a son, and they shall name him Emmanuel," which means, "God is with us." When Joseph awoke from sleep, he did as the angel of the Lord commanded him; he took her as his wife.

- When God breaks in to human affairs it causes surprises and not a little initial upset.
- What must Joseph's first reaction have been? How could he have known what mysteries were afoot? Can I follow in imagination the steps he must have gone through before humbly accommodating himself to God's plans?
- What does this reality of God's "breaking in" say to my life and experience?

Monday 20th December   Isaiah 7:10-14

Again the LORD spoke to Ahaz, saying, "Ask a sign of the LORD your God; let it be deep as Sheol or high as heaven." But Ahaz said, "I will not ask, and I will not put the LORD to the test." Then Isaiah said: "Hear then, O house of David! Is it too little for you to weary mortals, that you weary my God also? Therefore the Lord himself will give you a sign. Look, the young woman is with child and shall bear a son, and shall name him Immanuel."

- As we build towards the great event of the birth of the Son of God, it is good to remember the prophecy given long before by the Prophet Isaiah: "the young woman is with child ... "
- Can I situate myself in the great sweep of history where God planned from the beginning to take on flesh and share our lot, my lot?
- Immanuel means God is with us. How is that true for me?

Tuesday 21st December   Luke 1:39-45

In those days Mary set out and went with haste to a Judean town in the hill country, where she entered the house of Zechariah and greeted Elizabeth. When Elizabeth heard Mary's greeting, the child leaped in her womb. And Elizabeth was filled with the Holy Spirit and exclaimed with a loud cry, "Blessed are you among women, and blessed is the fruit of your womb. And why has this happened to me, that the mother of my Lord comes to me? For as soon as I heard the sound of your greeting, the child in my womb leaped for joy. And blessed is she who believed that there would be a fulfillment of what was spoken to her by the Lord."

- It is good to spend time gazing at this scene. Two women meet, both of them specially blessed and both called to cooperate in the unexpected designs of God.
- Elizabeth is given the special grace of an intimate insight and appreciation of what is happening and who is really present.
- In life do I always appreciate what is happening and who is really present?

Wednesday 22nd December   Luke 1:46-56

And Mary said, "My soul magnifies the Lord, and my spirit rejoices in God my Savior, for he has looked with favor on the lowliness of his servant. Surely, from now on all generations will call me blessed; for the Mighty One has done great things for me, and holy is his name. His mercy is for those who fear him from generation to generation. He has shown strength with his arm; he has scattered the proud in the thoughts of their hearts. He has brought down the powerful from their thrones, and lifted up the lowly; he has filled the hungry with good things, and sent the rich away empty. He has helped his servant Israel, in remembrance of his mercy, according to the promise he made to our ancestors, to Abraham and to his descendants forever." And Mary remained with Elizabeth about three months and then returned to her home.

- As the Mother of God moves towards the birth of her son these are her sentiments.
- Can I slowly pray over her words and ask for the grace to share in the vision?

Thursday 23rd December   Luke 1:57-66

Now the time came for Elizabeth to give birth, and she bore a son. Her neighbors and relatives heard that the Lord had shown his great mercy to her, and they rejoiced with her. On the eighth day they came to circumcise the child, and they were going to name him Zechariah after his father. But his mother said, "No; he is to be called John." They said to her, "None of your relatives has this name." Then they began motioning to his father to find out what name he wanted to give him. He asked for a writing tablet and wrote, "His name is John." And all of them were amazed. Immediately his mouth was opened and his tongue freed, and he began to speak, praising God. Fear came over all their neighbors, and all these things were talked about throughout the entire hill country of Judea. All who heard them pondered them and said, "What then will this child become?" For, indeed, the hand of the Lord was with him.

- It would be good to stop and spend some time watching developments in the house of Elizabeth—once childless—after she has given birth to her "miracle" child.
- How must Elizabeth be feeling? How has it all impacted on old Zechariah? What about the friends and neighbours? What do they make of it?
- And what about my world? Does God break in—or try to break in—to my life?

Friday 24th December   Luke 1:67-79

Then his father Zechariah was filled with the Holy Spirit and spoke this prophecy: "Blessed be the Lord God of Israel, for he has looked favorably on his people and redeemed them. He has raised up a mighty savior for us in the house of his servant David, as he spoke through the mouth of his holy prophets from of old, that we would be saved from our enemies and from the hand of all who hate us. Thus he has shown the mercy promised to our ancestors, and has remembered his holy covenant, the oath that he swore to our ancestor Abraham, to grant us that we, being rescued from the hands of our enemies, might serve him without fear, in holiness and righteousness before him all our days. And you, child, will be called the prophet of the Most High; for you will go before the Lord to prepare his ways, to give knowledge of salvation to his people by the forgiveness of their sins. By the tender mercy of our God, the dawn from on high will break upon us, to give light to those who sit in darkness and in the shadow of death, to guide our feet into the way of peace."

- The Benedictus is a prayer of prophecy about the coming of the Saviour. This "Most High" that Zechariah mentions comes not in a cloud of glory, but as a vulnerable child, with an ordinary family, in a cold stable. That is the kind of God we have.
- This babe in a manger brings light to those in darkness and takes away all my sins, doing away with the power of evil. What do I say to him, who loves me beyond all love?
- Am I ready this Christmas to invite Jesus into my heart and my home, giving all that I have over to him?

Saturday 25th December, Feast of the Nativity of the Lord
Luke 2:6-14

While they were in Bethlehem, the time came for Mary to deliver her child. And she gave birth to her first-born son and wrapped him in bands of cloth, and laid him in a manger, because there was no place for them in the inn. In that region there were shepherds living in the fields, keeping watch over their flock by night. Then an angel of the Lord stood before them, and the glory of the Lord shone around them, and they were terrified. But the angel said to them, "Do not be afraid; for see—I am bringing you good news of great joy for all the people: to you is born this day in the city of David a Savior, who is the Messiah, the Lord. This will be a sign for you: you will find a child wrapped in bands of cloth and lying in a manger." And suddenly there was with the angel a multitude of the heavenly host, praising God and saying, "Glory to God in the highest heaven, and on earth peace among those whom he favors!"

- Can I contemplate the mystery of Christmas?
- There is a baby, newly born in very poor circumstances, with very ordinary, simple people gathered round.
- This baby is the Son of God, the Saviour of the world.
- What is God up to? What mystery is afoot? What do I want to say to him today?

december 26 – january 1

Something to think and pray about each day this week:

Christmas week
Christians celebrate the birth of Jesus on the 25th of December. Though the birth of a child is a joyful event, our scripture passages this week have a hard edge. There are stories of both joy and pain.

We see the tragic results of good people who were willing to kill a man—Stephen—to protect their religion. We can imagine only too well the grief caused by a selfish man— Herod—fearful of losing his power. We understand the distraught feelings of parents—Mary and Joseph—who have lost a child. In 2000 years little has changed.

There are still people who will sacrifice others for "the cause." Countries and companies are willing to overlook the pain and sufferings their actions cause to retain power and profits.

As you pray over the scripture this week, you might like to ponder on the similarity between the stories in the scripture passages and the stories of your own world. You may pray that you bring joy rather than pain to the people in your world.

The Presence of God
God is with me, but more, God is within me.
Let me dwell for a moment on God's life-giving presence
in my body, in my mind, in my heart,
as I sit here, right now.

Freedom
A thick and shapeless tree-trunk would never believe
that it could become a statue, admired as a miracle of sculpture,
and would never submit itself to the chisel of the sculptor,
who sees by her genius what she can make of it. (St Ignatius)
I ask for the grace to let myself be shaped by my loving Creator.

Consciousness
Knowing that God loves me unconditionally,
I can afford to be honest about how I am.
How has the last day been, and how do I feel now?
I share my feelings openly with the Lord.

The Word
I read the Word of God slowly, a few times over, and I listen
to what God is saying to me. (Please turn to your scripture on
the following pages. Inspiration points are there should you
need them. When you are ready, return here to continue.)

Conversation
Do I notice myself reacting as I pray with the Word of God?
Do I feel challenged, comforted, angry?
Imagining Jesus sitting or standing by me,
I speak out my feelings, as one trusted friend to another.

Conclusion
Glory be to the Father, and to the Son, and to the Holy Spirit,
As it was in the beginning, is now and ever shall be,
World without end. Amen

Sunday 26th December, The Holy Family
Matthew 2:13-15, 19-23

Now after they had left, an angel of the Lord appeared to Joseph in a dream and said, "Get up, take the child and his mother, and flee to Egypt, and remain there until I tell you; for Herod is about to search for the child, to destroy him." Then Joseph got up, took the child and his mother by night, and went to Egypt, and remained there until the death of Herod. This was to fulfill what had been spoken by the Lord through the prophet, "Out of Egypt I have called my son." ... When Herod died, an angel of the Lord suddenly appeared in a dream to Joseph in Egypt and said, "Get up, take the child and his mother, and go to the land of Israel, for those who were seeking the child's life are dead." Then Joseph got up, took the child and his mother, and went to the land of Israel. But when he heard that Archelaus was ruling over Judea in place of his father Herod, he was afraid to go there. And after being warned in a dream, he went away to the district of Galilee. There he made his home in a town called Nazareth, so that what had been spoken through the prophets might be fulfilled, "He will be called a Nazorean."

- When I read this passage where is my mind and heart drawn? Is it to the fragility of the child, the Word of God, under threat of extinction? Is it the solid, reliability of Joseph in the father's role? God's inspiration coming in remarkable ways?
- God has something for me here. What is it?

Monday 27th December, St John, Apostle and Evangelist
John 20:2-8

So Mary Magdalene ran and went to Simon Peter and the other disciple, the one whom Jesus loved, and said to them, "They have taken the Lord out of the tomb, and we do not know where they have laid him." Then Peter and the other disciple set out and went toward the tomb. The two were running together, but the other disciple outran Peter and reached the tomb first. He bent down to look in and saw the linen wrappings lying there, but he did not go in. Then Simon Peter came, following him, and went into the tomb. He saw the linen wrappings lying there, and the cloth that had been on Jesus' head, not lying with the linen wrappings but rolled up in a place by itself. Then the other disciple, who reached the tomb first, also went in, and he saw and believed.

- Still celebrating the great feast of Christmas, we are invited to run with Peter and the beloved disciples to the empty tomb.
- The two disciples "saw and believed." Can I allow myself to be drawn into the same response of faith?
- They "knew" then, that Jesus was alive and would be with them forever. Looking at my life in late December 2004, can I open myself to the same reality?

Tuesday 28th December, Holy Innocents
Matthew 2:13-18

Now after the wise men had left, an angel of the Lord appeared to Joseph in a dream and said, "Get up, take the child and his mother, and flee to Egypt, and remain there until I tell you; for Herod is about to search for the child, to destroy him." Then Joseph got up, took the child and his mother by night, and went to Egypt, and remained there until the death of Herod. This was to fulfill what had been spoken by the Lord through the prophet, "Out of Egypt I have called my son." When Herod saw that he had been tricked by the wise men, he was infuriated, and he sent and killed all the children in and around Bethlehem who were two years old or under, according to the time that he had learned from the wise men. Then was fulfilled what had been spoken through the prophet Jeremiah: "A voice was heard in Ramah, wailing and loud lamentation, Rachel weeping for her children; she refused to be consoled, because they are no more."

- In this scene we see the newborn Saviour intimately linked with the weakest and most vulnerable.
- When I consider the misery and cruelty of this scene, how does it move me? Do I think first of my own pain, or the pain of others?
- Who are the "innocents" in our world? How is the Christ related to them? How do I think of them?

Wednesday 29th December   Luke 2:25-32

Now there was a man in Jerusalem whose name was Simeon; this man was righteous and devout, looking forward to the consolation of Israel, and the Holy Spirit rested on him. It had been revealed to him by the Holy Spirit that he would not see death before he had seen the Lord's Messiah. Guided by the Spirit, Simeon came into the temple; and when the parents brought in the child Jesus, to do for him what was customary under the law, Simeon took him in his arms and praised God, saying, "Master, now you are dismissing your servant in peace, according to your word; for my eyes have seen your salvation, which you have prepared in the presence of all peoples, a light for revelation to the Gentiles and for glory to your people Israel."

- All his life, Simeon had been waiting and hoping for something. Meanwhile, God was planning the incarnation. In this scene Simeon sees it all as the fulfillment of his hopes.
- What about my longing and waiting? What am I hoping for, deep down?

- How does the image of the Christ child in his mother's arms speak to my hopes?
- Can I join with Simeon in his song? What do I want to say to the Lord?

Thursday 30th December   Luke 2:36-40

There was also a prophet, Anna the daughter of Phanuel, of the tribe of Asher. She was of a great age, having lived with her husband seven years after her marriage, then as a widow to the age of eighty-four. She never left the temple but worshiped there with fasting and prayer night and day. At that moment she came, and began to praise God and to speak about the child to all who were looking for the redemption of Jerusalem. When they had finished everything required by the law of the Lord, they returned to Galilee, to their own town of Nazareth. The child grew and became strong, filled with wisdom; and the favor of God was upon him.

- In this scene, Mary and Joseph are in the Temple with their child performing the rites that a poor Jewish family would.
- Anna, the holy woman who had spent years in prayer and fasting, recognised that salvation had come in this child.
- What did Anna see? How did she see it? Do I see it?

Friday 31st December   John 1:14-18

And the Word became flesh and lived among us, and we have seen his glory, the glory as of a father's only son, full of grace and truth. (John testified to him and cried out, "This was he of whom I said, 'He who comes after me ranks ahead of me because he was before me.'") From his fullness we have all received, grace upon grace. The law indeed was given through Moses; grace and truth came through Jesus Christ. No one has ever seen God. It is God the only Son, who is close to the Father's heart, who has made him known.

- The Christmas season is not about big numbers (or warm Dickensian nostalgia or charming old traditions) but about this simple fact: the Word became flesh and lived among us.
- Our God is not cold or distant, but loves us this much— becoming a poor, vulnerable human being in order to save us.
- So we are all "close to the Father's heart." I am close to God's heart now, and am invited into ever-deeper closeness.

Saturday 1st January, Solemnity of Mary, Mother of God
Luke 2:15-21

When the angels had left them and gone into heaven, the shepherds said to one another, "Let us go now to Bethlehem and see this thing that has taken place, which the Lord has made known to us." So they went with haste and found Mary and Joseph, and the child lying in the manger. When they saw this, they made known what had been told them about this child; and all who heard it were amazed at what the shepherds told them. But Mary treasured all these words and pondered them in her heart. The shepherds returned, glorifying and praising God for all they had heard and seen, as it had been told them. After eight days had passed, it was time to circumcise the child; and he was called Jesus, the name given by the angel before he was conceived in the womb.

- Can I imagine myself as one of the group of shepherds who have just heard extraordinary news? We head off quickly towards Bethlehem.
- What do we find? What is happening? Who do I see here? How are they reacting?
- Can I simply allow this scene to touch me deeply?

Sacred Space

january 2–8

Something to think and pray about each day this week:

New Year

We are entering a new year, a new adventure. Our scripture passages at the start of the year have the sense of announcing a new beginning.

Most of us have a desire for a new adventure, a new beginning, in some area of our life. Too often we are satisfied with second best, or we lose sight of what is really important. Some people get depressed. They make New Year's resolutions and then a week later break them. They see changes they would like to make in their life, but they haven't the willpower to make them. If you do feel there is a change you would like to make, then ask God's help to work together on it. If you can't then change, perhaps God is saying, "accept yourself for who you are."

This New Year is a good time to allow the scriptures to speak to us, to challenge us, to help us become aware of what is most important in our lives. A time for new beginnings.

The Presence of God
As I sit here, the beating of my heart,
the ebb and flow of my breathing, the movements of my mind
are all signs of God's ongoing creation of me.
I pause for a moment, and become aware
of this presence of God within me.

Freedom
I ask for the grace
to let go of my own concerns
and be open to what God is asking of me,
to let myself be guided and formed by my loving Creator.

Consciousness
In the presence of my loving Creator,
I look honestly at my feelings over the last day,
the highs, the lows and the level ground.
Can I see where the Lord has been present?

The Word
I take my time to read the Word of God, slowly, a few times,
allowing myself to dwell on anything that strikes me. (Please
turn to your scripture on the following pages. Inspiration
points are there should you need them. When you are ready,
return here to continue.)

Conversation
Remembering that I am still in God's presence,
I imagine Jesus himself standing or sitting beside me,
and say whatever is on my mind, whatever is in my heart,
speaking as one friend to another.

Conclusion
Glory be to the Father, and to the Son, and to the Holy Spirit,
As it was in the beginning, is now and ever shall be,
World without end. Amen

january 2005

Sunday 2nd January, The Epiphany of the Lord

Matthew 2:1-12

In the time of King Herod, after Jesus was born in Beth-lehem of Judea, wise men from the East came to Jerusalem, asking, "Where is the child who has been born king of the Jews? For we observed his star at its rising, and have come to pay him homage." When King Herod heard this, he was frightened, and all Jerusalem with him; and calling together all the chief priests and scribes of the people, he inquired of them where the Messiah was to be born. They told him, "In Bethlehem of Judea; for so it has been written by the prophet: 'And you, Bethlehem, in the land of Judah, are by no means least among the rulers of Judah; for from you shall come a ruler who is to shepherd my people Israel.'" Then Herod secretly called for the wise men and learned from them the exact time when the star had appeared. Then he sent them to Bethlehem, saying, "Go and search diligently for the child; and when you have found him, bring me word so that I may also go and pay him homage." When they had heard the king, they set out; and there, ahead of them, went the star that they had seen at its rising, until it stopped over the place where the child was. When they saw that the star had stopped, they were overwhelmed with joy. On entering the house, they saw the child with Mary his mother; and they knelt down and paid him homage. Then, opening their treasure chests, they offered him gifts of gold, frankincense, and myrrh. And having been warned in a dream not to return to Herod, they left for their own country by another road.

- How do I imagine the three Wise Men? How clear was the inspiration from the star? Was the decision to set out easy? How long—and difficult—was the journey? Did they know what they would find at the end?

- Is there a star—perhaps a little one—in my sky? To what does it call me?

Monday 3rd January   Matthew 4:12-17

Now when Jesus heard that John had been arrested, he withdrew to Galilee. He left Nazareth and made his home in Capernaum by the sea, in the territory of Zebulun and Naphtali, so that what had been spoken through the prophet Isaiah might be fulfilled: "Land of Zebulun, land of Naphtali, on the road by the sea, across the Jordan, Galilee of the Gentiles—the people who sat in darkness have seen a great light, and for those who sat in the region and shadow of death light has dawned." From that time Jesus began to proclaim, "Repent, for the kingdom of heaven has come near."

- Over the past few weeks we have been watching the gradual unfolding of God's plans in the Word made flesh.
- Now we see Jesus come of age and realize that the plans have a purpose.
- How does this purpose affect me?

Tuesday 4th January   1 John 4:7-10

Beloved, let us love one another, because love is from God; everyone who loves is born of God and knows God. Whoever does not love does not know God, for God is love. God's love was revealed among us in this way: God sent his only Son into the world so that we might live through him. In this is love, not that we loved God but that he loved us and sent his Son to be the atoning sacrifice for our sins.

- Religious practice and doctrine may be a help in sustaining a community of believers, but the measure of my Christian commitment is not my adherence to these. The measure is: Do I love?

- Love can be expressed in many ways. Saying "I love you" is the easiest. But it is in what we do and how we treat other people that love is made real, just as God's love for us was expressed most clearly by what Jesus did.
- If I think of the people I have encountered in the last few days, and am likely to encounter today and tomorrow, how might this self-giving love be expressed in the way I deal with them?

Wednesday 5th January   1 John 4:11-16

Beloved, since God loved us so much, we also ought to love one another. No one has ever seen God; if we love one another, God lives in us, and his love is perfected in us. By this we know that we abide in him and he in us, because he has given us of his Spirit. And we have seen and do testify that the Father has sent his Son as the Savior of the world. God abides in those who confess that Jesus is the Son of God, and they abide in God. So we have known and believe the love that God has for us. God is love, and those who abide in love abide in God, and God abides in them.

- John seems to be writing from his personal experience of living in community in Ephesus.
- Can I imagine their relationships, built on love, that left them convinced that God lived among them?
- Is there something here for me?

Thursday 6th January   Luke 4:16-21

When Jesus came to Nazareth, where he had been brought up, he went to the synagogue on the sabbath day, as was his custom. He stood up to read, and the scroll of the prophet Isaiah was given to him. He unrolled the scroll and found the place where it was written: "The Spirit of the Lord is upon me, because he has anointed me to bring good news to the poor. He has sent me to proclaim release to the captives and recovery of sight to the blind, to let the oppressed go free, to proclaim the year of the Lord's favor." And he rolled up the scroll, gave it back to the attendant, and sat down. The eyes of all in the synagogue were fixed on him. Then he began to say to them, "Today this scripture has been fulfilled in your hearing."

- The "local boy" is speaking in public to his neighbours for the first time. How does he feel?
- He has a mission. How does this affect me?
- A beginning full of drama. Where will it go?

Friday 7th January   Luke 5:12-16

Once, when Jesus was in one of the cities, there was a man covered with leprosy. When he saw Jesus, he bowed with his face to the ground and begged him, "Lord, if you choose, you can make me clean." Then Jesus stretched out his hand, touched him, and said, "I do choose. Be made clean." Immediately the leprosy left him. And he ordered him to tell no one. "Go," he said, "and show yourself to the priest, and, as Moses commanded, make an offering for your cleansing, for a testimony to them." But now more than ever the word about Jesus spread abroad; many crowds would gather to hear him and to be cured of their diseases. But he would withdraw to deserted places and pray.

- Can I let myself be touched by this poor, broken man, in desperation at the feet of Jesus?
- What do they say to each other?
- What happens?

Saturday 8th January   John 3:22-30

After this Jesus and his disciples went into the Judean countryside, and he spent some time there with them and baptized. John also was baptizing at Aenon near Salim because water was abundant there; and people kept coming and were being baptized—John, of course, had not yet been thrown into prison. Now a discussion about purification arose between John's disciples and a Jew. They came to John and said to him, "Rabbi, the one who was with you across the Jordan, to whom you testified, here he is baptizing, and all are going to him." John answered, "No one can receive anything except what has been given from heaven. You yourselves are my witnesses that I said, 'I am not the Messiah, but I have been sent ahead of him.' He who has the bride is the bridegroom. The friend of the bridegroom, who stands and hears him, rejoices greatly at the bridegroom's voice. For this reason my joy has been fulfilled. He must increase, but I must decrease."

- The rise in popularity of Jesus was seen as a threat by John's disciples.
- Is John himself threatened?
- How can we account for John's reactions?
- Where does his joy come from?

Sacred Space

january 9–15

Something to think and pray about each day this week:

A virtual community
One of the insights of Mark's gospel is that I can be helped and healed by the faith of others, and can help others through my faith (see Mark 2:1-12). On the *Sacred Space* website I am told that I'm never alone when I pray. In the same way I am never alone as I pray with this book in my hands. While I can get so used to that idea that I ignore it, pause and think about it for a minute.

Every day, thousands of people pray at the *Sacred Space* website, in different languages, from over fifty different countries—a twelve-year-old boy in Boston, a young language student in Budapest, an office worker from Santiago, a nurse from Manila, a voluntary worker from Cork, a school principal in Australia, a retired man from Panama.

As you pray in your sacred space, at that very minute ten or twenty people, somewhere in the world, are praying with you. While you are praying, sitting with this book in your hands or sitting at a computer, think of one of those people doing the same, and pray for them. They have their own needs and difficulties to cope with: they also have their own dreams, their own potential, something to give. Your faith, your prayer, can help them.

The Presence of God
I pause for a moment
and reflect on God's life-giving presence
in every part of my body, in everything around me,
in the whole of my life.

Freedom
I ask for the grace to believe
in what I could be and do
if I only allowed God, my loving Creator,
to continue to create me, guide me and shape me.

Consciousness
Knowing that God loves me unconditionally,
I look honestly over the last day, its events and my feelings.
Do I have something to be grateful for? Then I give thanks.
Is there something I am sorry for? Then I ask forgiveness.

The Word
God speaks to each one of us individually. I need to listen
to hear what he is saying to me. Read the text a few times,
then listen. (Please turn to your scripture on the following
pages. Inspiration points are there should you need them.
When you are ready, return here to continue.)

Conversation
How has God's Word moved me? Has it left me cold?
Has it consoled me or moved me to act in a new way?
I imagine Jesus standing or sitting beside me,
I turn and share my feelings with him.

Conclusion
Glory be to the Father, and to the Son, and to the Holy Spirit,
As it was in the beginning, is now and ever shall be,
World without end. Amen

Sunday 9th January, The Baptism of the Lord
Matthew 3:13-17

Then Jesus came from Galilee to John at the Jordan, to be baptized by him. John would have prevented him, saying, "I need to be baptized by you, and do you come to me?" But Jesus answered him, "Let it be so now; for it is proper for us in this way to fulfill all righteousness." Then he consented. And when Jesus had been baptized, just as he came up from the water, suddenly the heavens were opened to him and he saw the Spirit of God descending like a dove and alighting on him. And a voice from heaven said, "This is my Son, the Beloved, with whom I am well pleased."

- The people who went to John for baptism felt the need for forgiveness and cleansing from their sins. Jesus—the sinless one—went and took his place among them.
- Can I get in touch with my own need for forgiveness and cleansing? Do I see Jesus standing near me?

Monday 10th January
Mark 1:14-20

Now after John was arrested, Jesus came to Galilee, proclaiming the good news of God, and saying, "The time is fulfilled, and the kingdom of God has come near; repent, and believe in the good news." As Jesus passed along the Sea of Galilee, he saw Simon and his brother Andrew casting a net into the sea—for they were fishermen. And Jesus said to them, "Follow me and I will make you fish for people." And immediately they left their nets and followed him. As he went a little farther, he saw James son of Zebedee and his brother John, who were in their boat mending the nets. Immediately he called them; and they left their father Zebedee in the boat with the hired men, and followed him.

- I imagine this stretch of shore along the Sea of Galilee, with boats moored and fishermen about their business.
- As Jesus went along he stopped at particular places and specifically and personally called these individuals.
- Can I get in touch with the fact that Jesus also calls me, personally? How does that sit with me?

Tuesday 11th January   Mark 1:21b-28

Jesus entered the synagogue and taught. They were astounded at his teaching, for he taught them as one having authority, and not as the scribes. Just then there was in their synagogue a man with an unclean spirit, and he cried out, "What have you to do with us, Jesus of Nazareth? Have you come to destroy us? I know who you are, the Holy One of God." But Jesus rebuked him, saying, "Be silent, and come out of him!" And the unclean spirit, convulsing him and crying with a loud voice, came out of him. They were all amazed, and they kept on asking one another, "What is this? A new teaching—with authority! He commands even the unclean spirits, and they obey him." At once his fame began to spread throughout the surrounding region of Galilee.

- Can I imagine myself sitting in the synagogue when Jesus comes in and begins to teach? Seemingly the effect was electric.
- What happens? What impression do I get of this man?
- How does he move me?

Wednesday 12th January   Mark 1:32-39

That evening, at sundown, they brought to him all who were sick or possessed with demons. And the whole city was gathered around the door. And he cured many who were sick with various diseases, and cast out many demons; and he

52

would not permit the demons to speak, because they knew him. In the morning, while it was still very dark, he got up and went out to a deserted place, and there he prayed. And Simon and his companions hunted for him. When they found him, they said to him, "Everyone is searching for you." He answered, "Let us go on to the neighboring towns, so that I may proclaim the message there also; for that is what I came out to do." And he went throughout Galilee, proclaiming the message in their synagogues and casting out demons.

- People seem to flock to Jesus ... Who is he? What kind of man is he?
- It would be good to mull over and picture each of the scenes in this short passage in turn. Each little scene shows a different side of Jesus.
- How does this man move me?

Thursday 13th January   Mark 1:40-45

A leper came to Jesus begging him, and kneeling he said to him, "If you choose, you can make me clean." Moved with pity, Jesus stretched out his hand and touched him, and said to him, "I do choose. Be made clean!" Immediately the leprosy left him, and he was made clean. After sternly warning him he sent him away at once, saying to him, "See that you say nothing to anyone; but go, show yourself to the priest, and offer for your cleansing what Moses commanded, as a testimony to them." But he went out and began to proclaim it freely, and to spread the word, so that Jesus could no longer go into a town openly, but stayed out in the country; and people came to him from every quarter.

- I need to appreciate first what a scourge leprosy was. It involved not just physical deformity but complete rejection and isolation.

- Now let's observe the encounter between this leper and Jesus. What happened? What do I imagine was the impact?
- Can I detect something of the isolation of leprosy within me, around me, in others? What does Jesus say to this?

Friday 14th January   **Mark 2:1-12**

When Jesus returned to Capernaum after some days, it was reported that he was at home. So many gathered around that there was no longer room for them, not even in front of the door; and he was speaking the word to them. Then some people came, bringing to him a paralyzed man, carried by four of them. And when they could not bring him to Jesus because of the crowd, they removed the roof above him; and after having dug through it, they let down the mat on which the paralytic lay. When Jesus saw their faith, he said to the paralytic, "Son, your sins are forgiven." Now some of the scribes were sitting there, questioning in their hearts, "Why does this fellow speak in this way? It is blasphemy! Who can forgive sins but God alone?" At once Jesus perceived in his spirit that they were discussing these questions among themselves; and he said to them, "Why do you raise such questions in your hearts? Which is easier, to say to the paralytic, 'Your sins are forgiven,' or to say, 'Stand up and take your mat and walk'? But so that you may know that the Son of Man has authority on earth to forgive sins"—he said to the paralytic— "I say to you, stand up, take your mat and go to your home." And he stood up, and immediately took the mat and went out before all of them; so that they were all amazed and glorified God, saying, "We have never seen anything like this!"

- If I close my eyes, can I imagine the street and house and the particular roof over the house? What is the scene inside the house?

54

- Who is this paralytic and who are these people carrying him to see Jesus? A determined bunch, it seems.
- What happened then?
- What do I think of the man in the middle of it all?

Saturday 15th January   Mark 2:13-17

Jesus went out again beside the sea; the whole crowd gathered around him, and he taught them. As he was walking along, he saw Levi son of Alphaeus sitting at the tax booth, and he said to him, "Follow me." And he got up and followed him. And as he sat at dinner in Levi's house, many tax collectors and sinners were also sitting with Jesus and his disciples—for there were many who followed him. When the scribes of the Pharisees saw that he was eating with sinners and tax collectors, they said to his disciples, "Why does he eat with tax collectors and sinners?" When Jesus heard this, he said to them, "Those who are well have no need of a physician, but those who are sick; I have come to call not the righteous but sinners."

- In the eyes of some, Jesus' new friend Levi was a particularly undesirable character.
- What is happening here? How does Jesus choose this individual? What does he see in him that the others don't see?
- What is Jesus teaching me here?

Sacred Space

january 16–22

Something to think and pray about each day this week:

Preparation pays

A former Archbishop of Canterbury was once asked how long he prayed each day, and he replied, "About three minutes, but it takes me half an hour to get there."

In your sacred space, the temptation, especially for the task-oriented person, is to read through to the scripture fairly quickly and then try to focus on that. Yet very few of us are able to enter into that kind of reflection fruitfully without spending some time becoming aware of God's presence, stilling our busy minds, and opening ourselves to a will other than our own.

We might not be able to spare half an hour to sit and pray, but a few minutes on the preparatory stages (the *Presence of God* and praying for *Freedom*), can make a big difference. It is this preparation, this "disposing ourselves" to God, that makes the rest of the prayer real and effective.

The Presence of God

The world is charged with the grandeur of God (Gerard Manley Hopkins).
I dwell for a moment on the presence of God around me, in every part of my body, and deep within my being.

Freedom

"In these days, God taught me as a schoolteacher teaches a pupil" (St Ignatius).
I remind myself that there are things God has to teach me yet, and ask for the grace to hear them and let them change me.

Consciousness

How do I find myself today?
Where am I with God? With others?
Do I have something to be grateful for? Then I give thanks.
Is there something I am sorry for? Then I ask forgiveness.

The Word

I read the Word of God slowly, a few times over, and I listen to what God is saying to me. (Please turn to your scripture on the following pages. Inspiration points are there should you need them. When you are ready, return here to continue.)

Conversation

What feelings are rising in me as I pry and reflect on God's Word?
I imagine Jesus himself sitting or standing near me and open my heart to him.

Conclusion

Glory be to the Father, and to the Son, and to the Holy Spirit,
As it was in the beginning, is now and ever shall be,
World without end. Amen

Sunday 16th January, 2nd Sunday of the Year
John 1:29-34

The next day John saw Jesus coming toward him and declared, "Here is the Lamb of God who takes away the sin of the world! This is he of whom I said, 'After me comes a man who ranks ahead of me because he was before me.' I myself did not know him; but I came baptizing with water for this reason, that he might be revealed to Israel." And John testified, "I saw the Spirit descending from heaven like a dove, and it remained on him. I myself did not know him, but the one who sent me to baptize with water said to me, 'He on whom you see the Spirit descend and remain is the one who baptizes with the Holy Spirit.' And I myself have seen and have testified that this is the Son of God."

- This is the culminating moment of John's life, the arrival of the One for whom he prepared the way.
- Can I hear John's account of himself? He knew he was to prepare the way, but until now, he didn't know the identity of the one he was preparing for.
- How do I understand John? Does he move me to look towards the one who was to come?

Monday 17th January
Mark 2:18-22

Now John's disciples and the Pharisees were fasting; and people came and said to him, "Why do John's disciples and the disciples of the Pharisees fast, but your disciples do not fast?" Jesus said to them, "The wedding guests cannot fast while the bridegroom is with them, can they? As long as they have the bridegroom with them, they cannot fast. The days will come when the bridegroom is taken away from them, and then they will fast on that day. "No one sews a piece of unshrunk cloth on an old cloak; otherwise, the patch pulls away from it, the new from the old, and a worse tear is made. And no one puts new wine into old wineskins; otherwise, the wine will burst the skins, and the wine is lost, and so are the skins; but one puts new wine into fresh wineskins."

- This is one of those slightly enigmatic scenes in the life of Jesus. Its the kind of story that we can tend to skip over fairly quickly.
- What do I think of the questions posed to Jesus? What do I think of Jesus' answer? Am I intrigued by the mystery of it? Am I frustrated by it? Am I satisfied with it?
- If there is dissatisfaction in me, a sense that I can't fully grasp what Jesus means, can I stay with that experience?

Tuesday 18th January   Mark 2:23-28

One sabbath Jesus was going through the grainfields; and as they made their way his disciples began to pluck heads of grain. The Pharisees said to him, "Look, why are they doing what is not lawful on the sabbath?" And he said to them, "Have you never read what David did when he and his companions were hungry and in need of food? He entered the house of God, when Abiathar was high priest, and ate the bread of the Presence, which it is not lawful for any but the priests to eat, and he gave some to his companions." Then he said to them, "The sabbath was made for humankind, and not humankind for the sabbath; so the Son of Man is lord even of the sabbath."

- This is an unsubtle confrontation of Jesus by a group of his critics.
- Can I imagine the scene? What is the atmosphere like? What is the tone of voice? How do Jesus' accusers look?
- How is Jesus, under fire?
- What do I have to learn from him?

Wednesday 19th January   Mark 3:1-6

Again Jesus entered the synagogue, and a man was there who had a withered hand. They watched him to see whether he would cure him on the sabbath, so that they might accuse him. And he said to the man who had the withered hand, "Come forward." Then he said to them, "Is it lawful to do good or to do harm on the sabbath, to save life or to kill?" But they were silent. He looked around at them with anger; he was grieved at their hardness of heart and said to the man, "Stretch out your hand." He stretched it out, and his hand was restored. The Pharisees went out and immediately conspired with the Herodians against him, how to destroy him.

- In my mind's eye, can I take a seat in this synagogue? Looking around I see the action unfold as Jesus arrives.
- Step by step, what happens? Who is involved? How do the various characters react?
- Especially, how does Jesus behave? How do I feel about Jesus' reactions—to the man with the withered hand, and to the Pharisees?
- Do I feel comfortable with the Jesus I see here?
- I can speak to him about my reactions.

Thursday 20th January   Mark 3:7-12

Jesus departed with his disciples to the sea, and a great multitude from Galilee followed him; hearing all that he was doing, they came to him in great numbers from Judea, Jerusalem, Idumea, beyond the Jordan, and the region around Tyre and Sidon. He told his disciples to have a boat ready for him because of the crowd, so that they would not crush him; for he had cured many, so that all who had diseases pressed upon him to touch him. Whenever the unclean spirits saw him, they fell down before him and shouted, "You are the Son of God!" But he sternly ordered them not to make him known.

- Now the crowds are coming after Jesus. What brings them out in such numbers? What is the mood among them?
- People reach out in great need. What moves them? What draws them?
- How do I find myself responding? Do I keep my distance or do I want to get closer to this Jesus?

Friday 21st January   Mark 3:13-19

Jesus went up the mountain and called to him those whom he wanted, and they came to him. And he appointed twelve, whom he also named apostles, to be with him, and to be sent out to proclaim the message, and to have authority to cast out demons. So he appointed the twelve: Simon (to whom he gave the name Peter); James son of Zebedee and John the brother of James (to whom he gave the name Boanerges, that is, Sons of Thunder); and Andrew, and Philip, and Bartholomew, and Matthew, and Thomas, and James son of Alphaeus, and Thaddaeus, and Simon the Cananaean, and Judas Iscariot, who betrayed him.

- It is good to consider this calling of the Apostles, a key moment in God's great plan of salvation and yet so ordinary.
- Who were these chosen ones? A handful of fisherfolk, at least one despised tax collector, and sundry others.
- What was so special about them? What was God up to?
- In the light of all this, what about the call of very ordinary people to work with Jesus today? What about me?

Saturday 22nd January, St Vincent, Deacon and Martyr
Matthew 10:16-22

Jesus sent out the Twelve, "See, I am sending you out like sheep into the midst of wolves; so be wise as serpents and innocent as doves. Beware of them, for they will hand you over to councils and flog you in their synagogues; and you will be dragged before governors and kings because of me, as a testimony to them and the Gentiles. When they hand you over, do not worry about how you are to speak or what you are to say; for what you are to say will be given to you at that time; for it is not you who speak, but the Spirit of your Father speaking through you. Brother will betray brother to death, and a father his child, and children will rise against parents and have them put to death; and you will be hated by all because of my name. But the one who endures to the end will be saved."

- Some Christians today still face the vicious opposition that Jesus describes, but most of us don't. If it were a criminal offence to be a Christian, would there be enough evidence to convict me?
- "Wise as serpents and innocent as doves" is not an obvious combination. What does it mean in my life today? Taking people as I find them? Giving them the benefit of the doubt, even when I'm a bit suspicious of them? Knowing the tricks that are played, without playing them myself?
- Does Jesus' behaviour in the Gospels shed some light on this for me? Can I talk to him about it?

Sacred Space

january 23–29

Something to think and pray about each day this week:

Doing, not reading

Whether I am new to *Sacred Space* or very familiar with it, I will get less out of it if I content myself with reading the prayer rather than doing it.

If this kind of prayer is new to me, it may be difficult to adjust to the idea that the *Sacred Space* texts are more like "exercises" than "prayers"—they are for doing, not for reading out.

If I am very familiar with it, I may find myself moving ever more quickly through the pages, thinking to myself "yeah, yeah, I know" as I move on, and praying less deeply every day.

If this is happening, I may need to slow down and spend a bit more time on the earlier stages, reminding myself that "The Lord is waiting to be gracious to me" (Isaiah 30:18) and is inviting me to enjoy the real, growing, loving relationship between us.

The Presence of God

As I sit here, God is present,
breathing life into me and into everything around me.
For a few moments, I sit silently,
and become aware of God's loving presence.

Freedom

If God were trying to tell me something, would I know?
If God were reassuring me or challenging me, would I notice?
I ask for the grace to be free of my own preoccupations
and open to what God may be saying to me.

Consciousness

In God's loving presence I unwind the past day,
starting from now and looking back, moment by moment.
I gather in all the goodness and light, in gratitude.
I attend to the shadows and what they say to me,
seeking healing, courage, forgiveness.

The Word

I take my time to read the Word of God, slowly, a few
times, allowing myself to dwell on anything that strikes me.
(Please turn to your scripture on the following pages. Inspiration points are there should you need them. When you
are ready, return here to continue.)

Conversation

What is stirring in me as I pray?
Am I consoled, troubled, left cold?
I imagine Jesus himself standing or sitting at my side,
and share my feelings with him.

Conclusion

Glory be to the Father, and to the Son, and to the Holy Spirit,
As it was in the beginning, is now and ever shall be,
World without end. Amen

Sunday 23th January, Third Sunday of the Year
Matthew 4:12-17

Now when Jesus heard that John had been arrested, he withdrew to Galilee. He left Nazareth and made his home in Capernaum by the sea, in the territory of Zebulun and Naphtali, so that what had been spoken through the prophet Isaiah might be fulfilled: "Land of Zebulun, land of Naphtali, on the road by the sea, across the Jordan, Galilee of the Gentiles—the people who sat in darkness have seen a great light, and for those who sat in the region and shadow of death light has dawned." From that time Jesus began to proclaim, "Repent, for the kingdom of heaven has come near."Now

- Can I resonate with the lines, "the people who sat … light has dawned"?
- In what ways am I one of those people?
- Where is the darkness in and around me?
- Where do I begin to see the light?

Monday 24th January, St Francis de Sales   John 15:9-17

Jesus said to his disciples, "As the Father has loved me, so I have loved you; abide in my love.

If you keep my commandments, you will abide in my love, just as I have kept my Father's commandments and abide in his love. I have said these things to you so that my joy may be in you, and that your joy may be complete. "This is my commandment, that you love one another as I have loved you. No one has greater love than this, to lay down one's life for one's friends. You are my friends if you do what I command you. I do not call you servants any longer, because the servant does not know what the master is doing; but I have called you friends, because I have made known to you everything that I have heard from my Father. You did not choose me but I chose you. And I appointed you to go and bear fruit, fruit that will last, so that the Father will give you whatever you ask him in my name. I am giving you these commands so that you may love one another.

- Can I relate to Jesus as my friend, as he invites me to do here, or do I feel it is disrespectful? Listen to him saying to you, "I call you my friend … "
- Jesus has chosen me. But it's not like a job interview, where I'm kind of hoping they'll think I'm better than I really am. He knows my all my strengths—and weaknesses—and still chooses me. Listen to him saying, to you, "I chose you … "
- Jesus has chosen me to be part of his mission. Can I talk to him about what it is he wants me to do?

Tuesday 25th January, Conversion of St Paul
Acts 22:3-11

I persecuted this Way up to the point of death by binding both men and women and putting them in prison, as the high priest and the whole council of elders can testify about me. From them I also received letters to the brothers in Damascus, and I went there in order to bind those who were there and to bring them back to Jerusalem for punishment. "While I was on my way and approaching Damascus, about noon a great light from heaven suddenly shone about me. I fell to the ground and heard a voice saying to me, 'Saul, Saul, why are you persecuting me?' I answered, 'Who are you, Lord?' Then he said to me, 'I am Jesus of Nazareth whom you are persecuting.' Now those who were with me saw the light but did not hear the voice of the one who was speaking to me. I asked, 'What am I to do, Lord?' The Lord said to me, 'Get up and go to Damascus; there you will be told everything that has been assigned to you to do.' Since I could not see because of the brightness of that light, those who were with me took my hand and led me to Damascus.

- This is one of the great testimonies in Christian history of the Risen Lord active among his people.
- Can I simply listen to Paul telling his experience of meeting the Lord?
- How does this tale of radical conversion touch me? Is it frightening? Consoling? Alienating?

Wednesday 26th January   Mark 4:1-9

Again he began to teach beside the sea. Such a very large crowd gathered around him that he got into a boat on the sea and sat there, while the whole crowd was beside the sea on the land. He began to teach them many things in parables, and in his teaching he said to them: "Listen! A sower went out to sow. And as he sowed, some seed fell on the path, and the birds came and ate it up. Other seed fell on rocky ground, where it did not have much soil, and it sprang up quickly, since it had no depth of soil. And when the sun rose, it was scorched; and since it had no root, it withered away. Other seed fell among thorns, and the thorns grew up and choked it, and it yielded no grain. Other seed fell into good soil and brought forth grain, growing up and increasing and yielding thirty and sixty and a hundredfold." And he said, "Let anyone with ears to hear listen!"

- There is a large crowd on this shore gathered around Jesus. I could be there.
- Jesus says: "Listen!"
- What do these words inspire in me?

Thursday 27th January   **Mark 4:21-25**

Jesus said to the crowd, "Is a lamp brought in to be put under the bushel basket, or under the bed, and not on the lampstand? For there is nothing hidden, except to be disclosed; nor is anything secret, except to come to light. Let anyone with ears to hear listen!" And he said to them, "Pay attention to what you hear; the measure you give will be the measure you get, and still more will be given you. For to those who have, more will be given; and from those who have nothing, even what they have will be taken away."

- "Hiding your light under a bushel" has become such a cliche that it is difficult to listen to, but the message is an important one. Do I give to others out of what I have, my resources and my talents, my time and my energy? Do I want to?
- Can I ask the Lord for the grace of generosity? I can use my own words, or if I prefer, there is a prayer attributed to St Ignatius:
  Dearest Jesus, teach me to be generous.
  Teach me to love and serve you as you deserve;
  to give and not to count the cost;
  to toil and not to seek for rest;
  to labour and to look for no reward,
  save that of knowing that I do your holy will.
  Amen.

Friday 28th January, St Thomas Aquinas

Matthew 23:8-12

Jesus said to the crowds, "But you are not to be called rabbi, for you have one teacher, and you are all students. And call no one your father on earth, for you have one Father—the one in heaven. Nor are you to be called instructors, for you have one instructor, the Messiah. The greatest among you will be your servant. All who exalt themselves will be humbled, and all who humble themselves will be exalted."

- If another person is my teacher, or father or instructor, it seems right that I should have respect for them and for their position. So, what is Jesus saying here: that we shouldn't respect our teachers, fathers and instructors?
- The second part of the passage helps to clarify the point. The best teacher, father or instructor is one who does not rely on his or her position, one who does not demand respect, but earns it through humble service and devotion to those in their care.
- Have you ever met anyone like that? A teacher, or a boss, or someone else in authority who had no regard for their office or rank, and would just "muck in" and try to help wherever they could?
- Do I want to have that kind of humility? Can I ask the Lord for that grace?

Saturday 29th January   Mark 4:35-41

On that day, when evening had come, Jesus said to the disciples, "Let us go across to the other side." And leaving the crowd behind, they took him with them in the boat, just as he was. Other boats were with him. A great windstorm arose, and the waves beat into the boat, so that the boat was already being swamped. But he was in the stern, asleep on the cushion; and they woke him up and said to him, "Teacher, do you not care that we are perishing?" He woke up and rebuked the wind, and said to the sea, "Peace! Be still!" Then the wind ceased, and there was a dead calm. He said to them, "Why are you afraid? Have you still no faith?" And they were filled with great awe and said to one another, "Who then is this, that even the wind and the sea obey him?"

- I should really let my powers of imagination get me a place in this boat. Jesus' invitation to his disciples is also addressed to me?
- What happens? Do I feel the force of it all? What feelings arise in me?
- Where is God? What is he up to?
- What happens then?
- Who is this Jesus?

january 30 – february 5

Something to think and pray about each day this week:

The call to discipleship
In the *Spiritual Exercises*, St Ignatius invites us to imagine a king calling his people to conquer the world with him, using these words: "Whoever wishes to come with me has to be content with the same food I eat, and the drink, and the clothing which I wear, and so forth. So too each one must labor with me during the day, and keep watch at night, and so on, so that later each may have a part with me in the victory, just as each has shared in the toil."

The scriptures this week tell of Jesus sending his disciples out on mission. What does he tell them? That it's going to be a walk in the park? That it's a great career move? That they will be admired, respected and rewarded for everything they do?

No. It's going to be tough. Their lives will often be poor and uncomfortable. Many people will misjudge them, reject them, even make fun of them. That's what it was like for Jesus, and that is what it will be like for us if we accept the call to continue his mission. It has its own reward, but it is not for the faint-hearted.

The Presence of God
As I sit here with my book, God is here.
Around me, in my sensations, in my thoughts and deep
within me.
I pause for a moment, and become aware
of God's life-giving presence.

Freedom
I need to close out the noise, to rise above the noise;
The noise that interrupts, that separates,
The noise that isolates.
I need to listen to God again.

Consciousness
I exist in a web of relationships—links to nature, people, God.
I trace out these links, giving thanks for the life that flows
through them.
Some links are twisted or broken: I may feel regret, anger,
disappointment.
I pray for the gift of acceptance and forgiveness.

The Word
God speaks to each one of us individually. I need to listen
to what he is saying to me. (Please turn to your scripture on
the following pages. Inspiration points are there should you
need them. When you are ready, return here to continue.)

Conversation
Do I notice myself reacting as I pray with the Word of God?
Do I feel challenged, comforted, angry?
Imagining Jesus sitting or standing by me,
I speak out my feelings, as one trusted friend to another.

Conclusion
Glory be to the Father, and to the Son, and to the Holy Spirit,
As it was in the beginning, is now and ever shall be,
World without end. Amen

74

Sunday 30th January, Fourth Sunday of the Year
Matthew 5:1-6

When Jesus saw the crowds, he went up the mountain; and after he sat down, his disciples came to him. Then he began to speak, and taught them, saying: "Blessed are the poor in spirit, for theirs is the kingdom of heaven. Blessed are those who mourn, for they will be comforted. Blessed are the meek, for they will inherit the earth. Blessed are those who hunger and thirst for righteousness, for they will be filled."

- I have probably read The Beatitudes often before. Can I stop and listen to Jesus speaking on the mountainside as if it was the very first time?
- Is he to be taken seriously?
- Do I value poverty and meekness and these other things?
- Given where I am at myself right now, what is Jesus calling me to?

Monday 31st January, St John Bosco   Matthew 18:1-5

At that time the disciples came to Jesus and asked, "Who is the greatest in the kingdom of heaven?" He called a child, whom he put among them, and said, "Truly I tell you, unless you change and become like children, you will never enter the kingdom of heaven. Whoever becomes humble like this child is the greatest in the kingdom of heaven. Whoever welcomes one such child in my name welcomes me.

- Jesus is "counter-cultural" in this passage. He challenges the values of his listeners and of their society, by prizing humility and simple trust above wealth, power and conventional "greatness."
- It is just as much a challenge today, to the priorities of our society.
- It is also a challenge to me. Why would I want to have child-like humility? Can I talk to the Lord about this?

Tuesday 1st February   Mark 5:25-34

Now there was a woman who had been suffering from hemorrhages for twelve years. She had endured much under many physicians, and had spent all that she had; and she was no better, but rather grew worse. She had heard about Jesus, and came up behind him in the crowd and touched his cloak, for she said, "If I but touch his clothes, I will be made well." Immediately her hemorrhage stopped; and she felt in her body that she was healed of her disease. Immediately aware that power had gone forth from him, Jesus turned about in the crowd and said, "Who touched my clothes?" And his disciples said to him, "You see the crowd pressing in on you; how can you say, 'Who touched me?'" He looked all around to see who had done it. But the woman, knowing what had happened to her, came in fear and trembling, fell down before him, and told him the whole truth. He said to her, "Daughter, your faith has made you well; go in peace, and be healed of your disease."

- Can I imagine the experience of this woman over twelve long years? The frustration, the loss of energy, the longing for a new beginning.
- Something prompts her to reach out and touch Jesus' clothes.
- What happens?
- What about my life? Does any of this resonate with me?

Wednesday 2nd February, The Presentation of the Lord
Luke 2:22-24

When the time came for their purification according to the law of Moses, they brought him up to Jerusalem to present him to the Lord (as it is written in the law of the Lord, "Every firstborn male shall be designated as holy to the Lord"), and they offered a sacrifice according to what is stated in the law of the Lord, "a pair of turtledoves or two young pigeons."

- Can I picture Mary, Joseph and their child, joining all the other families as they went about buying and presenting their offering? They would have been among the less well off, as a pair of turtledoves was the offering of the poor.
- When God comes into our midst, it is among the ordinary that he is to be found.
- What does this say to me about the presence of this same Jesus today, in my life, in our world?

Thursday 3rd February   Mark 6:7-13

Jesus called the twelve and began to send them out two by two, and gave them authority over the unclean spirits. He ordered them to take nothing for their journey except a staff; no bread, no bag, no money in their belts; but to wear sandals and not to put on two tunics. He said to them, "Wherever you enter a house, stay there until you leave the place. If any place will not welcome you and they refuse to hear you, as you leave, shake off the dust that is on your feet as a testimony against them." So they went out and proclaimed that all should repent. They cast out many demons, and anointed with oil many who were sick and cured them.

- Like *Mission Impossible*, I have a mission from Jesus, "should I choose to accept it." So, do I?
- Knowing that Jesus does have a job for me, can I imagine myself in this scene, as one of the twelve being sent by Jesus? What does it feel like?
- The Twelve are a team, and they are sent out to work in teams of two, not alone. Who are the other members of my "team"? Do I think of them in that way?

Friday 4th February   Mark 6:18-29

For John had been telling Herod, "It is not lawful for you to have your brother's wife." And Herodias had a grudge against him, and wanted to kill him. But she could not, for Herod feared John, knowing that he was a righteous and holy man, and he protected him. When he heard him, he was greatly perplexed; and yet he liked to listen to him. But an opportunity came when Herod on his birthday gave a banquet for his courtiers and officers and for the leaders of Galilee. When his daughter Herodias came in and danced, she pleased Herod and his guests; and the king said to the girl, "Ask me for whatever you wish, and I will give it." And he solemnly swore to her, "Whatever you ask me, I will give you, even half of my kingdom." She went out and said to her mother, "What should I ask for?" She replied, "The head of John the baptizer." Immediately she rushed back to the king and requested, "I want you to give me at once the head of John the Baptist on a platter." The king was deeply grieved; yet out of regard for his oaths and for the guests, he did not want to refuse her. Immediately the king sent a soldier of the guard with orders to bring John's head. He went and beheaded him in the prison, brought his head on a platter, and gave it to the girl. Then the girl gave it to her mother. When his disciples heard about it, they came and took his body, and laid it in a tomb.

- A story of human deviousness, arrogance, moral weakness and crass evil.
- Does the horror of this story seem totally alien to me or do I recognise some of these realities in my own experience?
- Can I think of one situation in my own life where I was tempted to respond like Herod or Herodias (mother or daughter)?
- I humbly acknowledge my need of God's mercy and grace.

Saturday 5th February   Mark 6:30-34

The apostles gathered around Jesus, and told him all that they had done and taught. He said to them, "Come away to a deserted place all by yourselves and rest a while." For many were coming and going, and they had no leisure even to eat. And they went away in the boat to a deserted place by themselves. Now many saw them going and recognized them, and they hurried there on foot from all the towns and arrived ahead of them. As he went ashore, he saw a great crowd; and he had compassion for them, because they were like sheep without a shepherd; and he began to teach them many things.

- I imagine the disciples just returned from this first missionary experience away from Jesus, weary, footsore and full of stories of what happened. Jesus invites them away to a quiet place where they can be together, catch their breath and catch up.
- How do I imagine the experience was for them, of this quiet time with Jesus?
- Does it speak to me of my own need for a "deserted place" in the midst of my busy-ness? Can I hear Jesus make the same invitation to me?

Sacred Space

february 6–12

Something to think and pray about each day this week:

The power of the Word

Feedback from the *Sacred Space* website shows that thousands of people are praying together in their own sacred space and letting the Word of God change their lives. While the internet may be something of an innovation, there is nothing new about the phenomenon. For many centuries, the Judaeo-Christian tradition has taught of the transforming power of God's Word:

> How sweet are your words to my taste, sweeter than honey to my mouth Through your precepts I get understanding; therefore I hate every false way. Your word is a lamp to my feet and a light to my path. (Psalm 119:103-105)

But a vital part of praying with the Word is preparing myself to hear it, "disposing the soul" you might say. That is why the preparatory stages are so important—recognizing the presence of God around me and in my everyday life, and desiring to be free to respond. The Word of God will be a light for my steps, if I let it.

The Presence of God
I pause for a moment, aware that God is here.
I think of how everything around me,
the air I breathe, my whole body,
is tingling with the presence of God.

Freedom
I will ask God's help,
to be free from my own preoccupations,
to be open to God in this time of prayer,
to come to love and serve him more.

Consciousness
How am I really feeling? Light-hearted? Heavy-hearted?
I may be very much at peace, happy to be here.
Equally, I may be frustrated, worried or angry.
I acknowledge how I really am. It is the real me that the
Lord loves.

The Word
I read the Word of God slowly, a few times over, and I listen
to what God is saying to me. (Please turn to your scripture on
the following pages. Inspiration points are there should you
need them. When you are ready, return here to continue.)

Conversation
Remembering that I am still in God's presence,
I imagine Jesus himself standing or sitting beside me,
and say whatever is on my mind, whatever is in my heart,
speaking as one friend to another.

Conclusion
Glory be to the Father, and to the Son, and to the Holy Spirit,
As it was in the beginning, is now and ever shall be,
World without end. Amen

Sunday 6th February, Fifth Sunday of the Year
Matthew 5:13-16

Jesus said to the crowds, "You are the salt of the earth; but if salt has lost its taste, how can its saltiness be restored? It is no longer good for anything, but is thrown out and trampled under foot. You are the light of the world. A city built on a hill cannot be hid. No one after lighting a lamp puts it under the bushel basket, but on the lampstand, and it gives light to all in the house. In the same way, let your light shine before others, so that they may see your good works and give glory to your Father in heaven."

- If we live according to the teachings of Jesus we will manifest the goodness of God.
- How do the words "You are the light of the world" make me feel? Do they put pressure on me? Or, do I trust God and rejoice?

Monday 7th February
Mark 6:53-56

When they had crossed over, they came to land at Gennesaret and moored the boat. When they got out of the boat, people at once recognized him, and rushed about that whole region and began to bring the sick on mats to wherever they heard he was. And wherever he went, into villages or cities or farms, they laid the sick in the market-places, and begged him that they might touch even the fringe of his cloak; and all who touched it were healed.

- Look at the scene in the little town of Gennesaret when the boat pulls up at the shore. What is the reaction as soon as the word hits the street that Jesus has come?
- What does this great outpouring of human need and vulnerability and faith spark in me? Am I frightened? Am I sceptical? Am I drawn to trust?

Tuesday 8th February   **Psalm 8:1-5**

O LORD, our Sovereign, how majestic is your name in all the earth! You have set your glory above the heavens. Out of the mouths of babes and infants you have founded a bulwark because of your foes, to silence the enemy and the avenger. When I look at your heavens, the work of your fingers, the moon and the stars that you have established; what are human beings that you are mindful of them, mortals that you care for them? Yet you have made them a little lower than God, and crowned them with glory and honor.

- Can I allow the words of the psalm to settle me down and help me look with wonder at creation and God's plan for it?
- Where do I fit into the plan? What do I want to say to God about it?

Wednesday 9th February, Ash Wednesday   **Joel 2:12-14**

Y et even now, says the Lord, return to me with all your heart, with fasting, with weeping, and with mourning; rend your hearts and not your clothing. Return to the Lord, your God, for he is gracious and merciful, slow to anger, and abounding in steadfast love, and relents from punishing. Who knows whether he will not turn and relent, and leave a blessing behind him, a grain offering and a drink offering for the Lord, your God?

- In churches all over the world today, people will receive ashes and be told, "Repent and believe the good news." That form of words might sound a bit blunt, a bit harsh today, but it is just a call to respond to this invitation from God: "Return to me with all your heart."
- "Rend your hearts and not your clothing." Lent is not about outward shows, or making myself suffer, but about renewing my relationship with God, opening myself to God's grace

february 2005

which, if I let it work in me, can do infinitely more than I can think or imagine.

Thursday 10th February   Deuteronomy 30:15-16, 19-20

See, I have set before you today life and prosperity, death and adversity. If you obey the commandments of the Lord your God that I am commanding you today, by loving the Lord your God, walking in his ways, and observing his commandments, decrees, and ordinances, then you shall live and become numerous, and the Lord your God will bless you in the land that you are entering to possess ... Choose life, so that you and your descendants may live, loving the Lord your God, obeying him, and holding fast to him; for that means life to you and length of days, so that you may live in the land that the Lord swore to give to your ancestors, to Abraham, to Isaac, and to Jacob. [P, ln 8]

- God offers life and happiness to humankind as a whole, and to me personally. And we can choose—and "I" can choose—whether to accept it or reject it.
- Can I read these words and listen to God making this offer, this promise, to "me"? How do I want to respond?
- What choices have I made today? What choices will I be making tomorrow? What would it mean for "me" to "choose life" in those situations?

Friday 11th February   Isaiah 58:5-9

Is such the fast that I choose, a day to humble oneself? Is it to bow down the head like a bulrush, and to lie in sackcloth and ashes? Will you call this a fast, a day acceptable to the Lord? Is not this the fast that I choose: to loose the bonds of injustice, to undo the thongs of the yoke, to let the oppressed go free, and to break every yoke? Is it not to share your bread with the hungry, and bring the homeless poor into your house; when you see the naked, to cover them, and not to hide yourself from your own kin? Then your light shall break forth like the dawn, and your healing shall spring up quickly; your vindicator shall go before you, the glory of the Lord shall be your rear guard. Then you shall call, and the Lord will answer; you shall cry for help, and he will say, Here I am.

- My relationship with God will be real and living not when I make a show of punishing myself, but when I respond to the needs of the people around me.
- Loosing the bonds of injustice, undoing the thongs of the yoke and letting the oppressed go free may sound romantic and ambitious, but Christianity is quite a romantic and ambitious faith—about God giving his own Son to transform the world through love.
- I am part of that ambitious mission. I am not taking on the needs and injustices of the world on my own.
- What are the needs around me? What are the wrongs that need to be confronted? What can I do about them?

Saturday 12th February   Luke 5:27-32

After this he went out and saw a tax collector named Levi, sitting at the tax booth; and he said to him, "Follow me." And he got up, left everything, and followed him. Then Levi gave a great banquet for him in his house; and there was a large crowd of tax collectors and others sitting at the table with them. The Pharisees and their scribes were complaining to his disciples, saying, "Why do you eat and drink with tax collectors and sinners?" Jesus answered, "Those who are well have no need of a physician, but those who are sick; I have come to call not the righteous but sinners to repentance."

- Jewish society at this time looked on tax-collectors as the lowest of the low. "Respectable" people would not associate with them, let alone eat with them.
- But Jesus has no regard for respectability. And even if a person has really done wrong—many tax collectors extorted money and were corrupt—he saw this as all the more reason to reach out to them.
- Who are the people or groups shunned by "respectable" people in my society? What can I do to reach out to them?
- Do I feel sinful, unworthy, not respectable? Have I ignored God for years, and now feel ashamed to come back? Then I am exactly who Jesus is looking for, waiting for, inviting into a new, living relationship with him.

Sacred Space

february 13–19

Something to think and pray about each day this week:

Lent
It's our annual Christian call to get back out onto the training fields. All over the world people are—metaphorically speaking of course—doing some light stretches before settling down to six or seven weeks of extra effort.

When the 46 days between Ash Wednesday and Easter Sunday are over, how will I know if I have had a "good" Lent? What would make it a "success"? If I keep the resolution to pray faithfully every day, that would be good. If I choose to give up something that I like as a sacrifice and don't slip up even once, that would be very good. But would it necessarily be a "successful" Lent?

Lent will be a success if, by the end of it, I recognise a little more deeply that I am utterly dependent on God. That realisation can be born out of my "failures" just as much as my "successes." *Sacred Space* invites me daily to depend entirely on the care of a loving Father.

The Presence of God

For a few moments, I think of God's veiled presence in things:
in the elements, giving them existence;
in plants, giving them life; in animals, giving them sensation;
and finally, in me, giving me all this and more,
making me a temple, a dwelling-place of the Spirit.

Freedom

God is not foreign to my freedom.
Instead the Spirit breathes life into my most intimate desires,
gently nudging me towards all that is good.
I ask for the grace to let myself be enfolded by the Spirit.

Consciousness

Knowing that God loves me unconditionally,
I can afford to be honest about how I am.
How has the last day been, and how do I feel now?
I share my feelings openly with the Lord.

The Word

I take my time to read the Word of God, slowly, a few
times, allowing myself to dwell on anything that strikes
me. (Please turn to your scripture on the following pages.
Inspiration points are there should you need them. When
you are ready, return here to continue.)

Conversation

How has God's Word moved me? Has it left me cold?
Has it consoled me or moved me to act in a new way?
I imagine Jesus standing or sitting beside me,
I turn and share my feelings with him.

Conclusion

Glory be to the Father, and to the Son, and to the Holy Spirit,
As it was in the beginning, is now and ever shall be,
World without end. Amen

Sunday 13th February, First Sunday of Lent

Matthew 4:1-11

Then Jesus was led up by the Spirit into the wilderness to be tempted by the devil. He fasted forty days and forty nights, and afterwards he was famished. The tempter came and said to him, "If you are the Son of God, command these stones to become loaves of bread." But he answered, "It is written, 'One does not live by bread alone, but by every word that comes from the mouth of God.'" Then the devil took him to the holy city and placed him on the pinnacle of the temple, saying to him, "If you are the Son of God, throw yourself down; for it is written, 'He will command his angels concerning you,' and 'On their hands they will bear you up, so that you will not dash your foot against a stone.'" Jesus said to him, "Again it is written, 'Do not put the Lord your God to the test.'" Again, the devil took him to a very high mountain and showed him all the kingdoms of the world and their splendor; and he said to him, "All these I will give you, if you will fall down and worship me." Jesus said to him, "Away with you, Satan! for it is written, 'Worship the Lord your God, and serve only him.'" Then the devil left him, and suddenly angels came and waited on him.

- Does it help me to think of Jesus weak from hunger and vulnerable to temptation?
- Jesus was being invited to a vainglorious abuse of his divine nature.
- What about me? Do I experience temptation to vanity and to abuse my position in life?

Monday 14th February, Sts Cyril and Methodius
Luke 10:1-9

After this the Lord appointed seventy others and sent them on ahead of him in pairs to every town and place where he himself intended to go. He said to them, "The harvest is plentiful, but the laborers are few; therefore ask the Lord of the harvest to send out laborers into his harvest. Go on your way. See, I am sending you out like lambs into the midst of wolves. Carry no purse, no bag, no sandals; and greet no one on the road. Whatever house you enter, first say, 'Peace to this house!' And if anyone is there who shares in peace, your peace will rest on that person; but if not, it will return to you. Remain in the same house, eating and drinking whatever they provide, for the laborer deserves to be paid. Do not move about from house to house. Whenever you enter a town and its people welcome you, eat what is set before you; cure the sick who are there, and say to them, 'The kingdom of God has come near to you.'

- Can I imagine myself being sent on ahead by Jesus as one of a pair? The instructions before setting out suggest a good deal of insecurity ahead and a big need for trust.
- He wants us to announce two messages especially: "Peace to this house" and "The Kingdom of God has come near to you".
- Do I feel prepared to proclaim those two realities? What do I need to say to Jesus about this mission?

Tuesday 15th February
Isaiah 55:10-12

For as the rain and the snow come down from heaven, and do not return there until they have watered the earth, making it bring forth and sprout, giving seed to the sower and bread to the eater, so shall my word be that goes out from my mouth; it shall not return to me empty, but it shall

92

accomplish that which I purpose, and succeed in the thing
for which I sent it. For you shall go out in joy, and be led
back in peace; the mountains and the hills before you shall
burst into song, and all the trees of the field shall clap their
hands.

- Isaiah has no doubt about the strength of purpose behind
  everything that God does, and God's confidence that this
  purpose will be fulfilled.
- What purpose does God have for me? What does God want
  me to accomplish? Can I talk to the Lord about this?
- Transforming the world through love may sound an ambitious
  mission to be a part of. Am I daunted by it? Can I ask the
  Lord for the grace of confidence and hope, for the kind of joy
  that Isaiah describes in this passage?

Wednesday 16th February
Psalm 50(51):1-3, 10-11, 16-17

Have mercy on me, O God, according to your steadfast
love; according to your abundant mercy blot out my
transgressions. Wash me thoroughly from my iniquity, and
cleanse me from my sin. For I know my transgressions, and
my sin is ever before me. Create in me a clean heart, O God,
and put a new and right spirit within me. Do not cast me
away from your presence, and do not take your holy spirit
from me. For you have no delight in sacrifice; if I were to
give a burnt offering, you would not be pleased. The sacrifice acceptable to God is a contrite spirit; a humbled and
contrite heart, O God, you will not spurn.

- Sin is a reality in the life of every one of us, but so is God's
  mercy and forgiveness.
- Sin is not a matter of committing one of a list of proscribed
  acts, but of turning away from God when I make a decision.

If I am honest with myself, I know when I am doing this.

- Is there some area of my life where this is going on, where I am keeping God out, because doing the right thing might be inconvenient?
- The Good News is this: all I have to do is turn back. If I really want it, I can have a clean slate right now. God is just waiting to offer me this fresh start.

Thursday 17th February   Matthew 7:7-11

Jesus said to the crowds, "Ask, and it will be given you; search, and you will find; knock, and the door will be opened for you. For everyone who asks receives, and everyone who searches finds, and for everyone who knocks, the door will be opened. Is there anyone among you who, if your child asks for bread, will give a stone? Or if the child asks for a fish, will give a snake? If you then, who are evil, know how to give good gifts to your children, how much more will your Father in heaven give good things to those who ask him!

- "Desire" is very important in my relationship with God— knowing what I really want, and asking for it.
- Talking through my desires with God can help me to discern what I really want, to distinguish the shallow, superficial wants from the things that will give me deep and lasting satisfaction.
- What do I most deeply desire in my life at the moment? Can I ask the Lord for this?

Friday 18th February Matthew 5:20-26

Jesus said to his disciples, "For I tell you, unless your right-eousness exceeds that of the scribes and Pharisees, you will never enter the kingdom of heaven. "You have heard that it was said to those of ancient times, 'You shall not murder'; and 'whoever murders shall be liable to judgment.' But I say to you that if you are angry with a brother or sister, you will be liable to judgment; and if you insult a brother or sister, you will be liable to the council; and if you say, 'You fool,' you will be liable to the hell of fire. So when you are offering your gift at the altar, if you remember that your brother or sister has something against you, leave your gift there before the altar and go; first be reconciled to your brother or sister, and then come and offer your gift. Come to terms quickly with your accuser while you are on the way to court with him, or your accuser may hand you over to the judge, and the judge to the guard, and you will be thrown into prison. Truly I tell you, you will never get out until you have paid the last penny."

- Jesus' instruction that we should literally break off our act of worship to go and make up with a friend suggests that our relationships are of immense importance to God.
- With whom do I need to be reconciled? Do I believe that our reconciliation is really important to God? Can I let this be an encouragement to action?
- If I can't recognise any great crises in my relationships with others, what is all this saying to me?

Saturday 19th February   Matthew 5:43-48

Jesus said to the disciples, "You have heard that it was said, 'You shall love your neighbour and hate your enemy.' But I say to you, Love your enemies and pray for those who persecute you, so that you may be children of your Father in heaven; for he makes his sun rise on the evil and on the good, and sends rain on the righteous and on the unrighteous. For if you love those who love you, what reward do you have? Do not even the tax collectors do the same? And if you greet only your brothers and sisters, what more are you doing than others? Do not even the Gentiles do the same? Be perfect, therefore, as your heavenly Father is perfect."

- "Be perfect" does sound a bit much to ask. Who could live up to a standard like that?
- But "keeping my head down" and "doing no harm" is not enough for anyone who is a follower of Jesus. More is asked of us than that.
- This "perfection" is not something I achieve for myself, in isolation. All the examples Jesus gives here are about showing love to others, to people I don't know, to people who do not show love to me.
- Am I satisfied with mediocrity? Is my aim just to fit in with the people around me, to behave as my friends, neighbors and colleagues behave? Or can I hear God's call to be fully alive, to fulfil my potential, to be the best I can be?

february 20–26

Something to think and pray about each day this week:

Turning back

"Then he came to his senses." This deceptively simple statement about the Prodigal Son poses a profound challenge to us all. None of us can claim to be without sin. "We all fall short of the glory of God." Lent can be that moment in which we "come to our senses," face facts about ourselves and make the appropriate adjustments.

After a brief romantic affair which threatened to destroy his marriage and alienate his family and friends, "John" "came to his senses." Before matters got worse, he had the courage to face his fault, admit his sin and turn back. He was fortunate to receive his wife's understanding, love and forgiveness.

During Lent we turn back to God and entrust ourselves once again to his immense mercy. We allow the Father to embrace us in our sinfulness and sorrow. In being forgiven much we discover the depths of God's love.

The Presence of God
I pause for a moment
and think of the love and the grace that God showers on me,
creating me in his image and likeness, making me his temple.

Freedom
Everything has the potential to draw forth from me a fuller love
and life.
Yet my desires are often fixed, caught, on illusions of fulfillment.
I ask that God, through my freedom, may orchestrate
my desires in a vibrant loving melody rich in harmony.

Consciousness
In the presence of my loving Creator,
I look honestly at my feelings over the last day,
the highs, the lows and the level ground.
Can I see where the Lord has been present?

The Word
God speaks to each one of us individually. I need to listen
to what he is saying to me. (Please turn to your scripture on
the following pages. Inspiration points are there should you
need them. When you are ready, return here to continue.)

Conversation
What feelings are rising in me
as I pray and reflect on God's Word?
I imagine Jesus himself sitting or standing beside me,
and open my heart to him.

Conclusion
Glory be to the Father, and to the Son, and to the Holy Spirit,
As it was in the beginning, is now and ever shall be,
World without end. Amen

Sunday 20th February, Second Sunday of Lent
Matthew 17:1-9

Six days later, Jesus took with him Peter and James and his brother John and led them up a high mountain, by themselves. And he was transfigured before them, and his face shone like the sun, and his clothes became dazzling white. Suddenly there appeared to them Moses and Elijah, talking with him. Then Peter said to Jesus, "Lord, it is good for us to be here; if you wish, I will make three dwellings here, one for you, one for Moses, and one for Elijah." While he was still speaking, suddenly a bright cloud overshadowed them, and from the cloud a voice said, "This is my Son, the Beloved; with him I am well pleased; listen to him!" When the disciples heard this, they fell to the ground and were overcome by fear. But Jesus came and touched them, saying, "Get up and do not be afraid." And when they looked up, they saw no one except Jesus himself alone. As they were coming down the mountain, Jesus ordered them, "Tell no one about the vision until after the Son of Man has been raised from the dead."

- Can I imagine the scene? Three fishermen disciples and their master resting in the hills.
- Suddenly, the amazing truth beneath the surface bursts out.
- What happens?
- What does it say to me?

Monday 21st February
Luke 6:36-38

Jesus said to the disciples, "Be merciful, just as your Father is merciful. "Do not judge, and you will not be judged; do not condemn, and you will not be condemned. Forgive, and you will be forgiven; give, and it will be given to you. A good measure, pressed down, shaken together, running over, will be put into your lap; for the measure you give will be the measure you get back."

- Jesus is talking about mercy, judgement and condemnation, forgiveness and giving.
- What is my experience of these realities?
- What is he trying to teach me?

Tuesday 22nd February, Chair of St Peter
Matthew 16:13-19

Now when Jesus came into the district of Caesarea Philippi, he asked his disciples, "Who do people say that the Son of Man is?" And they said, "Some say John the Baptist, but others Elijah, and still others Jeremiah or one of the prophets." He said to them, "But who do you say that I am?" Simon Peter answered, "You are the Messiah, the Son of the living God." And Jesus answered him, "Blessed are you, Simon son of Jonah! For flesh and blood has not revealed this to you, but my Father in heaven. And I tell you, you are Peter, and on this rock I will build my church, and the gates of Hades will not prevail against it. I will give you the keys of the kingdom of heaven, and whatever you bind on earth will be bound in heaven, and whatever you loose on earth will be loosed in heaven."

- This is the question that is always before us about Jesus: "Who do you say that I am?"
- By the grace of God Peter answered it correctly. But, the answer was not just once off. It was the beginning of a whole new life of relationship with this Son of God.
- Can I hear the question? Who is he? What differences will I allow it to make?

Wednesday 23rd February
Matthew 20:17-19

While Jesus was going up to Jerusalem, he took the twelve disciples aside by themselves, and said to them on the way, "See, we are going up to Jerusalem, and the Son of Man will be handed over to the chief priests and scribes, and they will condemn him to death; then they will hand him over to the Gentiles to be mocked and flogged and crucified; and on the third day he will be raised."

- Try imagining yourself as one of the disciples, enthusiastically following the Messiah, the Chosen One, who works miracles and will come with power to deliver God's people from their enemies.
- What does it feel like when Jesus predicts his humiliation, suffering and death?
- For his followers as well as for Jesus himself, serving God and doing the right thing can be tough. At times our only strength and support will be the knowledge that we are doing what God wants us to do.
- What kind of things would I find it difficult to do, even if I was sure that it was the right thing to do, and that God was asking it of me? Can I talk to the Lord about this?

Thursday 24th February   Jeremiah 17:5-8

Thus says the Lord: Cursed are those who trust in mere mortals and make mere flesh their strength, whose hearts turn away from the Lord. They shall be like a shrub in the desert, and shall not see when relief comes. They shall live in the parched places of the wilderness, in an uninhabited salt land. Blessed are those who trust in the Lord, whose trust is the Lord. They shall be like a tree planted by water, sending out its roots by the stream. It shall not fear when heat comes, and its leaves shall stay green; in the year of drought it is not anxious, and it does not cease to bear fruit.

- Do I know what Jeremiah is talking about here? Do I recognise that feeling of strength and "rootedness" that comes when my relationship with God is alive and constant?

- Have I ever had that "wilderness" feeling when, without that relationship, I am blown about like a paper bag in the wind, feeling good if things go well, feeling bad if things go badly, at the mercy of each day's events?
- If I want that rootedness back, if I want my relationship with God to be stronger, deeper and more alive, I can ask for it, and I will get it. Not wanting it is the only thing that can stop me.

Friday 25th February   Matthew 21:42-46

Jesus said to the chief priests and the elders, "Have you never read in the scriptures: 'The stone that the builders rejected has become the cornerstone; this was the Lord's doing, and it is amazing in our eyes'? Therefore I tell you, the kingdom of God will be taken away from you and given to a people that produces the fruits of the kingdom. The one who falls on this stone will be broken to pieces; and it will crush anyone on whom it falls." When the chief priests and the Pharisees heard his parables, they realized that he was speaking about them. They wanted to arrest him, but they feared the crowds, because they regarded him as a prophet.

- "The stone that the builders rejected … " encapsulates the revolutionary nature of the Christian faith. The people considered worthless by "mainstream, respectable" society, are the ones that God has chosen.
- Do I join in with that mainstream in rejecting and condemning those who don't fit into it?
- Jesus does not tell us that the kingdom will be given to those who profess to believe in all the right things. He says it will be given to those who produce the fruits of the kingdom. What do I think the fruits of the kingdom are? And what am I doing to produce them?

Saturday 26th February   Luke 15:20-24

But while he was still far off, his father saw him and was filled with compassion; he ran and put his arms around him and kissed him. Then the son said to him, 'Father, I have sinned against heaven and before you; I am no longer worthy to be called your son.' But the father said to his slaves, 'Quickly, bring out a robe—the best one—and put it on him; put a ring on his finger and sandals on his feet. And get the fatted calf and kill it, and let us eat and celebrate; for this son of mine was dead and is alive again; he was lost and is found!' And they began to celebrate.

- The father must have been searching the horizon to see his son coming "a long way off."
- Can I let this speak to me of God's patient waiting for me?
- When I think of God longing for my friendship what arises in me?

Sacred Space

february 27 – march 5

Something to think and pray about each day this week:

A time to take stock

St. Paul tells us that "the body is for the Lord." And so it is—destined to be transfigured like Christ's. But the body is also subject to sin, suffering and death. Illness or bereavement brings home to us in stark fashion the misery of our human condition while at the same time heightening our nostalgia for the destiny intended for us, that is, eternal life.

Lent is a time to take stock of our true situation, to remember that we are creatures—not gods—and so, utterly dependent on God's gratuitous love and mercy. This should not frighten or dismay us but rather fill us with gratitude for the miracle of salvation which God has wrought in our lives. "Come, let us bow and do reverence; kneel before Yahweh who made us!" (Psalm 95)

The Presence of God
I reflect for a moment on God's presence around me and in me.
Creator of the universe, the sun and the moon, the earth,
every molecule, every atom, everything that is:
God is in every beat of my heart. God is with me, now.

Freedom
A thick and shapeless tree-trunk would never believe
that it could become a statue, admired as a miracle of sculpture,
and would never submit itself to the chisel of the sculptor,
who sees by her genius what she can make of it. (St Ignatius)
I ask for the grace to let myself be shaped by my loving Creator.

Consciousness
Knowing that God loves me unconditionally,
I look honestly over the last day, its events and my feelings.
Do I have something to be grateful for? Then I give thanks.
Is there something I am sorry for? Then I ask forgiveness.

The Word
I read the Word of God slowly, a few times over, and I listen
to what God is saying to me. (Please turn to your scripture on
the following pages. Inspiration points are there should you
need them. When you are ready, return here to continue.)

Conversation
What is stirring in me as I pray?
Am I consoled, troubled, left cold?
I imagine Jesus himself standing or sitting at my side,
and share my feelings with him.

Conclusion
Glory be to the Father, and to the Son, and to the Holy Spirit,
As it was in the beginning, is now and ever shall be,
World without end. Amen

Sunday 27th February, Third Sunday of Lent
John 4:10-14

Jesus said to the Samaritan woman, "If you knew the gift of God, and who it is that is saying to you, 'Give me a drink,' you would have asked him, and he would have given you living water." The woman said to him, "Sir, you have no bucket, and the well is deep. Where do you get that living water? Are you greater than our ancestor Jacob, who gave us the well, and with his sons and his flocks drank from it?" Jesus said to her, "Everyone who drinks of this water will be thirsty again, but those who drink of the water that I will give them will never be thirsty. The water that I will give will become in them a spring of water gushing up to eternal life."

- Initially the Samaritan woman was far from open to receive the "living water" that Jesus offers.
- What is this "living water"?
- Am I open to receive it?

Monday 28th February Psalm 41(42):2-3 and 42(43):3-4

Like the deer that yearns for running streams
so my soul is yearning for you, my God.
My soul is thirsting for God, the God of my life;
When can I enter and see the face of God?
O send forth your light and your truth; let these be my guide.
Let them bring me to your holy mountain, to the place where you dwell.
And I will come to the altar of God, the God of my joy.
My redeemer, I will thank you on the harp, O God, my God.

- Do I recognise this feeling of dryness, of yearning and thirsting for God?
- Can I speak the words of this psalm, pondering on them, and meaning them?

- God is waiting to quench my thirst. But I cannot drink with my mouth closed. I have to open up to receive the refreshing grace that God is offering me.

Tuesday 1st March   Daniel 3:38-41

We now have no leader, no prophet, no Prince, no burnt offering, no sacrifice, no oblation, no incense, no place where we can make offerings to you and win your favour. But may the contrite soul, the humbled spirit, be as acceptable to you as burnt offerings of rams and bullocks, as thousands of fat lambs: such let our sacrifice be to you today, and may it please you that we follow you wholeheartedly, since those who trust in you will not be shamed. And now we put our whole heart into following you, into fearing you and seeking your face once more.

- Azariah makes this prayer when all seems lost, when he and his companions are facing death for refusing to worship false Gods. What is my prayer like when I hit rock-bottom? Has it happened recently?
- Sometimes I may feel I haven't got much to offer to God. I am not a big shot, not a success. Why would God be interested in me and my failings?
- But God, who knows me intimately, with all my strengths and weaknesses, is still more interested in me than in all the riches and lavish offerings other people might have to make.
- What would I do differently if I were "putting my whole heart" into following the Lord, and into seeking God's face?

Wednesday 2nd March   Deuteronomy 4:5-9

See, just as the Lord my God has charged me, I now teach you statutes and ordinances for you to observe in the land that you are about to enter and occupy. You must observe

them diligently, for this will show your wisdom and discern-
ment to the peoples, who, when they hear all these statutes,
will say, "Surely this great nation is a wise and discerning
people!" For what other great nation has a god so near to it
as the Lord our God is whenever we call? And what other
great nation has statutes and ordinances as just as this entire
law that I am setting before you today? But take care and
watch yourselves closely, so as neither to forget the things
that your eyes have seen nor to let them slip from your mind
all the days of your life; make them known to your children
and your children's children.

- All this "statutes and ordinances" language can sound legalistic
  and off-putting to us, but it is an expression of the close
  concern God has for the well-being of each one of us.
- Who else has a god so near to them as the Lord our God is
  whenever I call?
- It is easy to "forget the things that your eyes have seen" and
  "let them slip from your mind." What do I want to keep in
  mind today? Can I ask the Lord to help me?
- A good measure of whether I really believe something is
  whether I would teach it to my children, whose safety and
  well-being is paramount to me. What guidelines for life would
  I teach them? What guidelines do I teach them?

Thursday 3rd March   Jeremiah 7:23-28

But this command I gave them, "Obey my voice, and I
will be your God, and you shall be my people; and walk
only in the way that I command you, so that it may be well
with you." Yet they did not obey or incline their ear, but, in
the stubbornness of their evil will, they walked in their own
counsels, and looked backward rather than forward. From
the day that your ancestors came out of the land of Egypt

until this day, I have persistently sent all my servants the prophets to them, day after day; yet they did not listen to me, or pay attention, but they stiffened their necks. They did worse than their ancestors did. So you shall speak all these words to them, but they will not listen to you. You shall call to them, but they will not answer you. You shall say to them: This is the nation that did not obey the voice of the Lord their God, and did not accept discipline; truth has perished; it is cut off from their lips.

- At first glance, these words may sound harsh and "judgemental." A whole people seems to be condemned for not following the rules.
- But what is the reason behind God's "command ... so that it may be well with you"? God does not make arbitrary rules for me, but guides me towards what is good for me.
- I am free to reject that guidance, to stiffen my neck, walk in my own counsel, look backward rather than forward. I always have that choice. How am I going to use that freedom?
- What might the Lord be saying to me today that I am in danger of ignoring?

Friday 4th March   Hosea 14:2, 4-7

Take words with you and return to the Lord; say to him, "Take away all guilt; accept that which is good, and we will offer the fruit of our lips ... I will heal their disloyalty; I will love them freely, for my anger has turned from them. I will be like the dew to Israel; he shall blossom like the lily, he shall strike root like the forests of Lebanon. His shoots shall spread out; his beauty shall be like the olive tree, and his fragrance like that of Lebanon. They shall again live beneath my shadow, they shall flourish as a garden; they shall blossom like the vine, their fragrance shall be like the wine of Lebanon.

- "Take away all guilt." Is there some burden of guilt that I am carrying, that I want to be taken away?
- Can I talk to the Lord about this? Is there someone else to whom I need to talk, to apologise, to ask forgiveness?
- Can I listen to the Lord speaking this promise to "me"? I will love you freely; you shall blossom like the lily; you shall flourish as a garden …

Saturday 5th March   Luke 18:9-14

He also told this parable to some who trusted in themselves that they were righteous and regarded others with contempt: "Two men went up to the temple to pray, one a Pharisee and the other a tax collector. The Pharisee, standing by himself, was praying thus, 'God, I thank you that I am not like other people: thieves, rogues, adulterers, or even like this tax collector. I fast twice a week; I give a tenth of all my income.' But the tax collector, standing far off, would not even look up to heaven, but was beating his breast and saying, 'God, be merciful to me, a sinner!' I tell you, this man went down to his home justified rather than the other; for all who exalt themselves will be humbled, but all who humble themselves will be exalted."

- There is probably both a Pharisee and a Tax Collector right in my heart: at times arrogant, at times weak and uncertain.
- Do I have difficulty asking God for mercy on my sinfulness?
- Jesus says that the weak and vulnerable person who is honest about it is the one who is truly free.

Sacred Space

march 6–12

Something to think and pray about each day this week:

The Christian struggle

Can you imagine sailing against a head wind on a stormy sea? Tension is high. You've got to be alert, concentrated, steadfast and energetic in setting yourself against the ongoing challenge. It's tough but it's also exhilarating, exciting and deeply satisfying to know you're on course despite the elements' efforts to upturn you!

Lent invites us to re-engage with the Christian struggle, to face the enemy within (our tendency to sin) and without (elements of our culture that are un-loving, un-Christian) and boldly fix our eyes on the goal, the prize of true freedom. The struggle can be tough and demanding, but it brings with it a wonderful sense of wellbeing and fulfilment. God confirms our efforts and encourages us along the way—his Way, the way of truth.

Let us be attentive to the voice of our Captain this Lent. Let us listen to his Word, his advice, his instruction. It will surely bring wisdom, courage, consolation and great joy into our lives.

The Presence of God

In the silence of my innermost being,
in the fragments of my yearned-for wholeness,
can I hear the whispers of God's presence?
Can I remember when I felt God's nearness?
When we walked together and I let myself be embraced by
God's love.

Freedom

There are very few people
who realize what God would make of them
if they abandoned themselves into his hands,
and let themselves be formed by his grace. (St Ignatius)
I ask for the grace to trust myself totally to God's love.

Consciousness

How do I find myself today?
Where am I with God? With others?
Do I have something to be grateful for? Then I give thanks.
Is there something I am sorry for? Then I ask forgiveness.

The Word

I take my time to read the Word of God, slowly, a few times,
allowing myself to dwell on anything that strikes me. (Please
turn to your scripture on the following pages. Inspiration
points are there should you need them. When you are ready,
return here to continue.)

Conversation

Do I notice myself reacting as I pray with the Word of God?
Do I feel challenged, comforted, angry?
Imagining Jesus sitting or standing by me,
I speak out my feelings, as one trusted friend to another.

Conclusion

Glory be to the Father, and to the Son, and to the Holy Spirit,
As it was in the beginning, is now and ever shall be,
World without end. Amen

Sunday 6th March, Fourth Sunday of Lent
John 9:1,6-9,13-17

As Jesus walked along, he saw a man blind from birth. He spat on the ground and made mud with the saliva and spread the mud on the man's eyes, saying to him, "Go, wash in the pool of Siloam" (which means Sent). Then he went and washed and came back able to see. The neighbors and those who had seen him before as a beggar began to ask, "Is this not the man who used to sit and beg?" Some were saying, "It is he." Others were saying, "No, but it is someone like him." He kept saying, "I am the man." They brought to the Pharisees the man who had formerly been blind. Now it was a sabbath day when Jesus made the mud and opened his eyes. Then the Pharisees also began to ask him how he had received his sight. He said to them, "He put mud on my eyes. Then I washed, and now I see." Some of the Pharisees said, "This man is not from God, for he does not observe the sabbath." But others said, "How can a man who is a sinner perform such signs?" And they were divided. So they said again to the blind man, "What do you say about him? It was your eyes he opened." He said, "He is a prophet."

- Can I imagine this scene? Where was the man who was blind from birth and what was going on for him when Jesus arrived?
- What happened?
- What was the gift of sight like for someone who had never seen before?
- Is there anything I would like to say to Jesus?

Monday 7th March
John 9:1-3,6,7

As he walked along, he saw a man blind from birth. His disciples asked him, "Rabbi, who sinned, this man or his parents, that he was born blind?" Jesus answered,

"Neither this man nor his parents sinned; he was born blind so that God's works might be revealed in him … When he had said this, he spat on the ground and made mud with the saliva and spread the mud on the man's eyes, saying to him, "Go, wash in the pool of Siloam" (which means Sent). Then he went and washed and came back able to see.

- Picture yourself in the scene: See a man blind from birth, a travelling rabbi and his followers passing by, and bystanders full of prejudices. Where do I fit in?
- Look at the details of this very earthy encounter between Jesus and the blind man.
- Imagine how the various parties felt afterwards.

Tuesday 8th March   John 5:1-8

After this there was a festival of the Jews, and Jesus went up to Jerusalem. Now in Jerusalem by the Sheep Gate there is a pool, called in Hebrew Beth-zatha, which has five porticoes. In these lay many invalids—blind, lame, and paralyzed. One man was there who had been ill for thirty-eight years. When Jesus saw him lying there and knew that he had been there a long time, he said to him, "Do you want to be made well?" The sick man answered him, "Sir, I have no one to put me into the pool when the water is stirred up; and while I am making my way, someone else steps down ahead of me." Jesus said to him, "Stand up, take your mat and walk."

- I am asked here to consider the lives of many broken and wounded people, including one who was waiting, alone and unaided for 38 years.
- When asked "Do you want to be made well?", the paralysed man can't answer the question. Can I?
- The paralysed man had no one to put him into the pool. That evoked Jesus' compassion and action. Does it evoke mine?

Wednesday 9th March   John 5:24-25

Jesus said to the Jews, "Very truly, I tell you, anyone who hears my word and believes him who sent me has eternal life, and does not come under judgment, but has passed from death to life. Very truly, I tell you, the hour is coming, and is now here, when the dead will hear the voice of the Son of God, and those who hear will live."

- Here Jesus is letting me in on the secret. As well as being the man who heals and teaches, he is much more.
- Am I open to the knowledge that Jesus is the way to eternal life? If I have difficulty understanding it, I can ask for insight.
- With Jesus "eternal life" begins now!

Thursday 10th March   Psalm 105(106):19-23

They made a calf at Horeb and worshiped a cast image. They exchanged the glory of God for the image of an ox that eats grass. They forgot God, their Savior, who had done great things in Egypt, wondrous works in the land of Ham, and awesome deeds by the Red Sea. Therefore he said he would destroy them—had not Moses, his chosen one, stood in the breach before him, to turn away his wrath from destroying them. Then they despised the pleasant land, having no faith in his promise.

- I'd better not judge the Chosen People too harshly. As I wander through my particular desert, what golden calves have caught my eye?
- No point dwelling too long on Golden Calves! "They forgot the God who was their saviour."
- It is all about remembering.

Friday 11th March   **Wisdom 2:1, 12-15**

For the godless reasoned unsoundly, saying to themselves, "Short and sorrowful is our life, and there is no remedy when a life comes to its end, and no one has been known to return from Hades. Let us lie in wait for the righteous man, because he is inconvenient to us and opposes our actions; he reproaches us for sins against the law, and accuses us of sins against our training. He professes to have knowledge of God, and calls himself a child of the Lord. He became to us a reproof of our thoughts; the very sight of him is a burden to us, because his manner of life is unlike that of others, and his ways are strange."

- This is a hard picture from Wisdom of the inability of the godless to tolerate the virtuous.
- When I read it do I identify with the virtuous person or the godless?
- What does God want to teach me from this?

Saturday 12th March   **John 7:40-47**

When they heard these words, some in the crowd said, "This is really the prophet." Others said, "This is the Messiah." But some asked, "Surely the Messiah does not come from Galilee, does he? Has not the scripture said that the Messiah is descended from David and comes from Bethlehem, the village where David lived?" So there was a division in the crowd because of him. Some of them wanted to arrest him, but no one laid hands on him. Then the temple police went back to the chief priests and Pharisees, who asked them, "Why did you not arrest him?" The police answered, "Never has anyone spoken like this!" Then the Pharisees replied, "Surely you have not been deceived too, have you?

- Would the Messiah be from Anytown … ? Would the Messiah be black … Catholic … Protestant?
- Can I begin to see the face of Jesus in persons or places where I least expected it?
- Can I now begin to welcome him there? If I struggle with this, I can ask for help.

Sacred Space

march 13–19

Something to think and pray about each day this week:

Extraordinary love

"Neither do I condemn you." The utter completeness of Christ's forgiveness is hard to take in. The past is dead, snuffed out like a wick, forgotten.

St. Ignatius of Loyola speaks of "amazement" and "surging emotion" as he takes in the wonder and beauty of God's faithful love towards him, a sinner.

Let's ask for the grace to know our own sinfulness so that we may more fully appreciate Jesus' extraordinary love for us. Then we will be seized with a great desire to follow him more closely as beloved companions.

The Presence of God

I remind myself that, as I sit here now,
God is gazing on me with love and holding me in being.
I pause for a moment and think of this.

Freedom

I ask for the grace
to let go of my own concerns
and be open to what God is asking of me,
to let myself be guided and formed by my loving Creator.

Consciousness

In God's loving presence I unwind the past day,
starting from now and looking back, moment by moment.
I gather in all the goodness and light, in gratitude.
I attend to the shadows and what they say to me,
seeking healing, courage, forgiveness.

The Word

God speaks to each one of us individually. I need to listen
to what he is saying to me. (Please turn to your scripture
on the following pages. Inspiration points are there should
you need them. When you are ready, return here to
continue.)

Conversation

Remembering that I am still in God's presence,
I imagine Jesus himself standing or sitting beside me,
and say whatever is on my mind, whatever is in my heart,
speaking as one friend to another.

Conclusion

Glory be to the Father, and to the Son, and to the Holy Spirit,
As it was in the beginning, is now and ever shall be,
World without end. Amen

Sunday 13th March, Fifth Sunday of Lent
John 11:17, 20-26

When Jesus arrived at the house of Mary and Martha, he found that Lazarus had already been in the tomb four days. When Martha heard that Jesus was coming, she went and met him, while Mary stayed at home. Martha said to Jesus, "Lord, if you had been here, my brother would not have died. But even now I know that God will give you whatever you ask of him." Jesus said to her, "Your brother will rise again." Martha said to him, "I know that he will rise again in the resurrection on the last day." Jesus said to her, "I am the resurrection and the life. Those who believe in me, even though they die, will live, and everyone who lives and believes in me will never die. Do you believe this?"

- Can I resonate with the experience of Martha—who has just lost her brother—when Jesus arrives?
- Can I hear Jesus speak to me as he speaks to Martha?
- What does this promise of "life" mean to me?

Monday 14th March
John 11:25-27

Jesus said to Martha, "I am the resurrection and the life. Those who believe in me, even though they die, will live, and everyone who lives and believes in me will never die. Do you believe this?" She said to him, "Yes, Lord, I believe that you are the Messiah, the Son of God, the one coming into the world."

- Martha has just lost her brother Lazarus. Can I imagine myself in her shoes standing before Jesus?
- "I am the resurrection": mysterious words about death and life. Can I let myself be touched by them?

Tuesday 15th March — Numbers 21:4-9

From Mount Hor they set out by the way to the Red Sea, to go around the land of Edom; but the people became impatient on the way. The people spoke against God and against Moses, "Why have you brought us up out of Egypt to die in the wilderness? For there is no food and no water, and we detest this miserable food." Then the LORD sent poisonous serpents among the people, and they bit the people, so that many Israelites died. The people came to Moses and said, "We have sinned by speaking against the LORD and against you; pray to the LORD to take away the serpents from us." So Moses prayed for the people. And the LORD said to Moses, "Make a poisonous serpent, and set it on a pole; and everyone who is bitten shall look at it and live." So Moses made a serpent of bronze, and put it upon a pole; and whenever a serpent bit someone, that person would look at the serpent of bronze and live.

- I am in the caravan trudging through the desert. The thrill of the escape from Egypt has worn off and all I can see is sand.
- When I forget where I have come from and lose sight of where I am going, what thoughts and feelings rise up in me?
- How can I renew my sense of trust in God and confidence about my particular journey?

Wednesday 16th March — John 8:31-32

Then Jesus said to the Jews who had believed in him, "If you continue in my word, you are truly my disciples; and you will know the truth, and the truth will make you free."

- Can I get in touch with my longings for truth and freedom?
- Jesus guarantees them to those who make his word their "home".

Thursday 17th March, St Patrick   Luke 5:4-11

When Jesus had finished speaking to the crowds, he said to Simon, "Put out into the deep water and let down your nets for a catch." Simon answered, "Master, we have worked all night long but have caught nothing. Yet if you say so, I will let down the nets." When they had done this, they caught so many fish that their nets were beginning to break. So they signalled to their partners in the other boat to come and help them. And they came and filled both boats, so that they began to sink. But when Simon Peter saw it, he fell down at Jesus' knees, saying, "Go away from me, Lord, for I am a sinful man!" For he and all who were with him were amazed at the catch of fish that they had taken; and so also were James and John, sons of Zebedee, who were partners with Simon. Then Jesus said to Simon, "Do not be afraid; from now on you will be catching people." When they had brought their boats to shore, they left everything and followed him.

- Sometimes the standards, ideals and ambitions I find in the gospels can seem too high, too unrealistic.
- Doubts, cynicism, or just plain, practical realism can lead me to say, "What Jesus offers is an impossible dream."
- As happened with Simon, if we enter into a relationship with the Lord, with openness and trust, he will surprise us. God's grace working in us can do infinitely more than we can think or imagine.

Friday 18th March   Psalm 17(18) 1-3

I love you, O LORD, my strength. The LORD is my rock, my fortress, and my deliverer, my God, my rock in whom I take refuge, my shield, and the horn of my salvation, my stronghold. I call upon the LORD, who is worthy to be praised, so I shall be saved from my enemies.

- The author of the Psalms knew good times and bad. In my own situation can I make these words my own?

Saturday 19th March, St Joseph
Psalm 88(89): 1-4, 26-28

I will sing of your steadfast love, O Lord, forever; with my mouth I will proclaim your faithfulness to all generations. I declare that your steadfast love is established forever; your faithfulness is as firm as the heavens. You said, "I have made a covenant with my chosen one, I have sworn to my servant David: 'I will establish your descendants forever, and build your throne for all generations.'" He shall cry to me, 'You are my Father, my God, and the Rock of my salvation!' I will make him the firstborn, the highest of the kings of the earth. Forever I will keep my steadfast love for him, and my covenant with him will stand firm.

- I will not always be in the mood to say these words. At times my real feelings towards God may not be so positive (and there is no point pretending otherwise).
- But when I look back on my life, on the path I have taken up to this point, can I see where the Lord has been present, guiding me, caring for me?
- Can I relate to the images of God used here—Father, Rock of my salvation? What names and images speak to me of God?
- Do I realize how much I am treasured and precious in God's eyes? Can I listen to God speaking to "me" the words in this passage, "I have made a covenant with my chosen one … "?

march 20–26

Something to think and pray about each day this week:

Praying the Passion
As we contemplate the events of Christ's passion this week, we may find it distressing and painful to enter into those scenes of suffering and death. It may help to bear in mind the meaning that St Paul draws out of the Passion—the unconditional love that God has for us.

Our God is not a God who dominates and bullies and enforces his will, but one who, despite our failings, loves us passionately, with real, self-giving, self-sacrificing love.

Let the same mind be in you that was in Christ Jesus, who, though he was in the form of God, did not regard equality with God as something to be exploited, but emptied himself, taking the form of a slave, being born in human likeness. And being found in human form, he humbled himself and became obedient to the point of death—even death on a cross. (Philippians 2:5-8)

The Presence of God

God is with me, but more,
God is within me, giving me existence.
Let me dwell for a moment on God's life-giving presence
in my body, my mind, my heart
and in the whole of my life.

Freedom

I ask for the grace to believe
in what I could be and do
if I only allowed God, my loving Creator,
to continue to create me, guide me and shape me.

Consciousness

I exist in a web of relationships—links to nature, people, God.
I trace out these links, giving thanks for the life that flows
through them.
Some links are twisted or broken: I may feel regret, anger,
disappointment.
I pray for the gift of acceptance and forgiveness.

The Word

I read the Word of God slowly, a few times over, and I
listen to what God is saying to me. (Please turn to your
scripture on the following pages. Inspiration points are
there should you need them. When you are ready, return
here to continue.)

Conversation

How has God's Word moved me? Has it left me cold?
Has it consoled me or moved me to act in a new way?
I imagine Jesus standing or sitting beside me,
I turn and share my feelings with him.

Conclusion

Glory be to the Father, and to the Son, and to the Holy Spirit,
As it was in the beginning, is now and ever shall be,
World without end. Amen

march 2005

Sunday 20th March, Palm Sunday   Philippians 2:6-11

Let the same mind be in you that was in Christ Jesus, who, though he was in the form of God, did not regard equality with God as something to be exploited, but emptied himself, taking the form of a slave, being born in human likeness. And being found in human form, he humbled himself and became obedient to the point of death—even death on a cross. Therefore God also highly exalted him and gave him the name that is above every name, so that at the name of Jesus every knee should bend, in heaven and on earth and under the earth, and every tongue should confess that Jesus Christ is Lord, to the glory of God the Father.

- As Holy Week begins, I fix my eyes on Jesus. Simply mulling over the words of this beautiful early Christian hymn can help me appreciate the mystery of it.

Monday 21st March   John 12:1-9

Six days before the Passover Jesus came to Bethany, the home of Lazarus, whom he had raised from the dead. There they gave a dinner for him. Martha served, and Lazarus was one of those at the table with him. Mary took a pound of costly perfume made of pure nard, anointed Jesus' feet, and wiped them with her hair. The house was filled with the fragrance of the perfume. But Judas Iscariot, one of his disciples (the one who was about to betray him), said, "Why was this perfume not sold for three hundred denarii and the money given to the poor?" (He said this not because he cared about the poor, but because he was a thief; he kept the common purse and used to steal what was put into it.) Jesus said, "Leave her alone. She bought it so that she might keep it for the day of my burial. You always have the poor with you, but you do not always have me." When the great crowd of the Jews learned that he was there, they came not only because of Jesus but also to see Lazarus, whom he had raised from the dead.

- Stay with the scene.
- What tenderness moved Mary? What blindness confused Judas? How did Martha and Lazarus react?
- How do I react?

Tuesday 22nd March   **Isaiah 49:1-4**

Listen to me, O coastlands, pay attention, you peoples from far away! The LORD called me before I was born, while I was in my mother's womb he named me. He made my mouth like a sharp sword, in the shadow of his hand he hid me; he made me a polished arrow, in his quiver he hid me away. And he said to me, "You are my servant, Israel, in whom I will be glorified." But I said, "I have labored in vain, I have spent my strength for nothing and vanity; yet surely my cause is with the LORD, and my reward with my God."

- Little does Israel know, even in her darkest days, that the Lord called her by name even before she was born. The same is true of me.
- God has a plan for me, despite my weakness and failings.
- "My cause is with the Lord": Can I make these words my own?

Wednesday 23rd March   **Isaiah 50:4-7**

The Lord GOD has given me the tongue of a teacher, that I may know how to sustain the weary with a word. Morning by morning he wakens—wakens my ear to listen as those who are taught. The Lord GOD has opened my ear, and I was not rebellious, I did not turn backward. I gave my back to those who struck me, and my cheeks to those who pulled out the beard; I did not hide my face from insult and spitting. The Lord GOD helps me; therefore I have not been disgraced; therefore I have set my face like flint, and I know that I shall not be put to shame.

- The Suffering Servant knows full well the extent of the pain inflicted on him and doesn't deny it.
- Amid mockery and insult he can trust in the Lord.
- Over these next few days can I keep watch with Jesus, our Suffering Servant?

Thursday 24th March, Holy Thursday   John 13:12-16
After Jesus had washed their feet, had put on his robe, and had returned to the table, he said to them, "Do you know what I have done to you? You call me Teacher and Lord—and you are right, for that is what I am. So if I, your Lord and Teacher, have washed your feet, you also ought to wash one another's feet. For I have set you an example, that you also should do as I have done to you. Very truly, I tell you, servants are not greater than their master, nor are messengers greater than the one who sent them."

- I imagine washing the feet of twelve different people I know, including the one who is going to betray me.
- What feelings and reactions does this stir up in me?
- Can I respond to Jesus' call to follow his example today?

Friday 25th March, Good Friday   John 19:25-30
Meanwhile, standing near the cross of Jesus were his mother, and his mother's sister, Mary the wife of Clopas, and Mary Magdalene. When Jesus saw his mother and the disciple whom he loved standing beside her, he said to his mother, "Woman, here is your son." Then he said to the disciple, "Here is your mother." And from that hour the disciple took her into his own home. After this, when Jesus

knew that all was now finished, he said (in order to fulfill the scripture), "I am thirsty." A jar full of sour wine was standing there. So they put a sponge full of the wine on a branch of hyssop and held it to his mouth. When Jesus had received the wine, he said, "It is finished." Then he bowed his head and gave up his spirit.

- Just one point: I simply watch what is happening, in silence.

Saturday 26th March, Holy Saturday   John 19:38-42

After these things, Joseph of Arimathea, who was a disciple of Jesus, though a secret one because of his fear of the Jews, asked Pilate to let him take away the body of Jesus. Pilate gave him permission; so he came and removed his body. Nicodemus, who had at first come to Jesus by night, also came, bringing a mixture of myrrh and aloes, weighing about a hundred pounds. They took the body of Jesus and wrapped it with the spices in linen cloths, according to the burial custom of the Jews. Now there was a garden in the place where he was crucified, and in the garden there was a new tomb in which no one had ever been laid. And so, because it was the Jewish day of Preparation, and the tomb was nearby, they laid Jesus there.

- Today we are allowed to feel empty because the one in whom we hoped is dead.
- We watch the tomb, now sealed over, and wonder.

march 27 – april 2

Something to think and pray about each day this week:

Christ the Consoler

Reflecting on the scriptures of the Easter season, Ignatius encourages us to consider how Jesus acts towards his followers, consoling them just as one friend consoles another.

The disciples had just been through the worst experience of their lives. Their leader and their friend, in whom they had put all their hope, had been unjustly convicted and cruelly put to death. Their hopes and dreams were shattered. They were confused and afraid. The Risen Jesus comes among them and says, "Peace be with you." Their faith was not in vain. Their friend is alive. His consoling presence brings new hope to each one of them.

With us, just as with them, the Risen Christ disregards our failings, our weakness, our lack of faith. He does not accuse, he does not criticise. He gently offers consolation, encouragement and love.

The Presence of God

To be present is to arrive as one is and open up to the other. At this instant, as I arrive here, God is present waiting for me. God always arrives before me, desiring to connect with me even more than my most intimate friend.

I take a moment and greet my loving God.

Freedom

"In these days, God taught me
as a schoolteacher teaches a pupil" (St Ignatius).

I remind myself that there are things God has to teach me yet, and ask for the grace to hear them and let them change me.

Consciousness

How am I really feeling? Light-hearted? Heavy-hearted?

I may be very much at peace, happy to be here.

Equally, I may be frustrated, worried or angry.

I acknowledge how I really am. It is the real me that the Lord loves.

The Word

I take my time to read the Word of God, slowly, a few times, allowing myself to dwell on anything that strikes me. (Please turn to your scripture on the following pages. Inspiration points are there should you need them. When you are ready, return here to continue.)

Conversation

What feelings are rising in me
as I pray and reflect on God's Word?

I imagine Jesus himself sitting or standing beside me, and open my heart to him.

Conclusion

Glory be to the Father, and to the Son, and to the Holy Spirit, As it was in the beginning, is now and ever shall be, World without end. Amen

Sunday 27th March, Easter Sunday   **John 20:1-9**

Early on the first day of the week, while it was still dark, Mary Magdalene came to the tomb and saw that the stone had been removed from the tomb. So she ran and went to Simon Peter and the other disciple, the one whom Jesus loved, and said to them, "They have taken the Lord out of the tomb, and we do not know where they have laid him." Then Peter and the other disciple set out and went toward the tomb. The two were running together, but the other disciple outran Peter and reached the tomb first. He bent down to look in and saw the linen wrappings lying there, but he did not go in. Then Simon Peter came, following him, and went into the tomb. He saw the linen wrappings lying there, and the cloth that had been on Jesus' head, not lying with the linen wrappings but rolled up in a place by itself. Then the other disciple, who reached the tomb first, also went in, and he saw and believed; for as yet they did not understand the scripture, that he must rise from the dead.

- Can I imagine myself standing near to the tomb on the morning in question, before first light? I observe the comings and goings.
- How do the people look? First, the woman: Can I see her face? What does she do next? Then two men …
- What has happened here?

Monday 28th March   **Matthew 28:8-10**

So the women left the tomb quickly with fear and great joy, and ran to tell his disciples. Suddenly Jesus met them and said, "Greetings!" And they came to him, took hold of his feet, and worshiped him. Then Jesus said to them, "Do not be afraid; go and tell my brothers to go to Galilee; there they will see me."

- "Fear and great joy": It's very real.
- I may need to pinch myself as a reminder that the one who was dead is risen!
- He is saying to me "Do not be afraid" and "go and bring the good news to others".

Tuesday 29th March   John 20:11-17

As Mary wept, she bent over to look into the tomb; and she saw two angels in white, sitting where the body of Jesus had been lying, one at the head and the other at the feet. They said to her, "Woman, why are you weeping?" She said to them, "They have taken away my Lord, and I do not know where they have laid him." When she had said this, she turned around and saw Jesus standing there, but she did not know that it was Jesus. Jesus said to her, "Woman, why are you weeping? Whom are you looking for?" Supposing him to be the gardener, she said to him, "Sir, if you have carried him away, tell me where you have laid him, and I will take him away." Jesus said to her, "Mary!" She turned and said to him in Hebrew, "Rabbouni!" (which means Teacher). Jesus said to her, "Do not hold on to me, because I have not yet ascended to the Father. But go to my brothers and say to them, 'I am ascending to my Father and your Father, to my God and your God.'"

- Allow yourself to see Mary in great distress. The one she longs to see is there and she can't recognise him.
- The sound of her own name breaks through the cloud of her unknowing.
- Can I imagine Jesus calling me by my name? How does it sound?

136

Wednesday 30th March   Acts 3:1-8

One day Peter and John were going up to the temple at the hour of prayer, at three o'clock in the afternoon. And a man lame from birth was being carried in. People would lay him daily at the gate of the temple called the Beautiful Gate so that he could ask for alms from those entering the temple. When he saw Peter and John about to go into the temple, he asked them for alms. Peter looked intently at him, as did John, and said, "Look at us." And he fixed his attention on them, expecting to receive something from them. But Peter said, "I have no silver or gold, but what I have I give you; in the name of Jesus Christ of Nazareth, stand up and walk." And he took him by the right hand and raised him up; and immediately his feet and ankles were made strong. Jumping up, he stood and began to walk, and he entered the temple with them, walking and leaping and praising God.

- Jesus is alive and active here in a new way.
- We see two disciples, Peter and John, responding to a person in need. They act, with power, in Jesus' name.
- Can I see myself as part of this new reality?

Thursday 31st March   Luke 24:36-43

While they were talking about this, Jesus himself stood among them and said to them, "Peace be with you." They were startled and terrified, and thought that they were seeing a ghost. He said to them, "Why are you frightened, and why do doubts arise in your hearts? Look at my hands and my feet; see that it is I myself. Touch me and see; for a ghost does not have flesh and bones as you see that I have." And when he had said this, he showed them his hands and his feet. While in their joy they were disbelieving and still wondering, he said to them, "Have you anything here to eat?" They gave him a piece of broiled fish, and he took it and ate in their presence.

- The mood in this room is so full of fear and loss that people are tense and easily startled. Can I resonate with these people?
- Into their—our—my trauma comes Jesus, saying "Peace be with you!"
- This is a real flesh and blood, fish-eating Jesus, who has conquered the causes of our fears. Can I be present to Him?

Friday 1st April   John 21:2-8

Gathered there together were Simon Peter, Thomas called the Twin, Nathanael of Cana in Galilee, the sons of Zebedee, and two others of his disciples. Simon Peter said to them, "I am going fishing." They said to him, "We will go with you." They went out and got into the boat, but that night they caught nothing. Just after daybreak, Jesus stood on the beach; but the disciples did not know that it was Jesus. Jesus said to them, "Children, you have no fish, have you?" They answered him, "No." He said to them, "Cast the net to the right side of the boat, and you will find some." So they cast it, and now they were not able to haul it in because there were so many fish. That disciple whom Jesus loved said to Peter, "It is the Lord!" When Simon Peter heard that it was the Lord, he put on some clothes, for he was naked, and jumped into the sea. But the other disciples came in the boat, dragging the net full of fish, for they were not far from the land, only about a hundred yards off.

- Can you imagine yourself in the boat, after a fruitless night and it is still quite dark? What does it feel like?
- Jesus brings a new perspective. He asks us to try something else: "Cast your net to the right side of the boat ... " Am I

willing to be guided in a new way, even if I am not certain who is leading. (The disciples did not know for sure that it was Jesus.)

- Hear the awe in John's voice: "It is the Lord!"

Saturday 2nd April   Acts 4:18-21

So they called Peter and John and ordered them not to speak or teach at all in the name of Jesus. But Peter and John answered them, "Whether it is right in God's sight to listen to you rather than to God, you must judge; for we cannot keep from speaking about what we have seen and heard." After threatening them again, they let them go, finding no way to punish them because of the people, for all of them praised God for what had happened.

- When the love of God takes hold of people (Peter and John) they are changed: they just can't keep it to themselves.
- In these Easter days I am invited to admire the change that God's love brings about in people and to be open to it in my own life.

Sacred Space

april 3–9

Something to think and pray about each day this week:

Quiet joy
After forty days of Lent, and the anguish of the Holy Week narratives, I may find myself ready for a bit of rejoicing when it comes to Easter. It may help to imagine myself as one of the disciples, and trace my feelings through Jesus' suffering and death, my hopes and dreams dying with him, to understand what hearing the first news of the Resurrection would have been like. Right enough, there really is something to celebrate here.

But this does not mean I have to force myself to rejoice, or reproach myself if I am not feeling ecstatic for days on end after Easter. The Resurrection is more than just a one-off event, it is a sign for all humanity, God's pledge that death will not triumph over us.

The difficulties and pains of life do not stop just because it is Easter, but if I can accept this sign, and trust in God's love for me, then I can have a real sense of joy and peace. Outwardly, I am not necessarily bubbling over with joy, but deep inside me there is a reassurance and an enduring hope that is a solid foundation for my life.

The Presence of God

What is present to me is what has a hold on my becoming.
I reflect on the presence of God always there in love,
amidst the many things that have a hold on me.
I pause and pray that I may let God
affect my becoming in this precise moment.

Freedom

If God were trying to tell me something, would I know?
If God were reassuring me or challenging me, would I notice?
I ask for the grace to be free of my own preoccupations
and open to what God may be saying to me.

Consciousness

Knowing that God loves me unconditionally,
I can afford to be honest about how I am.
How has the last day been, and how do I feel now?
I share my feelings openly with the Lord.

The Word

God speaks to each one of us individually. I need to listen
to what he is saying to me. (Please turn to your scripture on
the following pages. Inspiration points are there should you
need them. When you are ready, return here to continue.)

Conversation

What is stirring in me as I pray?
Am I consoled, troubled, left cold?
I imagine Jesus himself standing or sitting at my side,
and share my feelings with him.

Conclusion

Glory be to the Father, and to the Son, and to the Holy Spirit,
As it was in the beginning, is now and ever shall be,
World without end. Amen

april 2005

Sunday 3rd April, Second Sunday of Easter
John 20:24-31

But Thomas (who was called the Twin), one of the twelve, was not with them when Jesus came. So the other disciples told him, "We have seen the Lord." But he said to them, "Unless I see the mark of the nails in his hands, and put my finger in the mark of the nails and my hand in his side, I will not believe." A week later his disciples were again in the house, and Thomas was with them. Although the doors were shut, Jesus came and stood among them and said, "Peace be with you." Then he said to Thomas, "Put your finger here and see my hands. Reach out your hand and put it in my side. Do not doubt but believe." Thomas answered him, "My Lord and my God!" Jesus said to him, "Have you believed because you have seen me? Blessed are those who have not seen and yet have come to believe."

• Can I imagine that I am Thomas and the others come and say: We have seen Jesus who died?
• What is my reaction?
• Can I move through the scene as it unfolds?
• Where does it bring me to?

Monday 4th April, Annunciation
Luke 1:26-32, 34-35, 38a

In the sixth month the angel Gabriel was sent by God to a town in Galilee called Nazareth, to a virgin whose name was Mary. And he came to her and said, "Greetings, favoured one! The Lord is with you." But she was much perplexed by his words and pondered what sort of greeting this might be. The angel said to her, "Do not be afraid, Mary, for you have found favour with God. And now, you will conceive in your womb and bear a son, and you will name him Jesus. He will be great, and will be called the Son of the Most High, and the Lord God will give to him the throne of his ancestor David. Mary said to the angel, "How can this be, since I am a virgin?" The angel said to her, "The Holy Spirit will come upon you, and the power of the Most High will overshadow you; therefore the child to be born will be holy; he will be called Son of God." Then Mary said, "Here am I, the servant of the Lord; let it be with me according to your word."

- Imagine what Mary felt as she was given this awesome news.
- Mary has questions and voices them, but she says "Yes" to God's will for her. Can I learn from her example?

Tuesday 5th April   Acts 4:32-35

Now the whole group of those who believed were of one heart and soul, and no one claimed private ownership of any possessions, but everything they owned was held in common. With great power the apostles gave their testimony to the resurrection of the Lord Jesus, and great grace was upon them all. There was not a needy person among them, for as many as owned lands or houses sold them and brought the proceeds of what was sold. They laid it at the apostles' feet, and it was distributed to each as any had need.

- The presence of the Risen Lord moves many people to try and live in a whole new way.
- Can I look at my life and give thanks for the ways (however small), in which it does give witness to the Risen Lord and be gently challenged for the ways in which it does not?

Wednesday 6th April   John 3:16-17

Jesus said to Nicodemus, "For God so loved the world that he gave his only Son, so that everyone who believes in him may not perish but may have eternal life. "Indeed, God did not send the Son into the world to condemn the world, but in order that the world might be saved through him.

- These sentences are a core statement of Christian belief. For me, here, today, do they sound uplifting, hollow, consoling, trite, or gloriously life-giving?
- I can be before the Lord as I am, without fear of condemnation.

Thursday 7th April   John 3:31-34a

John the Baptist said to his disciples, "The one who comes from above is above all; the one who is of the earth belongs to the earth and speaks about earthly things. The one who comes from heaven is above all. He testifies to what he has seen and heard, yet no one accepts his testimony. Whoever has accepted his testimony has certified this, that God is true. He whom God has sent speaks the words of God."

- I am invited to be in the presence of the one who "comes from above." Jesus shares our humanity and is close to us but he is of God.
- Perhaps I too find it hard to accept the full testimony of Jesus and the truth about him.
- Now I can simply ask to know him better.

Friday 8th April   John 6:5-11

When he looked up and saw a large crowd coming toward him, Jesus said to Philip, "Where are we to buy bread for these people to eat?" He said this to test him, for he himself knew what he was going to do. Philip answered him, "Six months' wages would not buy enough bread for each of them to get a little." One of his disciples, Andrew, Simon Peter's brother, said to him, "There is a boy here who has five barley loaves and two fish. But what are they among so many people?" Jesus said, "Make the people sit down." Now there was a great deal of grass in the place; so they sat down, about five thousand in all. Then Jesus took the loaves, and when he had given thanks, he distributed them to those who were seated; so also the fish, as much as they wanted.

- I imagine myself in the scene. Am I the little boy? Am I a frustrated Philip or one of the large crowd? Who am I?
- Five loaves and two fish seem so little as to be useless. But they have a place in a lavish plan. Can I apply this to my life?
- What is Jesus telling me about God in this miracle?

Saturday 9th April   John 6:16-21

When evening came, his disciples went down to the sea, got into a boat, and started across the sea to Capernaum. It was now dark, and Jesus had not yet come to them. The sea became rough because a strong wind was blowing. When they had rowed about three or four miles, they saw Jesus walking on the sea and coming near the boat, and they were terrified. But he said to them, "It is I; do not be afraid." Then they wanted to take him into the boat, and immediately the boat reached the land toward which they were going.

- Spend a moment recapturing the scene in the boat: there is a gale blowing, the sea is rough and above all it is dark and scary.
- The disciples are terrified at the sight of Jesus because they haven't fully understood who he is.
- The key words then and now: "It is I; do not be afraid".

april 10–16

Something to think and pray about each day this week:

I can't find words

Do I sometimes come to prayer feeling completely empty? No words, no thoughts, no feelings. Possibly I don't even have the desire to pray.

St Paul evidently had the exact same experience on occasion. The words he wrote to the Romans (8:26) have the ring of personal experience about them: "The Spirit too comes to help us in our weakness. For when we cannot choose words in order to pray properly, the Spirit himself expresses our plea in a way that could never be put into words."

When I come to pray it doesn't matter if I am "empty." What matters is that I am present. According to Paul, the Spirit will do the rest.

The Presence of God
God is with me, but more, God is within me.
Let me dwell for a moment on God's life-giving presence
in my body, in my mind, in my heart,
as I sit here, right now.

Freedom
I need to close out the noise, to rise above the noise;
The noise that interrupts, that separates,
The noise that isolates.
I need to listen to God again.

Consciousness
In the presence of my loving Creator,
I look honestly at my feelings over the last day,
the highs, the lows and the level ground.
Can I see where the Lord has been present?

The Word
I read the Word of God slowly, a few times over, and I listen
to what God is saying to me. (Please turn to your scripture
on the following pages. Inspiration points are there should you
need them. When you are ready, return here to continue.)

Conversation
Do I notice myself reacting as I pray with the Word of God?
Do I feel challenged, comforted, angry?
Imagining Jesus sitting or standing by me,
I speak out my feelings, as one trusted friend to another.

Conclusion
Glory be to the Father, and to the Son, and to the Holy Spirit,
As it was in the beginning, is now and ever shall be,
World without end. Amen

Sunday 10th April, Third Sunday of Easter
Luke 24:28-35

As they came near the village to which they were going, Jesus walked ahead as if he were going on. But the two disciples urged him strongly, saying, "Stay with us, because it is almost evening and the day is now nearly over." So he went in to stay with them. When he was at the table with them, he took bread, blessed and broke it, and gave it to them. Then their eyes were opened, and they recognized him; and he vanished from their sight. They said to each other, "Were not our hearts burning within us while he was talking to us on the road, while he was opening the scriptures to us?" That same hour they got up and returned to Jerusalem; and they found the eleven and their companions gathered together. They were saying, "The Lord has risen indeed, and he has appeared to Simon!" Then they told what had happened on the road, and how he had been made known to them in the breaking of the bread.

- The two disciples were walking away, confused, from an experience of complete loss. The Lord came to find them in the guise of a stranger.
- In my moments of loss and confusion has the Lord been there in disguise?
- Do I sometimes find myself "walking away"?
- Can I look again at those experiences? Is there something there that I have been missing?

Monday 11th April
John 6:26-29

Jesus answered them, "Very truly, I tell you, you are looking for me, not because you saw signs, but because you ate your fill of the loaves. Do not work for the food that perishes, but for the food that endures for eternal life, which the Son of Man will give you. For it is on him that God the Father has set his seal." Then they said to him, "What must we do to perform the works of God?" Jesus answered them, "This is the work of God, that you believe in him whom he has sent."

- The Lord is challenging me to go beyond what I am used to and comfortable with.
- For me what is the "food that perishes" and "the food that endures"?
- Remember, this is not something I can do on my own: "This is the work of God."

Tuesday 12th April   Acts 7:55-8:1

But filled with the Holy Spirit, he gazed into heaven and saw the glory of God and Jesus standing at the right hand of God. "Look," he said, "I see the heavens opened and the Son of Man standing at the right hand of God!" But they covered their ears, and with a loud shout all rushed together against him. Then they dragged him out of the city and began to stone him; and the witnesses laid their coats at the feet of a young man named Saul. While they were stoning Stephen, he prayed, "Lord Jesus, receive my spirit." Then he knelt down and cried out in a loud voice, "Lord, do not hold this sin against them." When he had said this, he died. And Saul approved of their killing him. That day a severe persecution began against the church in Jerusalem, and all except the apostles were scattered throughout the countryside of Judea and Samaria.

- Stephen is the first martyr. The Christians pass on the story more as a victory than a defeat.
- The victory is the power to forgive, to love even under duress.
- We are invited to marvel at the work of grace, not to be overpowered by it.

Wednesday 13th April   John 6:35-38

Jesus said to them, "I am the bread of life. Whoever comes to me will never be hungry, and whoever believes in me will never be thirsty. But I said to you that you have seen me and yet do not believe. Everything that the Father gives me will come to me, and anyone who comes to me I will never drive away; for I have come down from heaven, not to do my own will, but the will of him who sent me.

- Can I open myself to hear the invitation to the banquet of the "Bread of Life"?
- I can stumble and falter in faith, but the invitation is whole-hearted.

Thursday 14th April   Psalm 65(66):8-9, 16-17, 20

Bless our God, O peoples, let the sound of his praise be heard, who has kept us among the living, and has not let our feet slip. Come and hear, all you who fear God, and I will tell what he has done for me. I cried aloud to him, and he was extolled with my tongue. Blessed be God, because he has not rejected my prayer or removed his steadfast love from me.

- The Psalm invites me to shout out all the good that God has done for me. Can I own all the good that God has done for me?
- Does this lead me to want to give thanks?
- Or do I doubt all the good in me? Then I need to talk to God about that.
- Remember, God does not "reject my prayer".

Friday 15th April   John 6:56-59

Those who eat my flesh and drink my blood abide in me, and I in them. Just as the living Father sent me, and I live because of the Father, so whoever eats me will live because of me. This is the bread that came down from heaven, not like that which your ancestors ate, and they died. But the one who eats this bread will live forever." He said these things while he was teaching in the synagogue at Capernaum.

- We are invited to a profound communion with God. As we become more united with Christ, we become like him.
- Where am I on the communion scale? Do I feel close to Jesus? Do I feel I'm being nourished? Or not?
- I can talk to God about these things.

Saturday 16th April   **John 6:64-69**

But among you there are some who do not believe." For Jesus knew from the first who were the ones that did not believe, and who was the one that would betray him. And he said, "For this reason I have told you that no one can come to me unless it is granted by the Father." Because of this many of his disciples turned back and no longer went about with him. So Jesus asked the twelve, "Do you also wish to go away?" Simon Peter answered him, "Lord, to whom can we go? You have the words of eternal life. We have come to believe and know that you are the Holy One of God."

- Following Jesus is not just a matter of course. People are free to choose. So am I.
- It is good for me to hear the words: "What about you?" What is my response?
- To be able to say—"you have the words of eternal life"—and mean them, is a gift of God.

april 17–23

Something to think and pray about each day this week:

Everything is possible

It is a commonplace assertion in personal development circles that we "become what we think about." If we manage to keep our thoughts focused on positive things, especially some goal that we want to achieve, then—no surprise here—we are sure to succeed in whatever it is we want to do.

In Mark 9:23, Jesus says to the father who has brought his son, possessed by a mute spirit, for healing: "everything is possible to the one who believes." Faith is central and it is a pure gift from God. And yet! And yet, we seem to be able to make our contribution. We can choose to exercise our gift of faith. When we make that choice, "everything is possible."

Over these days in your sacred space, there is a great opportunity to choose faith in our wonderful God, with whom "everything is possible."

The Presence of God
As I sit here, the beating of my heart,
the ebb and flow of my breathing, the movements of my mind
are all signs of God's ongoing creation of me.
I pause for a moment, and become aware
of this presence of God within me.

Freedom
I will ask God's help,
to be free from my own preoccupations,
to be open to God in this time of prayer,
to come to love and serve him more.

Consciousness
Knowing that God loves me unconditionally,
I look honestly over the last day, its events and my feelings.
Do I have something to be grateful for? Then I give thanks.
Is there something I am sorry for? Then I ask forgiveness.

The Word
I take my time to read the Word of God, slowly, a few times,
allowing myself to dwell on anything that strikes me. (Please
turn to your scripture on the following pages. Inspiration
points are there should you need them. When you are ready,
return here to continue.)

Conversation
Remembering that I am still in God's presence,
I imagine Jesus himself standing or sitting beside me,
and say whatever is on my mind, whatever is in my heart,
speaking as one friend to another.

Conclusion
Glory be to the Father, and to the Son, and to the Holy Spirit,
As it was in the beginning, is now and ever shall be,
World without end. Amen

april 2005

154

Sunday 17th April, Fourth Sunday of Easter
John 10:1-10

Jesus said to the Pharisees, "Very truly, I tell you, anyone who does not enter the sheepfold by the gate but climbs in by another way is a thief and a bandit. The one who enters by the gate is the shepherd of the sheep. The gatekeeper opens the gate for him, and the sheep hear his voice. He calls his own sheep by name and leads them out. When he has brought out all his own, he goes ahead of them, and the sheep follow him because they know his voice. They will not follow a stranger, but they will run from him because they do not know the voice of strangers." Jesus used this figure of speech with them, but they did not understand what he was saying to them. So again Jesus said to them, "Very truly, I tell you, I am the gate for the sheep. All who came before me are thieves and bandits; but the sheep did not listen to them. I am the gate. Whoever enters by me will be saved, and will come in and go out and find pasture. The thief comes only to steal and kill and destroy. I came that they may have life, and have it abundantly.

- Can I stay with the image of the shepherd who calls each sheep by its own name and who leads them along safe paths?
- Do I allow Jesus to call me by name? Do I feel confidence in the sound of his voice?

Monday 18th April
John 10:9-10

Jesus said to the Pharisees, "I am the gate. Whoever enters by me will be saved, and will come in and go out and find pasture. The thief comes only to steal and kill and destroy. I came that they may have life, and have it abundantly.

- Jesus presumes here that we—I—have the potential for the abundance of life that he brings.

- Am I open to receive abundant life? Do I help those around me to accept this abundant life?
- If I have fears or reservations I can be open about them with the Lord.

Tuesday 19th April   Acts 11:19-26

Now those who were scattered because of the persecution that took place over Stephen traveled as far as Phoenicia, Cyprus, and Antioch, and they spoke the word to no one except Jews. But among them were some men of Cyprus and Cyrene who, on coming to Antioch, spoke to the Hellenists also, proclaiming the Lord Jesus. The hand of the Lord was with them, and a great number became believers and turned to the Lord. News of this came to the ears of the church in Jerusalem, and they sent Barnabas to Antioch. When he came and saw the grace of God, he rejoiced, and he exhorted them all to remain faithful to the Lord with steadfast devotion; for he was a good man, full of the Holy Spirit and of faith. And a great many people were brought to the Lord. Then Barnabas went to Tarsus to look for Saul, and when he had found him, he brought him to Antioch. So it was that for an entire year they met with the church and taught a great many people, and it was in Antioch that the disciples were first called "Christians."

- We watch how the Good News begins to spread out from the source. It is people on the run from persecution who bring the message as far as Antioch.
- It spread further still ... and it finally reached me.
- Do I see the "hand of the Lord" in that? Do I see myself in continuity with those who were first called "Christians"?

Wednesday 20th April   John 12:46-47

Jesus said to the crowds, "I have come as light into the world, so that everyone who believes in me should not remain in the darkness. I do not judge anyone who hears my words and does not keep them, for I came not to judge the world, but to save the world."

- Can I visualize the darkness as it exists in my life, and in the lives of those who are most oppressed and downtrodden?
- It is into this darkness that Jesus wants to come with a bright light.
- The purpose of the bright light is to save rather than judge.

Thursday 21st April   John 13:16-17

Jesus said to his disciples, "Very truly, I tell you, servants are not greater than their master, nor are messengers greater than the one who sent them. If you know these things, you are blessed if you do them."

- Since I am one who is sent, what am I sent to do?
- Jesus is saying here that I have a great master and a wonderful purpose. Can I ponder on this?

Friday 22nd April   John 14:1-3

Jesus said to his disciples, "Do not let your hearts be troubled. Believe in God, believe also in me. In my Father's house there are many dwelling places. If it were not so, would I have told you that I go to prepare a place for you? And if I go and prepare a place for you, I will come again and will take you to myself, so that where I am, there you may be also."

- These words of Jesus to his disciples are also directed to me personally. East time he says "you" or "your," he is talking to me.

- Am I consoled by his words? Am I challenged or encouraged?
- How do I respond to the promise of eternal life with God?

Saturday 23rd April   John 14:12-14

Jesus told the disciples, "Very truly, I tell you, the one who believes in me will also do the works that I do and, in fact, will do greater works than these, because I am going to the Father. I will do whatever you ask in my name, so that the Father may be glorified in the Son. If in my name you ask me for anything, I will do it."

- Jesus is determined that he will live and work in our world through us. Through me.
- It is the mystery of the Risen Lord that he sits at God's right hand AND he is intimately involved in the lives and struggles of his followers.
- What is my response? How can I let my life be a vehicle of Jesus' work in our world?

april 24–30

Something to think and pray about each day this week:

Speak Lord, your servant is listening
Picture the boy Samuel in the temple (1 Samuel 3). The general mood of the time was a little gloomy; it was uncommon for the Lord to reveal himself to the people. Then, unexpectedly, one night as he slept Samuel heard a voice calling his name: "Samuel, Samuel." The last thing he thought of was that it might be the Lord calling him. Only as a last resort, when the voice persisted, did he say: "Speak, Lord, your servant is listening." Samuel went on to play an important role as a prophet in Israel.

As I pray at *Sacred Space* in these days, if I listen I can hear the Lord call my name, ("Teresa, Teresa!" … "John, John!"). The Lord is calling me and there is a role for me to play. I need to be ready with my reply: "Speak, Lord, your servant is listening."

The Presence of God
I pause for a moment
and reflect on God's life-giving presence
in every part of my body, in everything around me,
in the whole of my life.

Freedom
God is not foreign to my freedom.
Instead the Spirit breathes life into my most intimate desires,
gently nudging me towards all that is good.
I ask for the grace to let myself be enfolded by the Spirit.

Consciousness
How do I find myself today?
Where am I with God? With others?
Do I have something to be grateful for? Then I give thanks.
Is there something I am sorry for? Then I ask forgiveness.

The Word
God speaks to each one of us individually. I need to listen
to what he is saying to me. (Please turn to your scripture on
the following pages. Inspiration points are there should you
need them. When you are ready, return here to continue.)

Conversation
How has God's Word moved me? Has it left me cold?
Has it consoled me or moved me to act in a new way?
I imagine Jesus standing or sitting beside me,
I turn and share my feelings with him.

Conclusion
Glory be to the Father, and to the Son, and to the Holy Spirit,
As it was in the beginning, is now and ever shall be,
World without end. Amen

Sunday 24th April, Fifth Sunday of Easter   John 14:4-8

Jesus said to his disciples, "You know the way to the place where I am going." Thomas said to him, "Lord, we do not know where you are going. How can we know the way?" Jesus said to him, "I am the way, and the truth, and the life. No one comes to the Father except through me. If you know me, you will know my Father also. From now on you do know him and have seen him."

- These words of Jesus to Thomas and the other disciples are also directed to me. Each time he says "you" or "your," he is talking to me.
- Do I accept Jesus as "the way" or do I want to follow other paths? Do I feel confronted by this choice? Would I rather look for an easier way? How do I respond?
- Have I known and seen the Father in my life?

Monday 25th April, St Mark the Evangelist
Mark 16:15-20

And Jesus said to the disciples, "Go into all the world and proclaim the good news to the whole creation. The one who believes and is baptized will be saved; but the one who does not believe will be condemned. And these signs will accompany those who believe: by using my name they will cast out demons; they will speak in new tongues; they will pick up snakes in their hands, and if they drink any deadly thing, it will not hurt them; they will lay their hands on the sick, and they will recover." So then the Lord Jesus, after he had spoken to them, was taken up into heaven and sat down at the right hand of God. And they went out and proclaimed the good news everywhere, while the Lord worked with them and confirmed the message by the signs that accompanied it.

- If I read this passage slowly I could, by turns, be challenged, frightened, amazed, distorted, inspired, consoled …
- Which reactions do I rest with spontaneously? Does that tell me something about myself?
- Both the first and the last sentence of the passage tell of "Good News." Can I situate my reactions within the context of this "Good News"?

Tuesday 26th April   John 14:27-29

Jesus said to the apostles, "Peace I leave with you; my peace I give to you. I do not give to you as the world gives. Do not let your hearts be troubled, and do not let them be afraid. You heard me say to you, 'I am going away, and I am coming to you.' If you loved me, you would rejoice that I am going to the Father, because the Father is greater than I. And now I have told you this before it occurs, so that when it does occur, you may believe."

- Jesus offers us a peace that is different from the peace that the world gives. What makes it different? How do I know if I have it?
- Jesus, now reunited with the Father, guarantees our peace. Can I open my heart to this truth and be touched by it?

Wednesday 27th April   John 15:7-8

Jesus said to his disciples, "If you abide in me, and my words abide in you, ask for whatever you wish, and it will be done for you. My Father is glorified by this, that you bear much fruit and become my disciples."

- To abide, or live, in Jesus means extraordinary intimacy. I possibly feel I am miles away from that.
- He offers me all I need to be fully alive in him. Even in the midst of my doubting, can I let myself be brought closer?

- My loving choices and actions, even small ones, are signs of God's life working in our world.

Thursday 28th April   John 15:9-11

Jesus said to his disciples, "As the Father has loved me, so I have loved you; abide in my love. If you keep my commandments, you will abide in my love, just as I have kept my Father's commandments and abide in his love. I have said these things to you so that my joy may be in you, and that your joy may be complete."

- Love expresses itself in action. God's love is real if it moves me to love concretely.
- How am I expressing God's love in these days?
- The call to love is not a burden. It is the road to joy.

Friday 29th April   John 15:12-15

Jesus said to his disciples, "This is my commandment, that you love one another as I have loved you. No one has greater love than this, to lay down one's life for one's friends. You are my friends if you do what I command you. I do not call you servants any longer, because the servant does not know what the master is doing; but I have called you friends, because I have made known to you everything that I have heard from my Father."

- We become more and more like the people we love.
- As I grow in friendship with Jesus, I will watch the pattern of his life and in time it will become mine.
- This is a process. Jesus doesn't expect me to be perfect on the first day.

Saturday 30th April   Psalm 99(100):1-3, 5

Make a joyful noise to the LORD, all the earth. Worship the LORD with gladness; come into his presence with singing. Know that the LORD is God. It is he that made us, and we are his; we are his people, and the sheep of his pasture. For the LORD is good; his steadfast love endures forever, and his faithfulness to all generations.

- The call is to make a "joyful noise," but it is not primarily about the feeling of the moment.
- I am called to acknowledge the greatness of God's love and care for me—for us—regardless of where I am right now.
- This is a chance for me to open up to the "bigger picture" and see how I can respond.

may 1–7

Something to think and pray about each day this week:

God has created me …
Cardinal Newman had a beautiful vision of the role that each one of us can play in the mysterious plans of God. The words of the following prayer were written over one hundred years ago, and yet they have the power to light up my life right now:

> God has created me to do him some definite service; he has committed some work to me which he has not committed to another. I have my mission—I may never know it in this life, but I shall be told it in the next. I am a link in a chain, a bond of connection between persons. He has not created me for naught. I shall do good, I shall do his work. I shall be a preacher of truth in my own place, while not intending it, if I do but keep his commandments and serve him in my calling.
>
> Therefore my God, I will put myself without reserve into your hands. What have I in heaven, and apart from you what do I want on earth? My flesh and my heart fail, but God is God of my heart, and my portion for ever.

The Presence of God

The world is charged with the grandeur of God (Gerard Manley Hopkins).
I dwell for a moment on the presence of God
around me, in every part of my body,
and deep within my being.

Freedom

Everything has the potential to draw forth from me a fuller love and life.
Yet my desires are often fixed, caught, on illusions of fulfillment.
I ask that God, through my freedom, may orchestrate
my desires in a vibrant loving melody rich in harmony.

Consciousness

In God's loving presence I unwind the past day,
starting from now and looking back, moment by moment.
I gather in all the goodness and light, in gratitude.
I attend to the shadows and what they say to me,
seeking healing, courage, forgiveness.

The Word

I read the Word of God slowly, a few times over, and I listen
to what God is saying to me. (Please turn to your scripture
on the following pages. Inspiration points are there should
you need them. When you are ready, return here to continue.)

Conversation

What feelings are rising in me
as I pray and reflect on God's Word?
I imagine Jesus himself sitting or standing beside me,
and open my heart to him.

Conclusion

Glory be to the Father, and to the Son, and to the Holy Spirit,
As it was in the beginning, is now and ever shall be,
World without end. Amen

may 2005

Sunday 1st May, Sixth Sunday of Easter   John 14:15-20

Jesus said to his disciples, "If you love me, you will keep my commandments. And I will ask the Father, and he will give you another Advocate, to be with you forever. This is the Spirit of truth, whom the world cannot receive, because it neither sees him nor knows him. You know him, because he abides with you, and he will be in you. I will not leave you orphaned; I am coming to you. In a little while the world will no longer see me, but you will see me; because I live, you also will live. On that day you will know that I am in my Father, and you in me, and I in you."

- Before he left Jesus promised us a special advocate or friend who would be with us always. Not everybody can experience the presence of this friend all of the time.
- Do I feel my self "alive" with the Spirit, in the way Jesus promised?
- Am I open to the experience?

Monday 2nd May   John 15:26-27

Jesus said to his disciples, "When the Advocate comes, whom I will send to you from the Father, the Spirit of truth who comes from the Father, he will testify on my behalf. You also are to testify because you have been with me from the beginning."

- Jesus is guaranteeing that the Holy Spirit will come and help us understand what God's plans are.
- Where do I imagine the Holy Spirit is working in my section of God's vineyard?

Tuesday 3rd May, Sts Philip and James   John 14:6-14

Jesus said to him, "I am the way, and the truth, and the life. No one comes to the Father except through me. If you know me, you will know my Father also. From now on you do know him and have seen him." Philip said to him, "Lord, show us the Father, and we will be satisfied." Jesus said to him, "Have I been with you all this time, Philip, and you still do not know me? Whoever has seen me has seen the Father. How can you say, 'Show us the Father'? Do you not believe that I am in the Father and the Father is in me? The words that I say to you I do not speak on my own; but the Father who dwells in me does his works. Believe me that I am in the Father and the Father is in me; but if you do not, then believe me because of the works themselves. Very truly, I tell you, the one who believes in me will also do the works that I do and, in fact, will do greater works than these, because I am going to the Father. I will do whatever you ask in my name, so that the Father may be glorified in the Son. If in my name you ask me for anything, I will do it.

- Can I allow these words, addressed to Philip, be spoken to me?
- Do these mysterious concepts about Jesus and his heavenly Father intrigue me, delight me, confuse me?
- The "one who believes in me" can, it seems, take part in the mystery too. Does this mean me? Am I open to that?

Wednesday 4th May   John 16:12-15

Jesus said to the disciples, "I still have many things to say to you, but you cannot bear them now. When the Spirit of truth comes, he will guide you into all the truth; for he will not speak on his own, but will speak whatever he hears, and he will declare to you the things that are to come. He will glorify me, because he will take what is mine and declare it to you. All that the Father has is mine. For this reason I said that he will take what is mine and declare it to you."

168

- Do the words "many things to say to you, but you cannot bear them now" ring any bells with me? Do I recognise mysteries that are still beyond my grasp?
- Can I trust myself to Jesus' promise that the Spirit will guide me "into all the truth"?
- What does the promise of the Spirit mean to me?

Thursday 5th May   John 16:20

Jesus said to his disciples, "Very truly, I tell you, you will weep and mourn, but the world will rejoice; you will have pain, but your pain will turn into joy."

- Jesus speaks these words to his disciples as a preparation for the coming trial.
- He addresses them to his followers in every age, including us.
- Am I moved to pray for any person or situation where there is great pain?

Friday 6th May   Psalm 46(47):2-7

Clap your hands, all you peoples; shout to God with loud songs of joy. For the LORD, the Most High, is awesome, a great king over all the earth. He subdued peoples under us, and nations under our feet. He chose our heritage for us, the pride of Jacob whom he loves. God has gone up with a shout, the LORD with the sound of a trumpet. Sing praises to God, sing praises; sing praises to our King, sing praises. For God is the king of all the earth; sing praises with a psalm.

- This psalm envisages a great crowd of the people of Israel delighting in the universal sovereignty of God.
- Can I enter into the spirit of it?
- When I look at human history—and at my own—what do I see as the great deeds of God?

Saturday 7th May   **John 16:23-24**

Jesus said to his disciples, "On that day you will ask nothing of me. Very truly, I tell you, if you ask anything of the Father in my name, he will give it to you. Until now you have not asked for anything in my name. Ask and you will receive, so that your joy may be complete."

- It is a huge promise that the Father will grant anything we ask in Jesus' name.
- Asking "in Jesus' name" implies a profound unity with Jesus.
- How can I open myself to this kind of unity with Jesus?

may 8–14

Something to think and pray about each day this week:

"Christians who pray together stay together"
This week is celebrated by nearly all the Christian churches in the world as a week of prayer for Christian Unity. Special joint services will be held in thousands of churches all over the globe. There is probably something going on near you—so why not find out from your local church and go along?

This week would also be a good time to think and pray about this dimension of *Sacred Space*. In a way, this book and the website are ecumenism in action: Christians of all denominations (and some of no denomination) praying together every day. Many have sent feedback via the website: Catholics, Lutherans, Anglicans and Episcopalians, Methodists, Baptists, Orthodox and others. And many have shared with us one of the fruits of that prayer—the realisation that "the faith that unites is much greater than what divides us."

The divisions in Christianity give a very poor example to the rest of the world, and undermine the credibility of the Christian message. Reconciling those divisions requires a conversion of heart in all of us. We need to try hard—and we need God's help—to open our hearts and overcome the resentment and prejudice that have sadly been a part of Christian culture for centuries. This week especially is a good time to ask for that grace.

The Presence of God
As I sit here, God is present,
breathing life into me and into everything around me.
For a few moments, I sit silently,
and become aware of God's loving presence.

Freedom
There are very few people
who realize what God would make of them
if they abandoned themselves into his hands,
and let themselves be formed by his grace. (St Ignatius)
I ask for the grace to trust myself totally to God's love.

Consciousness
I exist in a web of relationships—links to nature, people, God.
I trace out these links, giving thanks for the life that flows
through them.
Some links are twisted or broken: I may feel regret, anger,
disappointment.
I pray for the gift of acceptance and forgiveness.

The Word
I take my time to read the Word of God, slowly, a few times,
allowing myself to dwell on anything that strikes me. (Please
turn to your scripture on the following pages. Inspiration
points are there should you need them. When you are ready,
return here to continue.)

Conversation
What is stirring in me as I pray?
Am I consoled, troubled, left cold?
I imagine Jesus himself standing or sitting at my side,
and share my feelings with him.

Conclusion
Glory be to the Father, and to the Son, and to the Holy Spirit,
As it was in the beginning, is now and ever shall be,
World without end. Amen

Sunday 8th May, The Ascension of the Lord   Acts 1:6-11

So when they had come together, the disciples asked Jesus, "Lord, is this the time when you will restore the kingdom to Israel?" He replied, "It is not for you to know the times or periods that the Father has set by his own authority. But you will receive power when the Holy Spirit has come upon you; and you will be my witnesses in Jerusalem, in all Judea and Samaria, and to the ends of the earth." When he had said this, as they were watching, he was lifted up, and a cloud took him out of their sight. While he was going and they were gazing up toward heaven, suddenly two men in white robes stood by them. They said, "Men of Galilee, why do you stand looking up toward heaven? This Jesus, who has been taken up from you into heaven, will come in the same way as you saw him go into heaven."

- Because of Jesus' Ascension to the Father, humankind now has a place in heaven. We will no longer be out of place there. "One of our own" sits at God's right hand.
- If I have difficulty appreciating this I can look at the disciples in the scene. Even at the end they seem not to understand.

Monday 9th May   Psalm 67(68):3-6a

But let the righteous be joyful; let them exult before God; let them be jubilant with joy. Sing to God, sing praises to his name; lift up a song to him who rides upon the clouds—his name is the LORD—be exultant before him. Father of orphans and protector of widows is God in his holy habitation. God gives the desolate a home to live in; he leads out the prisoners to prosperity.

- It is Ascension time. Pentecost is not far off. We are invited to exult in the greatness of God.
- Whatever my mood, to repeat the words of the Psalm a few

times and enter into them—without forcing—can open me up to the wonder of life in God's world.

Tuesday 10th May   John 17:1-4

After Jesus had spoken these words, he looked up to heaven and said, "Father, the hour has come; glorify your Son so that the Son may glorify you, since you have given him authority over all people, to give eternal life to all whom you have given him. And this is eternal life, that they may know you, the only true God, and Jesus Christ whom you have sent. I glorified you on earth by finishing the work that you gave me to do."

- When the Father "glorifies" the Son, what does it mean?
- The "glory" of God shone through Jesus in every situation, especially in his passion.
- God's glory can shine through my life and in my world. I may have difficulty seeing it.

Wednesday 11th May   John 17:17-19

Jesus looked up to heaven and said, "Father, sanctify them in the truth; your word is truth. As you have sent me into the world, so I have sent them into the world. And for their sakes I sanctify myself, so that they also may be sanctified in truth."

- "Sanctify them in the truth" are words that may move me deeply OR leave me quite cold. Either way can I explore what sanctity and truth mean for me?
- Sanctity means immersing myself in "the One who is holy."
- The truth can sometimes be very uncomfortable. Do I really want to believe in the truth?

174

Thursday 12th May   **John 17:20-21**

J esus looked up to heaven and said, "Father, I ask not only
on behalf of these, but also on behalf of those who will
believe in me through their word, that they may all be one.
As you, Father, are in me and I am in you, may they also be
in us, so that the world may believe that you have sent me."

- The great Christian call to unity. So attractive and so difficult.
- Do I want to bring the various experiences of disunity both in
  my life and around my life to the Lord?
- The Lord does not call us to an ideal without offering us the
  grace necessary for it.

Friday 13th May   **Psalm 102:1-2, 11-12, 19-20**

B less the LORD, O my soul, and all that is within me,
bless his holy name. Bless the LORD, O my soul, and
do not forget all his benefits.
For as the heavens are high above the earth, so great is his
steadfast love toward those who fear him; as far as the east is
from the west, so far he removes our transgressions from us.
The LORD has established his throne in the heavens, and
his kingdom rules over all. Bless the LORD, O you his
angels, you mighty ones who do his bidding, obedient to his
spoken word.

- Is "all that is within me" ready to bless the Lord?
- Wherever I happen to be right now, can I allow the words of
  the Psalm to lead me and allow the Spirit to pray in me?

Saturday 14th May, St Matthias   **John 15:9-17**

J esus said to the apostles, "As the Father has loved me, so I
have loved you; abide in my love. If you keep my
commandments, you will abide in my love, just as I have
kept my Father's commandments and abide in his love.

I have said these things to you so that my joy may be in you, and that your joy may be complete. "This is my commandment, that you love one another as I have loved you. No one has greater love than this, to lay down one's life for one's friends. You are my friends if you do what I command you. I do not call you servants any longer, because the servant does not know what the master is doing; but I have called you friends, because I have made known to you everything that I have heard from my Father. You did not choose me but I chose you. And I appointed you to go and bear fruit, fruit that will last, so that the Father will give you whatever you ask him in my name. I am giving you these commands so that you may love one another."

- When I hear Jesus' commandment to love how do I feel? Is it encouraging or overwhelming?
- Do I hear the gentle invitation in the midst of the command: "You will abide in my love"?
- Do I hear the words "you are my friend" addressed to me?

Something to think and pray about each day this week:

Praying at Pentecost

At the feast of Pentecost, three thousand people joined the community and "devoted themselves to the apostles' teaching and fellowship, to the breaking of bread and the prayers. Awe came upon everyone, because many wonders and signs were being done by the apostles. All who believed were together and had all things in common; they would sell their possessions and goods and distribute the proceeds to all, as any had need. Day by day, as they spent much time together in the temple, they broke bread at home and ate their food with glad and generous hearts." (Acts 2:42-46)

It is a story of a community, consoled and encouraged in prayer and by each other, responding generously to God's promise by putting the Word into action: they give what they have to those who need it.

Many of us, too have experienced encouragement and consolation from God through *Sacred Space*. This might be a good time to reflect on how each of us, in our own ways and our own situations, can look at the needs around us and do something to put the Word into action.

The Presence of God
As I sit here with my book, God is here.
Around me, in my sensations, in my thoughts and deep
within me.
I pause for a moment, and become aware
of God's life-giving presence.

Freedom
A thick and shapeless tree-trunk would never believe
that it could become a statue, admired as a miracle of sculpture,
and would never submit itself to the chisel of the sculptor,
who sees by her genius what she can make of it. (St Ignatius)
I ask for the grace to let myself be shaped by my loving Creator.

Consciousness
How am I really feeling? Light-hearted? Heavy-hearted?
I may be very much at peace, happy to be here.
Equally, I may be frustrated, worried or angry.
I acknowledge how I really am. It is the real me that the
Lord loves.

The Word
God speaks to each one of us individually. I need to listen
to what he is saying to me. (Please turn to your scripture on
the following pages. Inspiration points are there should you
need them. When you are ready, return here to continue.)

Conversation
Do I notice myself reacting as I pray with the Word of God?
Do I feel challenged, comforted, angry?
Imagining Jesus sitting or standing by me,
I speak out my feelings, as one trusted friend to another.

Conclusion
Glory be to the Father, and to the Son, and to the Holy Spirit,
As it was in the beginning, is now and ever shall be,
World without end. Amen

Sunday 15th May, Pentecost   Acts 2:1-4

When the day of Pentecost had come, they were all together in one place. And suddenly from heaven there came a sound like the rush of a violent wind, and it filled the entire house where they were sitting. Divided tongues, as of fire, appeared among them, and a tongue rested on each of them. All of them were filled with the Holy Spirit and began to speak in other languages, as the Spirit gave them ability.

- Imagine the scene: the initial fear; the rush of wind; the shock; the confusion; the amazement; the power; the joy; the communication.
- We pray on behalf of all who come to *Sacred Space*: "come Holy Spirit."

Monday 16th May   Psalm 92(93)

The LORD is king, he is robed in majesty; the LORD is robed, he is girded with strength. He has established the world; it shall never be moved; your throne is established from of old; you are from everlasting. The floods have lifted up, O LORD, the floods have lifted up their voice; the floods lift up their roaring. More majestic than the thunders of mighty waters, more majestic than the waves of the sea, majestic on high is the LORD! Your decrees are very sure; holiness befits your house, O LORD, forevermore.

- As I sit here do I share in the Psalm's sense of thrill at the majesty of God in creation or in the goodness of things?
- If I do, then Praise God.
- If I don't feel the excitement, am I missing something? Or, is it simply that God is present to me in the ordinariness of things?
- How do I experience God's presence right now?

Tuesday 17th May   Mark 9:30-37

They went on from there and passed through Galilee. Jesus did not want anyone to know it; for he was teaching his disciples, saying to them, "The Son of Man is to be betrayed into human hands, and they will kill him, and three days after being killed, he will rise again." But they did not understand what he was saying and were afraid to ask him. Then they came to Capernaum; and when he was in the house he asked them, "What were you arguing about on the way?" But they were silent, for on the way they had argued with one another who was the greatest. He sat down, called the twelve, and said to them, "Whoever wants to be first must be last of all and servant of all." Then he took a little child and put it among them; and taking it in his arms, he said to them, "Whoever welcomes one such child in my name welcomes me, and whoever welcomes me welcomes not me but the one who sent me."

- This is a classic case of "crossed wires." It would be good to revisit each stage of this scene and see what was concerning Jesus and, on the other hand, what various things were filling the minds of the disciples.
- Jesus is challenging the disciples about what is really important for them.
- Can I let him challenge me?

Wednesday 18th May   Mark 9:38-40

John said to Jesus, "Teacher, we saw someone casting out demons in your name, and we tried to stop him, because he was not following us." But Jesus said, "Do not stop him; for no one who does a deed of power in my name will be able soon afterward to speak evil of me. Whoever is not against us is for us."

- John seems to have been hooked on the details here, while Jesus encourages him to take a bigger, more trusting view of things.
- How does this apply to my own life? (It is better to hear Jesus' challenge to me personally rather than others.)

Thursday 19th May   Mark 9:41-50

Jesus said to his disciples, "For truly I tell you, whoever gives you a cup of water to drink because you bear the name of Christ will by no means lose the reward. "If any of you put a stumbling block before one of these little ones who believe in me, it would be better for you if a great millstone were hung around your neck and you were thrown into the sea. If your hand causes you to stumble, cut it off; it is better for you to enter life maimed than to have two hands and to go to hell, to the unquenchable fire. And if your foot causes you to stumble, cut it off; it is better for you to enter life lame than to have two feet and to be thrown into hell. And if your eye causes you to stumble, tear it out; it is better for you to enter the kingdom of God with one eye than to have two eyes and to be thrown into hell, where their worm never dies, and the fire is never quenched. "For everyone will be salted with fire. Salt is good; but if salt has lost its saltiness, how can you season it? Have salt in yourselves, and be at peace with one another."

- How do I react to this really strong language? Do I ignore it? Does it upset and frighten me? Do I explain it all away?
- What is the truth, in my life, about bad example or about situations that lead me away from a life of love?
- How does Jesus, who loves me more than I can imagine, want to lead me into a richer and more loving life?

Friday 20th May   **Mark 10:1-9**

Jesus left that place and went to the region of Judea and beyond the Jordan. And crowds again gathered around him; and, as was his custom, he again taught them. Some Pharisees came, and to test him they asked, "Is it lawful for a man to divorce his wife?" He answered them, "What did Moses command you?" They said, "Moses allowed a man to write a certificate of dismissal and to divorce her." But Jesus said to them, "Because of your hardness of heart he wrote this commandment for you. But from the beginning of creation, 'God made them male and female.' 'For this reason a man shall leave his father and mother and be joined to his wife, and the two shall become one flesh.' So they are no longer two, but one flesh. Therefore what God has joined together, let no one separate."

- Central to this passage is Jesus' deep reverence for God's creation of male and female and for the union of man and woman in marriage.
- How do I hear Jesus' words? Are they consoling and encouraging? Do they touch into painful experiences—my own or others'?
- How am I moved to pray, now?

Saturday 21st May   **Mark 10:13-16**

People were bringing little children to Jesus in order that he might touch them; and the disciples spoke sternly to them. But when Jesus saw this, he was indignant and said to them, "Let the little children come to me; do not stop them; for it is to such as these that the kingdom of God belongs. Truly I tell you, whoever does not receive the kingdom of God as a little child will never enter it." And he took them up in his arms, laid his hands on them, and blessed them.

- When I see the disciples turning children away and Jesus welcoming them, what does it evoke in me? Tenderness? Sentimentality? Sneaking cynicism? What?
- When he says "to such as these the Kingdom of God belongs," what does he mean?
- How does it challenge me?

Sacred Space

Something to think and pray about each day this week:

The hard word

What do we do when someone we love speaks hard words? We don't like it. We feel wounded and misunderstood. Unloved. Later, when we have time to cool down we may come to recognize that there was some merit in the challenge which initially seemed so hurtful and unfair. Hard words can be the beginning of growth and new life.

What happens in me when I hear Jesus the Lord speak hard words? Do I imagine that he might be speaking to me? Can I take it? Do I shrink from it? Hide from it? Does his challenge make me feel unloved?

Over these few days we hear Jesus speak some very hard words. Can I stay with them, trusting that they come from someone who loves me without reserve?

The Presence of God
I pause for a moment, aware that God is here.
I think of how everything around me,
the air I breathe, my whole body,
is tingling with the presence of God.

Freedom
I ask for the grace
to let go of my own concerns
and be open to what God is asking of me,
to let myself be guided and formed by my loving Creator.

Consciousness
Knowing that God loves me unconditionally,
I can afford to be honest about how I am.
How has the last day been, and how do I feel now?
I share my feelings openly with the Lord.

The Word
I read the Word of God slowly, a few times over, and I listen
to what God is saying to me. (Please turn to your scripture
on the following pages. Inspiration points are there should
you need them. When you are ready, return here to continue.)

Conversation
Remembering that I am still in God's presence,
I imagine Jesus himself standing or sitting beside me,
and say whatever is on my mind, whatever is in my heart,
speaking as one friend to another.

Conclusion
Glory be to the Father, and to the Son, and to the Holy Spirit,
As it was in the beginning, is now and ever shall be,
World without end. Amen

186

Sunday 22nd May, Trinity Sunday John 3:16-17

Jesus said to Nicodemus, "For God so loved the world that he gave his only Son, so that everyone who believes in him may not perish but may have eternal life. Indeed, God did not send the Son into the world to condemn the world, but in order that the world might be saved through him."

- These sentences are a core statement of Christian belief. For me, here, today, do they sound uplifting, hollow, consoling, trite, or gloriously life-giving?
- I can be before the Lord as I am, without fear of condemnation.

Monday 23rd May Mark 10:17-22

As Jesus was setting out on a journey, a man ran up and knelt before him, and asked him, "Good Teacher, what must I do to inherit eternal life?" Jesus said to him, "Why do you call me good? No one is good but God alone. You know the commandments: 'You shall not murder; You shall not commit adultery; You shall not steal; You shall not bear false witness; You shall not defraud; Honor your father and mother.'" He said to him, "Teacher, I have kept all these since my youth." Jesus, looking at him, loved him and said, "You lack one thing; go, sell what you own, and give the money to the poor, and you will have treasure in heaven; then come, follow me." When he heard this, he was shocked and went away grieving, for he had many possessions.

- It is important to watch this scene closely and follow the reactions of the two men to one another. There are a few very intense moments in this short encounter.
- How do I feel as I watch this scene unfold? Can I imagine myself in the place of the rich man? In his place would I experience the love in Jesus' gaze at me?
- What is the Lord saying to me?

Tuesday 24th May — Mark 10:28-31

Peter began to say to him, "Look, we have left everything and followed you." Jesus said, "Truly I tell you, there is no one who has left house or brothers or sisters or mother or father or children or fields, for my sake and for the sake of the good news, who will not receive a hundredfold now in this age—houses, brothers and sisters, mothers and children, and fields with persecutions—and in the age to come eternal life. But many who are first will be last, and the last will be first."

- Sometimes Jesus speaks very bluntly. Following him will necessarily involve sacrifice—and also the sure promise of eternal life.
- Can I simply spend time and let either or both of these predictions sink in, according as I need to hear them?

Wednesday 25th May — Mark 10:35-45

James and John, the sons of Zebedee, came forward to Jesus and said to him, "Teacher, we want you to do for us whatever we ask of you." And he said to them, "What is it you want me to do for you?" And they said to him, "Grant us to sit, one at your right hand and one at your left, in your glory." But Jesus said to them, "You do not know what you are asking. Are you able to drink the cup that I drink, or be baptized with the baptism that I am baptized with?" They replied, "We are able." Then Jesus said to them, "The cup that I drink you will drink; and with the baptism with which I am baptized, you will be baptized; but to sit at my right hand or at my left is not mine to grant, but it is for those for whom it has been prepared." When the ten heard this, they began to be angry with James and John. So Jesus called them and said to them, "You know that among the Gentiles those whom they recognize as their rulers lord it over them, and

188

their great ones are tyrants over them. But it is not so among you; but whoever wishes to become great among you must be your servant, and whoever wishes to be first among you must be slave of all. For the Son of Man came not to be served but to serve, and to give his life a ransom for many."

- What is my reaction to the two brothers' approach to Jesus? Do I admire their initiative? Do I resent them for trying to get ahead of the other ten? Some other reaction? (My gut reaction to this scene tells me about my own relationship with Jesus.)
- How do I think Jesus dealt with them? How did they feel as they continued along the road to Jerusalem? More identified with Jesus? Misunderstood? More united with the group?
- I can speak to Jesus about my own position as his disciple.

Thursday 26th May   **Mark 10:46-52**

They came to Jericho. As he and his disciples and a large crowd were leaving Jericho, Bartimaeus son of Timaeus, a blind beggar, was sitting by the roadside. When he heard that it was Jesus of Nazareth, he began to shout out and say, "Jesus, Son of David, have mercy on me!" Many sternly ordered him to be quiet, but he cried out even more loudly, "Son of David, have mercy on me!" Jesus stood still and said, "Call him here." And they called the blind man, saying to him, "Take heart; get up, he is calling you." So throwing off his cloak, he sprang up and came to Jesus. Then Jesus said to him, "What do you want me to do for you?" The blind man said to him, "My teacher, let me see again."

52 Jesus said to him, "Go; your faith has made you well." Immediately he regained his sight and followed him on the way.

- Can I picture this scene on the road leading out of Jericho? What buildings are around? What is the road surface like? Where is Bartimaeus sitting?
- What is going on? Can I imagine myself present and watching the scene unfold? I might even imagine myself as a participant, even as Bartimaeus.
- When I see and hear and am touched by what happens, how does it move me?

Friday 27th May   Mark 11:15-19

Then they came to Jerusalem. And he entered the temple and began to drive out those who were selling and those who were buying in the temple, and he overturned the tables of the money changers and the seats of those who sold doves; and he would not allow anyone to carry anything through the temple. He was teaching and saying, "Is it not written, 'My house shall be called a house of prayer for all the nations'? But you have made it a den of robbers." And when the chief priests and the scribes heard it, they kept looking for a way to kill him; for they were afraid of him, because the whole crowd was spellbound by his teaching. And when evening came, Jesus and his disciples went out of the city.

- Can I imagine this scene as if it is happening in front of me? How does Jesus appear to me: If I was a bystander? If I was one of the money changers?
- When I see Jesus angry and assertive—aggressive even—how does that make me feel?
- Does it make me draw back from him in fear? Does it make me want to stand and cheer?
- What is Jesus teaching me here about situations of conflict and principle in my own life?

190

Saturday 28th May   Mark 11:27-33

Jesus and his disciples came to Jerusalem. As he was walking in the temple, the chief priests, the scribes, and the elders came to him and said, "By what authority are you doing these things? Who gave you this authority to do them?" Jesus said to them, "I will ask you one question; answer me, and I will tell you by what authority I do these things. Did the baptism of John come from heaven, or was it of human origin? Answer me." They argued with one another, "If we say, 'From heaven,' he will say, 'Why then did you not believe him?' But shall we say, 'Of human origin'?"—they were afraid of the crowd, for all regarded John as truly a prophet. So they answered Jesus, "We do not know." And Jesus said to them, "Neither will I tell you by what authority I am doing these things."

- More conflict in the life of Jesus. These people hated him and were looking for an excuse to have him killed!
- What impresses me about his response? His quick thinking? Calm under pressure? His courage?
- Who is this extraordinary man and by what power does he face this awful situation in this calm and peaceful way?

Sacred Space

Something to think and pray about each day this week:

Noticing my feelings
There will be times when praying leaves me cold, times when it comforts me and fills me with peace, and other times when it discomforts me, annoys me, leaves me feeling "disgruntled." St Ignatius teaches me to take note of these feelings, since they can tell me about what is happening deep within me.

He uses the terms "consolation" and "desolation" to describe two ways of feeling. Consolation is happening when I feel drawn closer to God, to unselfishness and generosity. This might be accompanied by gratitude or peace or new hope, but equally it could be an experience of grief or regret, or sympathy for somebody's suffering. Consolation is the feeling when barriers between myself and God are being broken down, and this can be initially painful.

Desolation is the opposite of all this. It is happening when I feel withdrawn or alienated from God and turned in on myself, when I am determined to "put my faith in earthly things" or shut God out of some area of my life. Again, this is not always felt as sadness, but may be accompanied by a shallow, self-satisfied kind of happiness.

With time, I can begin to notice the difference.

The Presence of God

For a few moments, I think of God's veiled presence in things:
in the elements, giving them existence;
in plants, giving them life; in animals, giving them sensation;
and finally, in me, giving me all this and more,
making me a temple, a dwelling-place of the Spirit.

Freedom

I ask for the grace to believe
in what I could be and do
if I only allowed God, my loving Creator,
to continue to create me, guide me and shape me.

Consciousness

In the presence of my loving Creator,
I look honestly at my feelings over the last day,
the highs, the lows and the level ground.
Can I see where the Lord has been present?

The Word

I take my time to read the Word of God, slowly, a few times,
allowing myself to dwell on anything that strikes me. (Please
turn to your scripture on the following pages. Inspiration
points are there should you need them. When you are ready,
return here to continue.)

Conversation

How has God's Word moved me? Has it left me cold?
Has it consoled me or moved me to act in a new way?
I imagine Jesus standing or sitting beside me,
I turn and share my feelings with him.

Conclusion

Glory be to the Father, and to the Son, and to the Holy Spirit,
As it was in the beginning, is now and ever shall be,
World without end. Amen

194

Sunday 29th May, Corpus Christi
(The Body and Blood of Christ)   John 6:51-58

Jesus said to the crowd, "I am the living bread that came down from heaven. Whoever eats of this bread will live forever; and the bread that I will give for the life of the world is my flesh." The Jews then disputed among themselves, saying, "How can this man give us his flesh to eat?" So Jesus said to them, "Very truly, I tell you, unless you eat the flesh of the Son of Man and drink his blood, you have no life in you. Those who eat my flesh and drink my blood have eternal life, and I will raise them up on the last day; for my flesh is true food and my blood is true drink. Those who eat my flesh and drink my blood abide in me, and I in them. Just as the living Father sent me, and I live because of the Father, so whoever eats me will live because of me. This is the bread that came down from heaven, not like that which your ancestors ate, and they died. But the one who eats this bread will live forever."

- Those who first heard Jesus speak like this were shocked and offended.
- Can I let the words in all their bluntness, speak to me? How do they move me?
- Do I hear an invitation to total oneness with Jesus?

Monday 30th May   Mark 12:1-12

Then Jesus began to speak to them in parables. "A man planted a vineyard, put a fence around it, dug a pit for the wine press, and built a watchtower; then he leased it to tenants and went to another country. When the season came, he sent a slave to the tenants to collect from them his share of the produce of the vineyard. But they seized him, and beat him, and sent him away empty-handed. And again he sent another slave to them; this one they beat over the head and insulted. Then he sent another, and that one they killed. And so it was with many others; some they beat, and others they killed. He had still one other, a beloved son. Finally he sent him to them, saying, 'They will respect my son.' But those tenants said to one another, 'This is the heir; come, let us kill him, and the inheritance will be ours.' So they seized him, killed him, and threw him out of the vineyard. What then will the owner of the vineyard do? He will come and destroy the tenants and give the vineyard to others. Have you not read this scripture: 'The stone that the builders rejected has become the cornerstone; this was the Lord's doing, and it is amazing in our eyes'?" When they realized that he had told this parable against them, they wanted to arrest him, but they feared the crowd. So they left him and went away.

- A grim parable of people whose blindness and greed leads them to reject and kill the source of their livelihood.
- The listeners realized uncomfortably that it was addressed to them.
- Is it addressed to me? How do I reject and resist the One who is the source of my life?

Tuesday 31st May, Visitation of the Blessed Virgin Mary   Luke 1:39-47

In those days Mary set out and went with haste to a Judean town in the hill country, where she entered the house of Zechariah and greeted Elizabeth. When Elizabeth heard Mary's greeting, the child leaped in her womb. And Elizabeth was filled with the Holy Spirit and exclaimed with a loud cry, "Blessed are you among women, and blessed is the fruit of your womb. And why has this happened to me, that the mother of my Lord comes to me? For as soon as I heard the sound of your greeting, the child in my womb leaped for joy. And blessed is she who believed that there would be a fulfillment of what was spoken to her by the Lord." And Mary said, "My soul magnifies the Lord, and my spirit rejoices in God my Savior."

- Stay with the scene. Both of the women are aware that something awesome is at work in them.
- In their meeting there is the ordinariness of friends meeting, and also a profound sense of destiny.
- Can I explore how they are responding?

Wednesday 1st June   Psalm 24:1-9

To you, O LORD, I lift up my soul. O my God, in you I trust; do not let me be put to shame; do not let my enemies exult over me. Do not let those who wait for you be put to shame; let them be ashamed who are wantonly treacherous. Make me to know your ways, O LORD; teach me your paths. Lead me in your truth, and teach me, for you are the God of my salvation; for you I wait all day long. Be mindful of your mercy, O LORD, and of your steadfast love, for they have been from of old. Do not remember the sins of my youth or my transgressions; according to your steadfast love remember me, for your goodness' sake, O LORD! Good and upright is the LORD; therefore he instructs sinners in the way. He leads the humble in what is right, and teaches the humble his way.

- Does any one sentence or phrase in this passage hook my attention?
- Can I sit with that "word" and see what it is saying to me?

Thursday 2nd June   Mark 12:28-34

One of the scribes came near and heard them disputing with one another, and seeing that he answered them well, he asked Jesus, "Which commandment is the first of all?" Jesus answered, "The first is, 'Hear, O Israel: the Lord our God, the Lord is one; you shall love the Lord your God with all your heart, and with all your soul, and with all your mind, and with all your strength.' The second is this, 'You shall love your neighbor as yourself.' There is no other commandment greater than these." Then the scribe said to him, "You are right, Teacher; you have truly said that 'he is one, and besides him there is no other'; and 'to love him with all the heart, and with all the understanding, and with all the strength,' and 'to love one's neighbor as oneself,'—this is much more important than all whole burnt offerings and sacrifices." When Jesus saw that he answered wisely, he said to him, "You are not far from the kingdom of God." After that no one dared to ask him any question.

- There is disputation and tension in the air when the scribe asks Jesus to tell them what is most important in life.
- The wisdom of Jesus' answer seems to quieten the disturbance around him.
- In my own life, in the midst of whatever might disturb me, do I need to ask Jesus the same question and listen to his answer?

Friday 3rd June, Feast of the Sacred Heart   Luke 15:3-7
Jesus told them this parable: "Which one of you, having a hundred sheep and losing one of them, does not leave the ninety-nine in the wilderness and go after the one that is lost until he finds it? When he has found it, he lays it on his shoulders and rejoices. And when he comes home, he calls together his friends and neighbors, saying to them, 'Rejoice with me, for I have found my sheep that was lost.' Just so, I tell you, there will be more joy in heaven over one sinner

who repents than over ninety-nine righteous persons who
need no repentance."

- "More joy in heaven ... " Can I let myself be surprised by this
  idea of God's delight when someone comes home?
- Do I imagine myself as the cause of this delighting?
- Do I think of myself as one of the ninety-nine? How does all
  of this move me?

Saturday 4th June, Immaculate Heart of Mary
Luke 2:41-51

Now every year his parents went to Jerusalem for the
festival of the Passover. And when he was twelve years
old, they went up as usual for the festival. When the festival
was ended and they started to return, the boy Jesus stayed
behind in Jerusalem, but his parents did not know it.
Assuming that he was in the group of travelers, they went a
day's journey. Then they started to look for him among their
relatives and friends. When they did not find him, they
returned to Jerusalem to search for him. After three days
they found him in the temple, sitting among the teachers,
listening to them and asking them questions. And all who
heard him were amazed at his understanding and his
answers. When his parents saw him they were astonished;
and his mother said to him, "Child, why have you treated us
like this? Look, your father and I have been searching for you
in great anxiety." He said to them, "Why were you searching
for me? Did you not know that I must be in my Father's
house?" But they did not understand what he said to them.
Then he went down with them and came to Nazareth, and
was obedient to them. His mother treasured all these things
in her heart.

- Can I use my imagination to visualize this scene? Mary and Joseph on the road with crowds all round. The boy Jesus—how do I imagine him?—in another place entirely.
- Can I follow the story? How do I respond to the different characters and the situations in which they find themselves?

june 5–11

Something to think and pray about each day this week:

The Sermon on the Mount
Many of the readings around this time are from the "Sermon on the Mount" (Chapters 5 to 7 of Matthew's Gospel). It is a long passage of uncompromising moral teaching, and part of the core of Christianity.

One possible reaction to such strong teaching is for me to condemn those around me for not heeding it. Jesus himself makes it clear that this is not what Christianity is about, saying, "Do not judge, so that you may not be judged" (Matthew 7:1).

Another possible reaction is to notice my own failure to live up to this teaching, and to feel condemned by Jesus, and incapable of the kind of virtue he requires. This, too, would be wrong. The God Jesus teaches us about is a God who understands our weakness and is full of compassion for our failings, "a God merciful and gracious, slow to anger, and abounding in steadfast love and faithfulness" (Exodus 34:6).

But this does not stop God from looking to the best in us and challenging us from time to time. Like a loving father (or a loving mother) God has high hopes for his children.

The Presence of God
I pause for a moment
and think of the love and the grace that God showers on me,
creating me in his image and likeness, making me his temple.

Freedom
"In these days, God taught me
as a schoolteacher teaches a pupil" (St Ignatius).
I remind myself that there are things God has to teach me yet,
and ask for the grace to hear them and let them change me.

Consciousness
Knowing that God loves me unconditionally,
I look honestly over the last day, its events and my feelings.
Do I have something to be grateful for? Then I give thanks.
Is there something I am sorry for? Then I ask forgiveness.

The Word
God speaks to each one of us individually. I need to listen
to what he is saying to me. (Please turn to your scripture on
the following pages. Inspiration points are there should you
need them. When you are ready, return here to continue.)

Conversation
What feelings are rising in me
as I pray and reflect on God's Word?
I imagine Jesus himself sitting or standing beside me,
and open my heart to him.

Conclusion
Glory be to the Father, and to the Son, and to the Holy Spirit,
As it was in the beginning, is now and ever shall be,
World without end. Amen

202

Sunday 5th June, 10th Sunday of the Year

Matthew 9:9-13

As Jesus was walking along, he saw a man called Matthew sitting at the tax booth; and he said to him, "Follow me." And he got up and followed him. And as he sat at dinner in the house, many tax collectors and sinners came and were sitting with him and his disciples. When the Pharisees saw this, they said to his disciples, "Why does your teacher eat with tax collectors and sinners?" But when he heard this, he said, "Those who are well have no need of a physician, but those who are sick. Go and learn what this means, 'I desire mercy, not sacrifice.' For I have come to call not the righteous but sinners."

- Some people run a mile from "tax collectors and sinners." Jesus seems to seek them out, to make friends with them.
- Why is that?
- Do I know any "tax collectors and sinners"?

Monday 6th June

Matthew 5:1-6

When Jesus saw the crowds, he went up the mountain; and after he sat down, his disciples came to him. Then he began to speak, and taught them, saying: "Blessed are the poor in spirit, for theirs is the kingdom of heaven. "Blessed are those who mourn, for they will be comforted. "Blessed are the meek, for they will inherit the earth. Blessed are those who hunger and thirst for righteousness, for they will be filled."

- Am I tempted to go "Yeah, yeah, the Beatitudes"? Maybe I need to stop and listen carefully.
- Is Jesus to be taken seriously?
- Do I value poverty and meekness and these other things?
- Given where I am at myself right now, what is Jesus calling me to?

Tuesday 7th June   Matthew 5:13-16

Jesus said to the disciples, "You are the salt of the earth; but if salt has lost its taste, how can its saltiness be restored? It is no longer good for anything, but is thrown out and trampled under foot. "You are the light of the world. A city built on a hill cannot be hid. No one after lighting a lamp puts it under the bushel basket, but on the lampstand, and it gives light to all in the house. In the same way, let your light shine before others, so that they may see your good works and give glory to your Father in heaven."

- Do I feel salty? Do I feel inspired?
- Do I feel like a light? Am I often in the dark?
- Does it all depend on my talents or efforts?
- If I get exhausted just thinking about it all, can I talk to the One who is the Light of the World and the Salt of the Earth?

Wednesday 8th June   Matthew 5:17-19

Jesus said to his disciples, "Do not think that I have come to abolish the law or the prophets; I have come not to abolish but to fulfill. For truly I tell you, until heaven and earth pass away, not one letter, not one stroke of a letter, will pass from the law until all is accomplished. Therefore, whoever breaks one of the least of these commandments, and teaches others to do the same, will be called least in the kingdom of heaven; but whoever does them and teaches them will be called great in the kingdom of heaven."

- Strangely, the idea arose for some people that the "way of love" proposed by Jesus was "soft" compared to what went before.
- How do I react to the demands that being a follower of Jesus puts on me? Do I avoid anything that might be demanding, dismissing it as "legalism"? Or, perhaps I am too hard on

myself? Do I lay unnecessary burdens on myself that don't come from Jesus?

- Can I look Jesus in the eye and ask him to show me what his "way" means concretely for me?

Thursday 9th June   Matthew 5:21-26

Jesus said to the disciples, "You have heard that it was said to those of ancient times, 'You shall not murder'; and 'whoever murders shall be liable to judgment.' But I say to you that if you are angry with a brother or sister, you will be liable to judgment; and if you insult a brother or sister, you will be liable to the council; and if you say, 'You fool,' you will be liable to the hell of fire. So when you are offering your gift at the altar, if you remember that your brother or sister has something against you, leave your gift there before the altar and go; first be reconciled to your brother or sister, and then come and offer your gift. Come to terms quickly with your accuser while you are on the way to court with him, or your accuser may hand you over to the judge, and the judge to the guard, and you will be thrown into prison. Truly I tell you, you will never get out until you have paid the last penny."

- What is my relationship with anger? Do I express it too readily or not enough?
- How does Jesus' challenge about reconciliation touch me?
- Does any particular experience come to mind? What steps can I take to bring about reconciliation?

Friday 10th June   Matthew 5:27-30

Jesus said to his disciples, "You have heard that it was said, 'You shall not commit adultery.' But I say to you that everyone who looks at a woman with lust has already committed adultery with her in his heart. If your right eye causes you to sin, tear it out and throw it away; it is better for you to lose one of your members than for your whole body to be thrown into hell. And if your right hand causes you to sin, cut it off and throw it away; it is better for you to lose one of your members than for your whole body to go into hell.

- It's hard to put a nice "spin" on this. What is Jesus trying to highlight by these shocking words?
- Is he challenging me about any tendency to live on the surface and be satisfied with it?
- When we are united with God we will be pure in our heart and in our whole being.
- Am I challenged to move in that direction now?

Saturday 11th June   Matthew 5:33-37

Jesus said to his disciples, "Again, you have heard that it was said to those of ancient times, 'You shall not swear falsely, but carry out the vows you have made to the Lord.' But I say to you, Do not swear at all, either by heaven, for it is the throne of God, or by the earth, for it is his footstool, or by Jerusalem, for it is the city of the great King. And do not swear by your head, for you cannot make one hair white or black. Let your word be 'Yes, Yes' or 'No, No'; anything more than this comes from the evil one."

- What significance do I give to my "word"?
- What significance do I imagine Jesus gives to my word?
- Why is my word so important to Jesus?

Something to think and pray about each day this week:

Holiness is for everyone
Again this week, many of the readings come from the "Sermon on the Mount" in Matthew's Gospel. Jesus sets out the high ideals that God has for his people, the values of simplicity, humility, prayerfulness, courage and trust that God wants us to live by. He even goes as far as to say, "be perfect, as your heavenly Father is perfect." (Matt 5:48)

Faced with such high standards, and knowing our own weakness, we can be tempted to give up, thinking it is all beyond our reach. But it isn't. God knows our weakness, loves us nonetheless, and calls every one of us to grow in holiness. Jesus shows us the ideal so that we know what to grow towards.

What God is asking of me now is to take one step towards him. God reassures me that this is not beyond my reach: "Surely, this commandment that I am commanding you today is not too hard for you, nor is it too far away. It is not in heaven, that you should say, 'Who will go up to heaven for us, and get it for us so that we may hear it and observe it?' Neither is it beyond the sea, that you should say, 'Who will cross to the other side of the sea for us, and get it for us so that we may hear it and observe it?' No, the word is very near to you; it is in your mouth and in your heart for you to observe." (Deuteronomy 30:11-14)

The Presence of God
I reflect for a moment on God's presence around me and in me.
Creator of the universe, the sun and the moon, the earth,
every molecule, every atom, everything that is:
God is in every beat of my heart. God is with me, now.

Freedom
If God were trying to tell me something, would I know?
If God were reassuring me or challenging me, would I notice?
I ask for the grace to be free of my own preoccupations
and open to what God may be saying to me.

Consciousness
How do I find myself today?
Where am I with God? With others?
Do I have something to be grateful for? Then I give thanks.
Is there something I am sorry for? Then I ask forgiveness.

The Word
I read the Word of God slowly, a few times over, and I listen
to what God is saying to me. (Please turn to your scripture
on the following pages. Inspiration points are there should you
need them. When you are ready, return here to continue.)

Conversation
What is stirring in me as I pray?
Am I consoled, troubled, left cold?
I imagine Jesus himself standing or sitting at my side,
and share my feelings with him.

Conclusion
Glory be to the Father, and to the Son, and to the Holy Spirit,
As it was in the beginning, is now and ever shall be,
World without end. Amen

208

Sunday 12th June, 11th Sunday of the Year

Matthew 9:36-10:8

When Jesus saw the crowds, he had compassion for them, because they were harassed and helpless, like sheep without a shepherd. Then he said to his disciples, "The harvest is plentiful, but the laborers are few; therefore ask the Lord of the harvest to send out laborers into his harvest." Then Jesus summoned his twelve disciples and gave them authority over unclean spirits, to cast them out, and to cure every disease and every sickness. These are the names of the twelve apostles: first, Simon, also known as Peter, and his brother Andrew; James son of Zebedee, and his brother John; Philip and Bartholomew; Thomas and Matthew the tax collector; James son of Alphaeus, and Thaddaeus; Simon the Cananaean, and Judas Iscariot, the one who betrayed him. These twelve Jesus sent out with the following instructions: "Go nowhere among the Gentiles, and enter no town of the Samaritans, but go rather to the lost sheep of the house of Israel. As you go, proclaim the good news, 'The kingdom of heaven has come near.' Cure the sick, raise the dead, cleanse the lepers, cast out demons. You received without payment; give without payment."

- It seems as if the whole missionary thrust flows out of Jesus' compassion for the crowds.
- Do I—do we—seem "harassed and helpless" as Jesus looks at me—at us—today?
- Do I want to be part of the mission that flows out of God's compassion?

Monday 13th June, St Anthony of Padua

Isaiah 61:1-3a

The spirit of the Lord GOD is upon me, because the LORD has anointed me; he has sent me to bring good news to the oppressed, to bind up the brokenhearted, to proclaim liberty to the captives, and release to the prisoners; to proclaim the year of the Lord's favor, and the day of vengeance of our God; to comfort all who mourn; to provide for those who mourn in Zion—to give them a garland instead of ashes, the oil of gladness instead of mourning, the mantle of praise instead of a faint spirit.

- If I could say with the same verve: "The Spirit of the Lord is upon 'ME' ... and has sent 'ME'"... I would have powerful focus and energy in my life.
- Can I stop and get in touch with the Spirit in my life?
- How am I being sent?

Tuesday 14th June   Matthew 5:43-48

J esus said to his disciples, "You have heard that it was said, 'You shall love your neighbor and hate your enemy.' But I say to you, Love your enemies and pray for those who persecute you, so that you may be children of your Father in heaven; for he makes his sun rise on the evil and on the good, and sends rain on the righteous and on the unrighteous. For if you love those who love you, what reward do you have? Do not even the tax collectors do the same? And if you greet only your brothers and sisters, what more are you doing than others? Do not even the Gentiles do the same? Be perfect, therefore, as your heavenly Father is perfect."

- Love my enemy. But, why?
- What is God's point of view that makes this a reasonable demand?
- Where am I in relation to loving enemies? How do I respond to this?

Wednesday 15th June   Matthew 6:4-6

Jesus said to the disciples, "And whenever you pray, do not be like the hypocrites; for they love to stand and pray in the synagogues and at the street corners, so that they may be seen by others. Truly I tell you, they have received their reward. But whenever you pray, go into your room and shut the door and pray to your Father who is in secret; and your Father who sees in secret will reward you."

- Am I doing, right now, exactly what Jesus suggests?
- Does it encourage me to know I am trying to respond to his challenge?
- He says God is watching me right now ... Does that feel good?

Thursday 16th June   Matthew 6:7-15

Jesus said to his disciples, "When you are praying, do not heap up empty phrases as the Gentiles do; for they think that they will be heard because of their many words. Do not be like them, for your Father knows what you need before you ask him. Pray then in this way: Our Father in heaven, hallowed be your name. Your kingdom come. Your will be done, on earth as it is in heaven. Give us this day our daily bread. And forgive us our debts, as we also have forgiven our debtors. And do not bring us to the time of trial, but rescue us from the evil one. For if you forgive others their trespasses, your heavenly Father will also forgive you; but if you do not forgive others, neither will your Father forgive your trespasses."

- It has been said: If I ask for more than is in the Our Father, I ask for too much. If I ask for less than is in the Our Father, I ask for too little!
- What is Jesus teaching me about my relationship of trust in God through this prayer? Too much? Too little?
- How do you want me to grow towards you, Lord?

Friday 17th June   Matthew 6:19-23

Jesus said to his disciples, "Do not store up for yourselves treasures on earth, where moth and rust consume and where thieves break in and steal; but store up for yourselves treasures in heaven, where neither moth nor rust consumes and where thieves do not break in and steal. For where your treasure is, there your heart will be also. "The eye is the lamp of the body. So, if your eye is healthy, your whole body will be full of light; but if your eye is unhealthy, your whole body will be full of darkness. If then the light in you is darkness, how great is the darkness!"

- This "lamp" shines light outwards as well as inwards.
- What sort of an "eye on the world" do I have? Does the world come into my life through the joyful filter of the Gospel? Or, do I have other, negative, filters through which I see the world?
- What sort of attitudes would I like to have in relation to my world?
- What sort of light might Jesus be calling me to have in my "eyes"?

Saturday 18th June   Matthew 6:24-34

Jesus said to his disciples, "No one can serve two masters; for a slave will either hate the one and love the other, or be devoted to the one and despise the other. You cannot serve God and wealth. "Therefore I tell you, do not worry about your life, what you will eat or what you will drink, or about your body, what you will wear. Is not life more than food, and the body more than clothing? Look at the birds of the air; they neither sow nor reap nor gather into barns, and yet your heavenly Father feeds them. Are you not of more value than they? And can any of you by worrying add a

212

single hour to your span of life? And why do you worry about clothing? Consider the lilies of the field, how they grow; they neither toil nor spin, yet I tell you, even Solomon in all his glory was not clothed like one of these. But if God so clothes the grass of the field, which is alive today and tomorrow is thrown into the oven, will he not much more clothe you—you of little faith? Therefore do not worry, saying, 'What will we eat?' or 'What will we drink?' or 'What will we wear?' For it is the Gentiles who strive for all these things; and indeed your heavenly Father knows that you need all these things. But strive first for the kingdom of God and his righteousness, and all these things will be given to you as well. "So do not worry about tomorrow, for tomorrow will bring worries of its own. Today's trouble is enough for today."

- As I hear Jesus say, "Do not worry about tomorrow," how does it affect me? Does it console me? Does it make me want to scream in frustration? Does it leave me cold?
- Can I get in touch with my honest feelings right now and talk to Jesus about them?

Sacred Space

june 19–25

Something to think and pray about each day this week:

Dealing with Desolation

Sometimes, during or after prayer, I may feel a certain dissatisfaction, and notice that I am not getting the feeling of God's presence, or the sense of peace, serenity, or reassurance that I often get when I pray.

St Ignatius identifies as "desolation" this feeling of being withdrawn or alienated from God and turned in on myself. It often happens when I am determined to "put my faith in earthly things" or shut God out of some area of my life, but it can happen for other reasons, too.

In the Spiritual Exercises (317–322), Ignatius gives some sound advice about dealing with desolation. Three important points are:

1. Don't make decisions in times of desolation.
2. I may feel less inclined to pray, but it is more important than ever to keep praying at these times.
3. I will need to be patient and resolute during this time: it may even help to treat it as a test of my resolve.

The Presence of God

In the silence of my innermost being,
in the fragments of my yearned-for wholeness,
can I hear the whispers of God's presence?
Can I remember when I felt God's nearness?
When we walked together and I let myself be embraced by
God's love.

Freedom

I need to close out the noise, to rise above the noise;
The noise that interrupts, that separates,
The noise that isolates.
I need to listen to God again.

Consciousness

In God's loving presence I unwind the past day,
starting from now and looking back, moment by moment.
I gather in all the goodness and light, in gratitude.
I attend to the shadows and what they say to me,
seeking healing, courage, forgiveness.

The Word

I take my time to read the Word of God, slowly, a few times,
allowing myself to dwell on anything that strikes me. (Please
turn to your scripture on the following pages. Inspiration
points are there should you need them. When you are ready,
return here to continue.)

Conversation

Do I notice myself reacting as I pray with the Word of God?
Do I feel challenged, comforted, angry?
Imagining Jesus sitting or standing by me,
I speak out my feelings, as one trusted friend to another.

Conclusion

Glory be to the Father, and to the Son, and to the Holy Spirit,
As it was in the beginning, is now and ever shall be,
World without end. Amen

Sunday 19th June, 12th Sunday of the Year
Matthew 10:26-33

Jesus said to the disciples, "So have no fear of them; for nothing is covered up that will not be uncovered, and nothing secret that will not become known. What I say to you in the dark, tell in the light; and what you hear whispered, proclaim from the housetops. Do not fear those who kill the body but cannot kill the soul; rather fear him who can destroy both soul and body in hell. Are not two sparrows sold for a penny? Yet not one of them will fall to the ground apart from your Father. And even the hairs of your head are all counted. So do not be afraid; you are of more value than many sparrows. Everyone therefore who acknowledges me before others, I also will acknowledge before my Father in heaven; but whoever denies me before others, I also will deny before my Father in heaven."

- Jesus preaches two messages here. One involves fear of the consequences of sin. The other is a word of confidence in a father who watches over me with infinite tenderness.
- Where is my mind drawn? Towards the fear? Or, towards confidence?
- What is the Lord's special word for me?

Monday 20th June
Genesis 12:1-7

Now the LORD said to Abram, "Go from your country and your kindred and your father's house to the land that I will show you. I will make of you a great nation, and I will bless you, and make your name great, so that you will be a blessing. I will bless those who bless you, and the one who curses you I will curse; and in you all the families of the earth shall be blessed." So Abram went, as the LORD had told him; and Lot went with him. Abram was seventy-five years old when he departed from Haran. Abram took his wife Sarai and his brother's son Lot, and all the possessions that they had gathered, and the persons whom they had acquired in Haran; and they set forth to go to the land of Canaan. When they had come to the land of Canaan, Abram passed through the land to the place at Shechem, to the oak of Moreh. At that time the Canaanites were in the land. Then the LORD appeared to Abram, and said, "To your offspring I will give this land." So he built there an altar to the LORD, who had appeared to him.

- "Leave behind everything familiar and secure and head out into the unknown—at the age of 75!"
- Does God's call to Abram strike a chord with me?
- Do I recognise the call to go out in trust?
- Do I hear the promise of blessing and prosperity addressed to me?

Tuesday 21st June, St Aloysius Gonzaga   Mark 10:23-27
Then Jesus looked around and said to his disciples, "How hard it will be for those who have wealth to enter the kingdom of God!" And the disciples were perplexed at these words. But Jesus said to them again, "Children, how hard it is to enter the kingdom of God! It is easier for a camel to go through the eye of a needle than for someone who is rich to enter the kingdom of God." They were greatly astounded and said to one another, "Then who can be saved?" Jesus looked at them and said, "For mortals it is impossible, but not for God; for God all things are possible."

- Why is it so hard for wealthy people?
- To whom is Jesus referring?
- Am I included?
- Do I find this challenging or confusing? Do I need to speak to Jesus about it?

Wednesday 22nd June   **Matthew 7:15-20**

Jesus said to his disciples, "Beware of false prophets, who come to you in sheep's clothing but inwardly are ravenous wolves. You will know them by their fruits. Are grapes gathered from thorns, or figs from thistles? In the same way, every good tree bears good fruit, but the bad tree bears bad fruit. A good tree cannot bear bad fruit, nor can a bad tree bear good fruit. Every tree that does not bear good fruit is cut down and thrown into the fire. Thus you will know them by their fruits."

* Here we hear a Jesus who speaks directly and frankly.
* How do I respond to his consideration of deception and strong words about good and evil?
* Does it stir me with an attitude of self-righteousness or panicky scrupulosity?
* Or, does Jesus want me to be clear-headed and realistic about the challenge to live authentically?
* What is he calling me to?

Thursday 23rd June   **Matthew 7:21-29**

Jesus said to his disciples, "Not everyone who says to me, 'Lord, Lord,' will enter the kingdom of heaven, but only the one who does the will of my Father in heaven. On that day many will say to me, 'Lord, Lord, did we not prophesy in your name, and cast out demons in your name, and do many deeds of power in your name?' Then I will declare to them, 'I never knew you; go away from me, you evildoers.' "Everyone then who hears these words of mine and acts on them will be like a wise man who built his house on rock. The rain fell, the floods came, and the winds blew and beat on that house, but it did not fall, because it had been founded on rock. And everyone who hears these words of mine and does not act on them will be like a foolish man who built his house on sand. The rain fell, and the floods came, and the winds blew and beat against that house, and it fell—and great was its fall!" Now when Jesus had finished saying these things, the crowds were astounded at his teaching, for he taught them as one having authority, and not as their scribes.

- Love is expressed better in deeds than in words.
- How does Jesus' challenge about doing the will of the Father catch me?
- Is there anything concrete that I feel I need to look at?

Friday 24th June, The Birth of John the Baptist
Luke 1:57-64

Now the time came for Elizabeth to give birth, and she bore a son. Her neighbors and relatives heard that the Lord had shown his great mercy to her, and they rejoiced with her. On the eighth day they came to circumcise the child, and they were going to name him Zechariah after his father. But his mother said, "No; he is to be called John." They said to her, "None of your relatives has this name." Then they began motioning to his father to find out what name he wanted to give him. He asked for a writing tablet and wrote, "His name is John." And all of them were amazed. Immediately his mouth was opened and his tongue freed, and he began to speak, praising God.

- Watch this remarkable little scene.
- God has intervened in the affairs of this family in an unexpected way.
- How do the different parties react? Elizabeth? The relatives? Zechariah?
- What can I learn from this?

220

Saturday 25th June Matthew 8:5-13

When Jesus entered Capernaum, a centurion came to him, appealing to him and saying, "Lord, my servant is lying at home paralyzed, in terrible distress." And he said to him, "I will come and cure him." The centurion answered, "Lord, I am not worthy to have you come under my roof; but only speak the word, and my servant will be healed. For I also am a man under authority, with soldiers under me; and I say to one, 'Go,' and he goes, and to another, 'Come,' and he comes, and to my slave, 'Do this,' and the slave does it." When Jesus heard him, he was amazed and said to those who followed him, "Truly I tell you, in no one in Israel have I found such faith. I tell you, many will come from east and west and will eat with Abraham and Isaac and Jacob in the kingdom of heaven, while the heirs of the kingdom will be thrown into the outer darkness, where there will be weeping and gnashing of teeth." And to the centurion Jesus said, "Go; let it be done for you according to your faith." And the servant was healed in that hour.

- Imagine this scene. A band of Jews with their travelling rabbi are entering the town. Up comes a Roman centurion.
- What do these two men look like? How do they compare with each other?
- Do I hear what is said?
- What is my attitude to Jesus?

Sacred Space

june 26 – july 2

Something to think and pray about each day this week:

Tough love
Responding to God's call is not always easy. Sometimes there are many obstacles and a lot of fear to overcome.

In my everyday life, doing the right thing—doing what God asks of me—will sometimes be tough. Perhaps it will involve a lot of work or inconvenience. Perhaps it will make me uncomfortable or unpopular. But if I want to live a life that is worth living, it has to involve some sacrifice. If I go from day to day taking the easy options, my life will be pretty unremarkable.

The courage required to respond to God's call is a theme in many of this week's readings, culminating in the words of Sunday's Gospel: "Those who find their life will lose it, and those who lose their life for my sake will find it."(Matthew 10:39)

This may sound like a warning or a challenge. But it is also a promise—a promise of the real freedom, true fulfillment and deep joy that flow from a life of self-giving love.

The Presence of God
I remind myself that, as I sit here now,
God is gazing on me with love and holding me in being.
I pause for a moment and think of this.

Freedom
I will ask God's help,
to be free from my own preoccupations,
to be open to God in this time of prayer,
to come to love and serve him more.

Consciousness
I exist in a web of relationships—links to nature, people, God.
I trace out these links, giving thanks for the life that flows
through them.
Some links are twisted or broken: I may feel regret, anger,
disappointment.
I pray for the gift of acceptance and forgiveness.

The Word
God speaks to each one of us individually. I need to listen
to what he is saying to me. (Please turn to your scripture on
the following pages. Inspiration points are there should you
need them. When you are ready, return here to continue.)

Conversation
Remembering that I am still in God's presence,
I imagine Jesus himself standing or sitting beside me,
and say whatever is on my mind, whatever is in my heart,
speaking as one friend to another.

Conclusion
Glory be to the Father, and to the Son, and to the Holy Spirit,
As it was in the beginning, is now and ever shall be,
World without end. Amen

Sunday 26th June, 13th Sunday of the Year
Matthew 10:37-39

Jesus said to his disciples, "Whoever loves father or mother more than me is not worthy of me; and whoever loves son or daughter more than me is not worthy of me; and whoever does not take up the cross and follow me is not worthy of me. Those who find their life will lose it, and those who lose their life for my sake will find it."

- These hard words are in fact an offer of life.
- What might the call to "take up the cross" or "lose my life" mean in my context?
- Do I believe that this kind of "losing" will lead to true life?

Monday 27th June   Psalm 102(103):1-4, 8-11

Bless the LORD, O my soul, and all that is within me, bless his holy name. Bless the LORD, O my soul, and do not forget all his benefits—who forgives all your iniquity, who heals all your diseases, who redeems your life from the Pit, who crowns you with steadfast love and mercy. The LORD is merciful and gracious, slow to anger and abounding in steadfast love. He will not always accuse, nor will he keep his anger forever. He does not deal with us according to our sins, nor repay us according to our iniquities. For as the heavens are high above the earth, so great is his steadfast love toward those who fear him;

- As I mull over the words "blessings," "forgives," "compassion," where do I find myself?
- Do they resonate in me or do they seem distant from me?
- Taking myself where I am, can I begin to allow God's words to echo in me?

Tuesday 28th June   **Matthew 8:23-27**

A nd when Jesus got into the boat, his disciples followed him. A windstorm arose on the sea, so great that the boat was being swamped by the waves; but he was asleep. And they went and woke him up, saying, "Lord, save us! We are perishing!" And he said to them, "Why are you afraid, you of little faith?" Then he got up and rebuked the winds and the sea; and there was a dead calm. They were amazed, saying, "What sort of man is this, that even the winds and the sea obey him?"

- Has there been a time in my life when I have felt like screaming: "Lord, save me! I am perishing!" Perhaps I resonate with those feelings on behalf of someone else.
- Can I go, with my feelings, into the boat and share in the fears of the disciples that they are going to be lost. And, where is Jesus? Asleep!
- I follow the scene as it unfolds.

Wednesday 29th June, Sts Peter and Paul
                                  Matthew 16:13-19

N ow when Jesus came into the district of Caesarea Philippi, he asked his disciples, "Who do people say that the Son of Man is?" And they said, "Some say John the Baptist, but others Elijah, and still others Jeremiah or one of the prophets." He said to them, "But who do you say that I am?" Simon Peter answered, "You are the Messiah, the Son of the living God." And Jesus answered him, "Blessed are you, Simon son of Jonah! For flesh and blood has not revealed this to you, but my Father in heaven. And I tell you, you are Peter, and on this rock I will build my church, and the gates of Hades will not prevail against it. I will give you the keys of the kingdom of heaven, and whatever you bind on earth will be bound in heaven, and whatever you loose on earth will be loosed in heaven."

- This is the big question that every follower is asked, again and again: "Who do you say I am?"
- What is my answer?
- Does my answer depend mainly on me, or on my Father in heaven?

Thursday 30th June   Matthew 9:1-8

A nd after getting into a boat Jesus crossed the sea and came to his own town. And just then some people were carrying a paralyzed man lying on a bed. When Jesus saw their faith, he said to the paralytic, "Take heart, son; your sins are forgiven." Then some of the scribes said to themselves, "This man is blaspheming." But Jesus, perceiving their thoughts, said, "Why do you think evil in your hearts? For which is easier, to say, 'Your sins are forgiven,' or to say, 'Stand up and walk'? But so that you may know that the Son of Man has authority on earth to forgive sins"—he then said to the paralytic—"Stand up, take your bed and go to your home." And he stood up and went to his home. When the crowds saw it, they were filled with awe, and they glorified God, who had given such authority to human beings.

- The words "your sins are forgiven" liberate a paralysed body as well as a wounded soul.
- Do I want to hear those words addressed to me? Do I feel the need to hear them?
- Can I put myself in the place of the paralysed man and be open to Jesus' healing words?

Friday 1st July   Matthew 9:9-13

A s Jesus was walking along, he saw a man called Matthew sitting at the tax booth; and he said to him, "Follow me." And he got up and followed him. And as he sat at dinner in the house, many tax collectors and sinners came and were sitting with him and his disciples. When the Pharisees saw this, they said to his disciples, "Why does your teacher eat with tax collectors and sinners?" But when he heard this, he said, "Those who are well have no need of a physician, but those who are sick. Go and learn what this means, 'I desire mercy, not sacrifice.' For I have come to call not the righteous but sinners."

- Can I imagine myself in Matthew's situation? I'm in my usual place, doing my usual things, when, all unexpected, I hear the words, "Follow me."
- How do I respond?
- What does he want?
- What does "I desire mercy, not sacrifice" mean for me?

Saturday 2nd July   Matthew 9:14-17

Then the disciples of John came to Jesus, saying, "Why do we and the Pharisees fast often, but your disciples do not fast?" And Jesus said to them, "The wedding guests cannot mourn as long as the bridegroom is with them, can they? The days will come when the bridegroom is taken away from them, and then they will fast. No one sews a piece of unshrunk cloth on an old cloak, for the patch pulls away from the cloak, and a worse tear is made. Neither is new wine put into old wineskins; otherwise, the skins burst, and the wine is spilled, and the skins are destroyed; but new wine is put into fresh wineskins, and so both are preserved."

- What makes the Pharisees react to Jesus in the way they do? What is it about him? What is it about them?
- Is there any pharisaism in me?
- Can I allow Jesus to help me change?

july 3–9

Something to think and pray about each day this week:

Allowing myself to "dwell"
Writing about praying slowly through the words of the *Our Father* or *Lord's Prayer*, Ignatius says, "If one finds in one or two words matter which yields thought, relish and consolation, one should not be anxious to move forward, even if the whole hour is consumed on what is being found."

This applies to any passage of scripture. If I am struck by a word or phrase that has meaning for me, there is no need to hurry on and finish the passage. I can dwell on that word or phrase for as long as I like, allowing myself to savor it, and enter more deeply into whatever stirring, insight or feeling it has caused in me.

These stirrings in the mind and heart are one of the ways that God speaks to us. Noticing them and staying with them is my effort to listen to what God is saying to me.

The Presence of God
God is with me, but more,
God is within me, giving me existence.
Let me dwell for a moment on God's life-giving presence
in my body, my mind, my heart
and in the whole of my life.

Freedom
God is not foreign to my freedom.
Instead the Spirit breathes life into my most intimate desires,
gently nudging me towards all that is good.
I ask for the grace to let myself be enfolded by the Spirit.

Consciousness
How am I really feeling? Light-hearted? Heavy-hearted?
I may be very much at peace, happy to be here.
Equally, I may be frustrated, worried or angry.
I acknowledge how I really am. It is the real me that the
Lord loves.

The Word
I read the Word of God slowly, a few times over, and I listen
to what God is saying to me. (Please turn to your scripture on
the following pages. Inspiration points are there should you
need them. When you are ready, return here to continue.)

Conversation
How has God's Word moved me? Has it left me cold?
Has it consoled me or moved me to act in a new way?
I imagine Jesus standing or sitting beside me,
I turn and share my feelings with him.

Conclusion
Glory be to the Father, and to the Son, and to the Holy Spirit,
As it was in the beginning, is now and ever shall be,
World without end. Amen

Sunday 3rd July, 14th Sunday of the Year
Matthew 11:28-30

Jesus said, "Come to me, all you that are weary and are carrying heavy burdens, and I will give you rest. Take my yoke upon you, and learn from me; for I am gentle and humble in heart, and you will find rest for your souls. For my yoke is easy, and my burden is light."

- I imagine Jesus beside me, speaking these words to me as if for the first time.
- I look at my journey—am I carrying heavy burdens or am I sailing along? I can talk to Jesus about this.
- Are there certain steps I need to take if I am burdened? I rest assured that Jesus is happy to help.

Monday 4th July
Matthew 9:18-26

While Jesus was saying these things to them, suddenly a leader of the synagogue came in and knelt before him, saying, "My daughter has just died; but come and lay your hand on her, and she will live." And Jesus got up and followed him, with his disciples. Then suddenly a woman who had been suffering from hemorrhages for twelve years came up behind him and touched the fringe of his cloak, for she said to herself, "If I only touch his cloak, I will be made well." Jesus turned, and seeing her he said, "Take heart, daughter; your faith has made you well." And instantly the woman was made well. When Jesus came to the leader's house and saw the flute players and the crowd making a commotion, he said, "Go away; for the girl is not dead but sleeping." And they laughed at him. But when the crowd had been put outside, he went in and took her by the hand, and the girl got up. And the report of this spread throughout that district.

- Can I picture this scene, as if I was an onlooker, perhaps one of Jesus' disciples?
- First I see the synagogue leader throw himself at Jesus' feet and then the woman simply reach out to touch the hem of his cloak.
- What is going on in their minds and hearts?
- What is it about Jesus that draws them to him?
- When I watch Jesus dealing with these two adults and then with the little girl, what does it tell me about him?

Tuesday 5th July   Matthew 9:32-38

After they had gone away, a demoniac who was mute was brought to Jesus. And when the demon had been cast out, the one who had been mute spoke; and the crowds were amazed and said, "Never has anything like this been seen in Israel." But the Pharisees said, "By the ruler of the demons he casts out the demons." Then Jesus went about all the cities and villages, teaching in their synagogues, and proclaiming the good news of the kingdom, and curing every disease and every sickness. When he saw the crowds, he had compassion for them, because they were harassed and helpless, like sheep without a shepherd. Then he said to his disciples, "The harvest is plentiful, but the laborers are few; therefore ask the Lord of the harvest to send out laborers into his harvest."

- Can I imagine this scene? The man who was once dumb and closed up within himself is set free? How do I react to this?
- The Pharisees assume that this must be the work of the devil. How can they look for evil in something so good?
- Is there a lesson for me in this?
- When Jesus looks on the crowd with compassion? Do I imagine that I am among them?

Wednesday 6th July   Matthew 10:1-7

Then Jesus summoned his twelve disciples and gave them authority over unclean spirits, to cast them out, and to cure every disease and every sickness. These are the names of the twelve apostles: first, Simon, also known as Peter, and his brother Andrew; James son of Zebedee, and his brother John; Philip and Bartholomew; Thomas and Matthew the tax collector; James son of Alphaeus, and Thaddaeus; Simon the Cananaean, and Judas Iscariot, the one who betrayed him. These twelve Jesus sent out with the following instructions: "Go nowhere among the Gentiles, and enter no town of the Samaritans, but go rather to the lost sheep of the house of Israel. As you go, proclaim the good news, 'The kingdom of heaven has come near.'"

- It is good to mull over the names of these particular characters that Jesus chose to do his work. They weren't very impressive as individuals, yet Jesus chose them and shared his authority and power to heal with them.
- Can I reflect on the fact that he has some particular work for me to do also? How does that thought strike me? Am I honoured and delighted? Does it make me nervous or feel unworthy?
- How might Jesus be sharing his power to heal with me? Am I open to being called and sent?

Thursday 7th July   Matthew 10:7-15

Jesus said to the twelve, "As you go, proclaim the good news, 'The kingdom of heaven has come near.' Cure the sick, raise the dead, cleanse the lepers, cast out demons. You received without payment; give without payment. Take no gold, or silver, or copper in your belts, no bag for your journey, or two tunics, or sandals, or a staff; for laborers deserve their food. Whatever town or village you enter, find out who in it is worthy, and stay there until you leave. As you enter the house, greet it. If the house is worthy, let your peace come upon it; but if it is not worthy, let your peace return to you. If anyone will not welcome you or listen to your words, shake off the dust from your feet as you leave that house or town. Truly I tell you, it will be more tolerable for the land of Sodom and Gomorrah on the day of judgment than for that town."

- Can I imagine the twelve, gathered round the master before going out as missionaries, hanging on his every word?
- The core message is: "The Kingdom of Heaven has come near."
- As they stand there listening to him, what do those words mean to them?
- What do they mean to me? How do I hear the command to go out into the unknown to make this message known?

Friday 8th July   Matthew 10:16-23

Jesus said to the twelve, "See, I am sending you out like sheep into the midst of wolves; so be wise as serpents and innocent as doves. Beware of them, for they will hand you over to councils and flog you in their synagogues; and you will be dragged before governors and kings because of me, as a testimony to them and the Gentiles. When they hand you over, do not worry about how you are to speak or what you are to say; for what you are to say will be given to you at that time; for it is not you who speak, but the Spirit of your Father speaking through you. Brother will betray brother to death, and a father his child, and children will rise against parents and have them put to death; and you will be hated by all because of my name. But the one who endures to the end will be saved. When they persecute you in one town, flee to the next; for truly I tell you, you will not have gone through all the towns of Israel before the Son of Man comes."

- The twelve, gathered around Jesus were being sent out to preach the greatest good news of all time.
- Then, they hear what awaits them: flogging, dragging, betrayal, universal hatred and persecution.
- This all seems very confusing. Why should it be like this?
- How can I hold on to the conviction that "the Kingdom of Heaven is near" in the face of all this negativity?
- What does Jesus have to say about it?

Saturday 9th July   Matthew 10:26-31

Jesus taught the twelve as follows: "So have no fear of them; for nothing is covered up that will not be uncovered, and nothing secret that will not become known. What I say to you in the dark, tell in the light; and what you hear whispered, proclaim from the housetops. Do not fear those who kill the body but cannot kill the soul; rather fear him who can destroy both soul and body in hell. Are not two sparrows sold for a penny? Yet not one of them will fall to the ground apart from your Father. And even the hairs of your head are all counted. So do not be afraid; you are of more value than many sparrows.

- Jesus has always been very frank about the possible trials and tribulations that his followers will face. Yet, he says, again and again: "Have no fear."
- Do I allow his words to speak strongly and clearly to me?
- What are the trials that I fear? What is Jesus saying to me?

Sacred Space

july 10–16

Something to think and pray about each day this week:

More about "dwelling"

Just as we may draw what Ignatius would call "great spiritual relish" from dwelling on just one word or phrase from a scripture passage, there may be times when one of the other stages of *Sacred Space* is worth dwelling on.

Some days, it might not be the scripture at all, but a sudden awareness of God's presence around me which moves me deeply. Or it might be a realization of my need for freedom, or reflecting on the experience of the last day.

If this happens, I don't have to move on immediately and start reading the scripture. I can allow myself to dwell for a while on whatever it was that caused that feeling in me. Such feelings are one of the ways in which God can speak to us, and I can bring them into "conversation" with the Lord.

The Presence of God

To be present is to arrive as one is and open up to the other.
At this instant, as I arrive here, God is present waiting for me.
God always arrives before me, desiring to connect with me
even more than my most intimate friend.
I take a moment and greet my loving God.

Freedom

Everything has the potential to draw forth from me a fuller
love and life.
Yet my desires are often fixed, caught, on illusions of
fulfillment.
I ask that God, through my freedom, may orchestrate
my desires in a vibrant loving melody rich in harmony.

Consciousness

Knowing that God loves me unconditionally,
I can afford to be honest about how I am.
How has the last day been, and how do I feel now?
I share my feelings openly with the Lord.

The Word

I take my time to read the Word of God, slowly, a few times,
allowing myself to dwell on anything that strikes me. (Please
turn to your scripture on the following pages. Inspiration
points are there should you need them. When you are ready,
return here to continue.)

Conversation

What feelings are rising in me
as I pray and reflect on God's Word?
I imagine Jesus himself sitting or standing beside me,
and open my heart to him.

Conclusion

Glory be to the Father, and to the Son, and to the Holy Spirit,
As it was in the beginning, is now and ever shall be,
World without end. Amen

Sunday 10th July, 15th Sunday of the Year

Matthew 13:3-9

And Jesus told them many things in parables, saying: "Listen! A sower went out to sow. And as he sowed, some seeds fell on the path, and the birds came and ate them up. Other seeds fell on rocky ground, where they did not have much soil, and they sprang up quickly, since they had no depth of soil. But when the sun rose, they were scorched; and since they had no root, they withered away. Other seeds fell among thorns, and the thorns grew up and choked them. Other seeds fell on good soil and brought forth grain, some a hundredfold, some sixty, some thirty. Let anyone with ears listen!"

- What is the rocky ground in me? In what areas of my life does God's word have no chance?
- What thorns are there that choke the faith and hope in me?
- Do I nurture the faith of others? Am I a watering can for them, or a scorching sun?
- Where have I seen good soil, and plentiful harvest, in my life or in others around me?

Monday 11th July, St Benedict   Matthew 19:27-29

Then Peter said in reply, "Look, we have left everything and followed you. What then will we have?" Jesus said to them, "Truly I tell you, at the renewal of all things, when the Son of Man is seated on the throne of his glory, you who have followed me will also sit on twelve thrones, judging the twelve tribes of Israel. And everyone who has left houses or brothers or sisters or father or mother or children or fields, for my name's sake, will receive a hundredfold, and will inherit eternal life."

- Jesus had just been saying how difficult it is for the "rich" people who cling to things to enter the Kingdom of Heaven. Peter says: What about us?
- Does this talk of leaving things—and even people—behind strike any resonance with me?
- Have I been asked to let go of things? Are there things I need to let go of but find it hard?
- Can I talk to Jesus about these things?

Tuesday 12th July   Matthew 11:20-24

Then he began to reproach the cities in which most of his deeds of power had been done, because they did not repent. "Woe to you, Chorazin! Woe to you, Bethsaida! For if the deeds of power done in you had been done in Tyre and Sidon, they would have repented long ago in sackcloth and ashes. But I tell you, on the day of judgment it will be more tolerable for Tyre and Sidon than for you. And you, Capernaum, will you be exalted to heaven? No, you will be brought down to Hades. For if the deeds of power done in you had been done in Sodom, it would have remained until this day. But I tell you that on the day of judgment it will be more tolerable for the land of Sodom than "Woe" is a word of lament cried out over the dead. Those towns and their people were spiritually dead and didn't respond to Jesus.

- Am I able to see—and respond to—any miracles of Jesus around me?
- Do I need help with this?

Wednesday 13th July   Matthew 11:25-27

At that time Jesus said, "I thank you, Father, Lord of heaven and earth, because you have hidden these things from the wise and the intelligent and have revealed them to infants; yes, Father, for such was your gracious will. All

240

things have been handed over to me by my Father; and no one knows the Son except the Father, and no one knows the Father except the Son and anyone to whom the Son chooses to reveal him.

- Jesus found that the "wise and the intelligent" couldn't respond to him but that "infants" could.
- Which group do I belong to: "the wise and the intelligent" or the "infants"?
- What change would I need to make in order to become an "infant"?

Thursday 14th July — Matthew 11:28-30

"Come to me, all you that are weary and are carrying heavy burdens, and I will give you rest. Take my yoke upon you, and learn from me; for I am gentle and humble in heart, and you will find rest for your souls. For my yoke is easy, and my burden is light."

- The yoke and burden are simple metaphors for friendship with Jesus and his Father.
- What further invitation do I need?

Friday 15th July — Matthew 12:1-8

At that time Jesus went through the grainfields on the sabbath; his disciples were hungry, and they began to pluck heads of grain and to eat. When the Pharisees saw it, they said to him, "Look, your disciples are doing what is not lawful to do on the sabbath." He said to them, "Have you not read what David did when he and his companions were hungry? He entered the house of God and ate the bread of the Presence, which it was not lawful for him or his companions to eat, but only for the priests. Or have you not read in the law that on the sabbath the priests in the temple break the sabbath and yet are guiltless? I tell you, something greater than the temple is here. But if you had known what this means, 'I desire mercy and not sacrifice,' you would not have condemned the guiltless. For the Son of Man is lord of the sabbath."

- The Pharisees probably believed they were justified in harassing Jesus.
- How could people with good intentions get it so wrong?
- What can I learn from this?

Saturday 16th July   Matthew 12:14-21

But the Pharisees went out and conspired against him, how to destroy him. When Jesus became aware of this, he departed. Many crowds followed him, and he cured all of them, and he ordered them not to make him known. This was to fulfill what had been spoken through the prophet Isaiah: "Here is my servant, whom I have chosen, my beloved, with whom my soul is well pleased. I will put my Spirit upon him, and he will proclaim justice to the Gentiles. He will not wrangle or cry aloud, nor will anyone hear his voice in the streets. He will not break a bruised reed or quench a smoldering wick until he brings justice to victory. And in his name the Gentiles will hope."

- This is a crucial moment where his enemies take a truly desperate path.
- How do I see Jesus, the object of all this bitterness and hatred? Who is he? The Prophet Isaiah foretold the coming of a Servant of God whose victory would come through humility and suffering.

july 17–23

Something to think and pray about each day this week:

The heart, not the head

At this stage, it's important to remember that prayer is about the heart. It's not about trying to have wonderful new ideas in my head. St. Ignatius advises us simply to let ourselves "savor" just one or two things deeply and personally. So, that's why it is very important to move slowly through those steps which don't change from day to day. The best part of the prayer for me might be to sit for a long time in the Presence of God, or on one of the other steps.

The Presence of God
What is present to me is what has a hold on my becoming.
I reflect on the presence of God always there in love,
amidst the many things that have a hold on me.
I pause and pray that I may let God
affect my becoming in this precise moment.

Freedom
There are very few people
who realize what God would make of them
if they abandoned themselves into his hands,
and let themselves be formed by his grace. (St Ignatius)
I ask for the grace to trust myself totally to God's love.

Consciousness
In the presence of my loving Creator,
I look honestly at my feelings over the last day,
the highs, the lows and the level ground.
Can I see where the Lord has been present?

The Word
God speaks to each one of us individually. I need to listen
to what he is saying to me. (Please turn to your scripture on
the following pages. Inspiration points are there should you
need them. When you are ready, return here to continue.)

Conversation
What is stirring in me as I pray?
Am I consoled, troubled, left cold?
I imagine Jesus himself standing or sitting at my side,
and share my feelings with him.

Conclusion
Glory be to the Father, and to the Son, and to the Holy Spirit,
As it was in the beginning, is now and ever shall be,
World without end. Amen

244

Sunday 17th July, 16th Sunday of the Year
Matthew 13:31-35

Jesus put before them another parable: "The kingdom of heaven is like a mustard seed that someone took and sowed in his field; it is the smallest of all the seeds, but when it has grown it is the greatest of shrubs and becomes a tree, so that the birds of the air come and make nests in its branches." He told them another parable: "The kingdom of heaven is like yeast that a woman took and mixed in with three measures of flour until all of it was leavened." Jesus told the crowds all these things in parables; without a parable he told them nothing. This was to fulfill what had been spoken through the prophet: "I will open my mouth to speak in parables; I will proclaim what has been hidden from the foundation of the world."

- Can I think of examples of "mustard seeds" … tiny insignificant things or persons, who make a huge impact?
- I might need to ask for a special grace to see how mustard seeds work.

Monday 18th July   Matthew 12:38-42

Then some of the scribes and Pharisees said to Jesus, "Teacher, we wish to see a sign from you." But he answered them, "An evil and adulterous generation asks for a sign, but no sign will be given to it except the sign of the prophet Jonah. For just as Jonah was three days and three nights in the belly of the sea monster, so for three days and three nights the Son of Man will be in the heart of the earth. The people of Nineveh will rise up at the judgment with this generation and condemn it, because they repented at the proclamation of Jonah, and see, something greater than Jonah is here! The queen of the South will rise up at the judgment with this generation and condemn it, because she came from the ends of the earth to listen to the wisdom of Solomon, and see, something greater than Solomon is here!"

- "We wish to see a sign from you." There already have been many miracles and signs and the ordinary people have turned to Jesus in crowds. His enemies ask for a sign but won't ever accept him, because they want things on their own terms.
- As I listen to Jesus in this setting, what arises in me?

Tuesday 19th July   Matthew 12:46-50

While Jesus was still speaking to the crowds, his mother and his brothers were standing outside, wanting to speak to him. Someone told him, "Look, your mother and your brothers are standing outside, wanting to speak to you." But to the one who had told him this, Jesus replied, "Who is my mother, and who are my brothers?" And pointing to his disciples, he said, "Here are my mother and my brothers! For whoever does the will of my Father in heaven is my brother and sister and mother."

- Can I imagine this scene: Jesus is busy with the work of preaching and his beloved family come by.
- When he points to the group of disciples can I imagine that I am standing among them?

Wednesday 20th July   Matthew 13:1-9

That same day Jesus went out of the house and sat beside the sea. Such great crowds gathered around him that he got into a boat and sat there, while the whole crowd stood on the beach. And he told them many things in parables, saying: "Listen! A sower went out to sow. And as he sowed, some seeds fell on the path, and the birds came and ate them up. Other seeds fell on rocky ground, where they did not have much soil, and they sprang up quickly, since they had no depth of soil. But when the sun rose, they were scorched; and since they had no root, they withered away. Other seeds fell among thorns, and the thorns grew up and choked them. Other seeds fell on good soil and brought forth grain, some a hundredfold, some sixty, some thirty. Let anyone with ears listen!"

- What is my standard way of thinking and praying about this parable?
- Do I apply it to myself and analyze whether I am "rocky" or "thorny" in nature?
- Do I think of the sower, scattering seed liberally, with confidence and hope?
- Can I try and come at this parable afresh and allow Jesus to speak to me in a new way right now?

Thursday 21st July   Matthew 13:10-17

Then the disciples came and asked Jesus, "Why do you speak to them in parables?" He answered, "To you it has been given to know the secrets of the kingdom of heaven, but to them it has not been given. For to those who have, more will be given, and they will have an abundance; but from those who have nothing, even what they have will be taken away. The reason I speak to them in parables is that 'seeing they do not perceive, and hearing they do not listen, nor do they understand.' With them indeed is fulfilled the prophecy of Isaiah that says: 'You will indeed listen, but never understand, and you will indeed look, but never perceive. For this people's heart has grown dull, and their ears are hard of hearing, and they have shut their eyes; so that they might not look with their eyes, and listen with their ears, and understand with their heart and turn—and I would heal them.' But blessed are your eyes, for they see, and your ears, for they hear. Truly I tell you, many prophets and right-eous people longed to see what you see, but did not see it, and to hear what you hear, but did not hear it.

- Jesus' message—his call to a self-sacrificing love—was falling on deaf ears. People were turning their backs on him; he had even been driven out of his home town!
- Can I feel, with him, his sense of frustration? He only wants people to have the fullness of life and they don't get it.
- Where am I in this? What might Jesus be wanting to say to me, now?

Friday 22nd July, St Mary Magdalene   John 20:11-18

But Mary stood weeping outside the tomb. As she wept, she bent over to look into the tomb; and she saw two angels in white, sitting where the body of Jesus had been lying, one at the head and the other at the feet. They said to her, "Woman, why are you weeping?" She said to them, "They have taken away my Lord, and I do not know where they have laid him." When she had said this, she turned around and saw Jesus standing there, but she did not know that it was Jesus. Jesus said to her, "Woman, why are you weeping? Whom are you looking for?" Supposing him to be the gardener, she said to him, "Sir, if you have carried him away, tell me where you have laid him, and I will take him away." Jesus said to her, "Mary!" She turned and said to him in Hebrew, "Rabbouni!" (which means Teacher). Jesus said to her, "Do not hold on to me, because I have not yet ascended to the Father. But go to my brothers and say to them, 'I am ascending to my Father and your Father, to my God and your God.'" Mary Magdalene went and announced to the disciples, "I have seen the Lord"; and she told them that he had said these things to her.

- Allow yourself to see Mary in great distress. The one she longs to see is there and she can't recognise him.
- The sound of her own name breaks through the cloud of her unknowing.
- Can I imagine Jesus calling me by my name? How does it sound?

Saturday 23rd July, St Bridget   John 15:7-8

Jesus said to his disciples, "If you abide in me, and my words abide in you, ask for whatever you wish, and it will be done for you. My Father is glorified by this, that you bear much fruit and become my disciples."

- To abide, or live, in Jesus means extraordinary intimacy. I possibly feel I am miles away from that.
- He offers me all I need to be fully alive in him. Even in the midst of my doubting, can I let myself be brought closer?
- My loving choices and actions, even small ones, are signs of God's life working in our world.

Sacred Space

july 24–30

Something to think and pray about each day this week:

How would I know?

If God were asking something of me, would I notice? If there was some change in my life that God was asking me to make, how would I know?

Wanting to hear is the first condition. There may be areas of my life that I want to keep as no-go areas for God, issues where I just don't want to hear that there is any need for change. I may feel discomfort when an area or issue like this comes up in conversation, and especially during my prayer. I may be itching to move on.

If I notice that feeling, it could be that I need to pray for the grace of freedom and openness to God's will for me, knowing that God always wants what is genuinely good for me. Praying for freedom, and really meaning it, will increase my sensitivity to what God is saying to me. If I am honest with myself, I will know when I am truly open to whatever God wants for me.

The Presence of God
God is with me, but more, God is within me.
Let me dwell for a moment on God's life-giving presence
in my body, in my mind, in my heart,
as I sit here, right now.

Freedom
A thick and shapeless tree-trunk would never believe
that it could become a statue, admired as a miracle of sculpture,
and would never submit itself to the chisel of the sculptor,
who sees by her genius what she can make of it. (St Ignatius)
I ask for the grace to let myself be shaped by my loving Creator.

Consciousness
Knowing that God loves me unconditionally,
I look honestly over the last day, its events and my feelings.
Do I have something to be grateful for? Then I give thanks.
Is there something I am sorry for? Then I ask forgiveness.

The Word
I read the Word of God slowly, a few times over, and I listen
to what God is saying to me. (Please turn to your scripture on
the following pages. Inspiration points are there should you
need them. When you are ready, return here to continue.)

Conversation
Do I notice myself reacting as I pray with the Word of God?
Do I feel challenged, comforted, angry?
Imagining Jesus sitting or standing by me,
I speak out my feelings, as one trusted friend to another.

Conclusion
Glory be to the Father, and to the Son, and to the Holy Spirit,
As it was in the beginning, is now and ever shall be,
World without end. Amen

252

Sunday 24th July, 17th Sunday of the Year
Matthew 13:44-46

Jesus said to the disciples, "The kingdom of heaven is like treasure hidden in a field, which someone found and hid; then in his joy he goes and sells all that he has and buys that field. "Again, the kingdom of heaven is like a merchant in search of fine pearls; on finding one pearl of great value, he went and sold all that he had and bought it."

- What is my "treasure"? For what would I sell everything?
- Pearls can be deceptive. We cannot always tell "fine pearls" from false ones.
- How does the Kingdom of Heaven challenge my "treasure" or my notion of "fine pearls"?

Monday 25th July, St James, Apostle   Matthew 20:20-28

Then the mother of the sons of Zebedee came to him with her sons, and kneeling before him, she asked a favor of him. And he said to her, "What do you want?" She said to him, "Declare that these two sons of mine will sit, one at your right hand and one at your left, in your kingdom." But Jesus answered, "You do not know what you are asking. Are you able to drink the cup that I am about to drink?" They said to him, "We are able." He said to them, "You will indeed drink my cup, but to sit at my right hand and at my left, this is not mine to grant, but it is for those for whom it has been prepared by my Father." When the ten heard it, they were angry with the two brothers. But Jesus called them to him and said, "You know that the rulers of the Gentiles lord it over them, and their great ones are tyrants over them. It will not be so among you; but whoever wishes to be great among you must be your servant, and whoever wishes to be first among you must be your slave; just as the

Son of Man came not to be served but to serve, and to give his life a ransom for many."

- Jesus had just finished speaking in terrible detail about the awful suffering that awaited him when this scene transpired.
- It seems the disciples and their mother wanted to avoid any suffering on the road to glory.
- What does Jesus say?

Tuesday 26th July, Sts Joachim and Anne
Matthew 13:16-17

Jesus said to the disciples, "But blessed are your eyes, for they see, and your ears, for they hear. Truly I tell you, many prophets and righteous people longed to see what you see, but did not see it, and to hear what you hear, but did not hear it."

- Jesus was deeply aware that many people who heard him didn't grasp what was going on. Then he turned to his followers and delighted in their response.
- Do I feel that I am blessed and privileged?
- What do I need to say to the Lord about this?

Wednesday 27th July
Matthew 13:44-46

Jesus said to the crowds, "The kingdom of heaven is like treasure hidden in a field, which someone found and hid; then in his joy he goes and sells all that he has and buys that field. "Again, the kingdom of heaven is like a merchant in search of fine pearls; on finding one pearl of great value, he went and sold all that he had and bought it."

- What is my image of the Kingdom of Heaven?
- Have I come to see that the Kingdom of Heaven is the most important thing?

- If I'm not at that stage yet, am I open to suggestions from the Lord?

Thursday 28th July   Exodus 40:34-38

Then the cloud covered the tent of meeting, and the glory of the LORD filled the tabernacle. Moses was not able to enter the tent of meeting because the cloud settled upon it, and the glory of the LORD filled the tabernacle. Whenever the cloud was taken up from the tabernacle, the Israelites would set out on each stage of their journey; but if the cloud was not taken up, then they did not set out until the day that it was taken up. For the cloud of the LORD was on the tabernacle by day, and fire was in the cloud by night, before the eyes of all the house of Israel at each stage of their journey.

- As they were trudging through the desert the people of Israel know that God was in their midst to guide them.
- Can I let these images remind me of God's guiding presence in the journey of my life?

Friday 29th July, St Martha   John 11:19-27

Many of the Jews had come to Martha and Mary to console them about their brother. When Martha heard that Jesus was coming, she went and met him, while Mary stayed at home. Martha said to Jesus, "Lord, if you had been here, my brother would not have died. But even now I know that God will give you whatever you ask of him." Jesus said to her, "Your brother will rise again." Martha said to him, "I know that he will rise again in the resurrection on the last day." Jesus said to her, "I am the resurrection and the life. Those who believe in me, even though they die, will live, and everyone who lives and believes in me will never die. Do you believe this?" She said to him, "Yes, Lord, I believe that you are the Messiah, the Son of God, the one coming into the world."

- In her moment of grief Martha, the woman of faith, still believes in Jesus' power to do something for her dead brother. But Jesus is going to lead her to an even deeper knowledge of himself.
- "I am the resurrection and the life," he says. This is an awesome claim. What can it mean?
- When Jesus asks, "Do you believe this?" Martha makes her response. What is my response? Remember: I don't have to compare myself with Martha or anyone else.

Saturday 30th July   Matthew 14:1-12

At that time Herod the ruler heard reports about Jesus; and he said to his servants, "This is John the Baptist; he has been raised from the dead, and for this reason these powers are at work in him." For Herod had arrested John, bound him, and put him in prison on account of Herodias, his brother Philip's wife, because John had been telling him, "It is not lawful for you to have her." Though Herod wanted to put him to death, he feared the crowd, because they regarded him as a prophet. But when Herod's birthday came, the daughter of Herodias danced before the company, and she pleased Herod so much that he promised on oath to grant her whatever she might ask. Prompted by her mother, she said, "Give me the head of John the Baptist here on a platter." The king was grieved, yet out of regard for his oaths and for the guests, he commanded it to be given; he sent and had John beheaded in the prison. The head was brought on a platter and given to the girl, who brought it to her mother. His disciples came and took the body and buried it; then they went and told Jesus.

- This is a story of innocent suffering, of a great wrong, the fruit of spite and cowardice.
- Where is God in the midst of this shabby and sordid picture?
- How is God present in the "shabby" elements of my life and world?

Sacred Space

july 31 – august 6

Something to think and pray about each day this week:

The "Limit" experience

Some contemporary theologians emphasize the importance of those moments in our lives when we hit against our own limits or limitations. Realities like sickness and death, evils of every kind, things over which we have no control can make us despair. They can also open us up to the holy Mystery, who is the source of our lives and the fulfillment for which we long.

In these days we must be very aware of our "limits." Feelings of fear and insecurity haunt many of us like specters. The even tenor of our lives is upended and we find ourselves plummeting into bitterness and hatred. The "limits" are always there and they will be different for each one.

When I pray I come into the presence of the Mystery who holds me in being and calls me forward. The first step is to acknowledge myself as limited.

The Presence of God
As I sit here, the beating of my heart,
the ebb and flow of my breathing, the movements of my mind
are all signs of God's ongoing creation of me.
I pause for a moment, and become aware
of this presence of God within me.

Freedom
I ask for the grace
to let go of my own concerns
and be open to what God is asking of me,
to let myself be guided and formed by my loving Creator.

Consciousness
How do I find myself today?
Where am I with God? With others?
Do I have something to be grateful for? Then I give thanks.
Is there something I am sorry for? Then I ask forgiveness.

The Word
I take my time to read the Word of God, slowly, a few
times, allowing myself to dwell on anything that strikes
me. (Please turn to your scripture on the following pages.
Inspiration points are there should you need them. When
you are ready, return here to continue.)

Conversation
Remembering that I am still in God's presence,
I imagine Jesus himself standing or sitting beside me,
and say whatever is on my mind, whatever is in my heart,
speaking as one friend to another.

Conclusion
Glory be to the Father, and to the Son, and to the Holy Spirit,
As it was in the beginning, is now and ever shall be,
World without end. Amen

july 2005

Sunday 31st July, 18th Sunday of the Year
Romans 8:35-39

Who will separate us from the love of Christ? Will hardship, or distress, or persecution, or famine, or nakedness, or peril, or sword? As it is written, "For your sake we are being killed all day long; we are accounted as sheep to be slaughtered." No, in all these things we are more than conquerors through him who loved us. For I am convinced that neither death, nor life, nor angels, nor rulers, nor things present, nor things to come, nor powers, nor height, nor depth, nor anything else in all creation, will be able to separate us from the love of God in Christ Jesus our Lord.

- What hardship has there been—is there—in my life?
- Where has God been in that experience?
- How does Paul's conviction that "nothing" can separate from the love of God sound to me?

Monday 1st August
Matthew 14:13-21

Now when Jesus heard this, he withdrew from there in a boat to a deserted place by himself. But when the crowds heard it, they followed him on foot from the towns. When he went ashore, he saw a great crowd; and he had compassion for them and cured their sick. When it was evening, the disciples came to him and said, "This is a deserted place, and the hour is now late; send the crowds away so that they may go into the villages and buy food for themselves." Jesus said to them, "They need not go away; you give them something to eat." They replied, "We have nothing here but five loaves and two fish." And he said, "Bring them here to me." Then he ordered the crowds to sit down on the grass. Taking the five loaves and the two fish, he looked up to heaven, and blessed and broke the loaves, and gave them to the disciples, and the disciples gave them to the crowds. And all ate and were filled; and they took up what was left over of the broken pieces, twelve baskets full. And those who ate were about five thousand men, besides women and children.

- Give yourself free rein to imagine this scene: What kind of a place is it? Who are all the people? What is happening? Just close your eyes and take a couple of brief minutes and let a picture form. Go on! It will only take a couple of minutes.
- Now, imagine that you are one of the characters involved. There are lots of persons present. If you were one of them, who would you be? Let your imagination go …
- So, who were you? One of the crowd? One of the disciples? Jesus himself? The person who provided the loaves and fishes? An outside observer?
- It is really valuable to consider the following question: when God is doing extraordinary things with—and for—human beings, where do I see myself fitting in?

Tuesday 2nd August   Matthew 14:23-33

When evening came, Jesus was on the mountains alone, but by this time the boat, battered by the waves, was far from the land, for the wind was against them.
And early in the morning Jesus came walking toward the disciples on the sea. But when the disciples saw him walking on the sea, they were terrified, saying, "It is a ghost!" And they cried out in fear. But immediately Jesus spoke to them and said, "Take heart, it is I; do not be afraid." Peter answered him, "Lord, if it is you, command me to come to you on the water." He said, "Come." So Peter got out of the boat, started walking on the water, and came toward Jesus. But when he noticed the strong wind, he became frightened, and beginning to sink, he cried out, "Lord, save me!" Jesus

immediately reached out his hand and caught him, saying to him, "You of little faith, why did you doubt?" When they got into the boat, the wind ceased. And those in the boat worshiped him, saying, "Truly you are the Son of God."

- Can I imagine myself as one of the crew on Peter's boat?
- What happens? How do people react? How do I react?
- Does this scene have parallels in my own life?

Wednesday 3rd August   Matthew 15:21-28

Jesus left that place and went away to the district of Tyre and Sidon. Just then a Canaanite woman from that region came out and started shouting, "Have mercy on me, Lord, Son of David; my daughter is tormented by a demon." But he did not answer her at all. And his disciples came and urged him, saying, "Send her away, for she keeps shouting after us." He answered, "I was sent only to the lost sheep of the house of Israel." But she came and knelt before him, saying, "Lord, help me." He answered, "It is not fair to take the children's food and throw it to the dogs." She said, "Yes, Lord, yet even the dogs eat the crumbs that fall from their masters' table." Then Jesus answered her, "Woman, great is your faith! Let it be done for you as you wish." And her daughter was healed instantly.

- Can I picture this woman? A despised outsider, mother of a disturbed child, at the end of her tether? Who does she make me think of?
- As I follow the steps of her encounter with Jesus what impression does it make on me?

Thursday 4th August   Matthew 16:13-20

Now when Jesus came into the district of Caesarea Philippi, he asked his disciples, "Who do people say that the Son of Man is?" And they said, "Some say John the Baptist, but others Elijah, and still others Jeremiah or one of the prophets." He said to them, "But who do you say that I am?" Simon Peter answered, "You are the Messiah, the Son of the living God." And Jesus answered him, "Blessed are you, Simon son of Jonah! For flesh and blood has not revealed this to you, but my Father in heaven. And I tell you, you are Peter, and on this rock I will build my church, and the gates of Hades will not prevail against it. I will give you the keys of the kingdom of heaven, and whatever you bind on earth will be bound in heaven, and whatever you loose on earth will be loosed in heaven." Then he sternly ordered the disciples not to tell anyone that he was the Messiah.

- Am I open to Jesus' question, "Who do YOU say that I am?" How do I answer it?
- I listen to Jesus' confirmation of Peter's special call and mission in the church.
- Do I believe that Jesus has a unique role and place for me in his plans? Can I hear him speak to me?

Friday 5th August   **Matthew 16:24-28**

Then Jesus told his disciples, "If any want to become my followers, let them deny themselves and take up their cross and follow me. For those who want to save their life will lose it, and those who lose their life for my sake will find it. For what will it profit them if they gain the whole world but forfeit their life? Or what will they give in return for their life? "For the Son of Man is to come with his angels in the glory of his Father, and then he will repay everyone for what has been done. Truly I tell you, there are some standing here who will not taste death before they see the Son of Man coming in his kingdom."

- When Ignatius Loyola was guiding Francis Xavier in the early days of his discovery of God's love, he repeated, over and over, that sentence: "Francis, what will it profit …?" He obviously felt that Francis was stuck in some un-freedom and needed a bit of prodding.
- What about me? What holds me back from giving myself in trust and love to the Lord?
- What am I afraid of losing? Has it to do with comforts, other people's opinion of me, my need to be in control? Something else?
- Do I want to be prodded into freedom?

Saturday 6th August, The Transfiguration of the Lord
Luke 9:28b-36

Jesus took with him Peter and John and James, and went up on the mountain to pray. And while he was praying, the appearance of his face changed, and his clothes became dazzling white. Suddenly they saw two men, Moses and Elijah, talking to him. They appeared in glory and were speaking of his departure, which he was about to accomplish at Jerusalem. Now Peter and his companions were weighed down with sleep; but since they had stayed awake, they saw his glory and the two men who stood with him. Just as they were leaving him, Peter said to Jesus, "Master, it is good for us to be here; let us make three dwellings, one for you, one for Moses, and one for Elijah—not knowing what he said. While he was saying this, a cloud came and overshadowed them; and they were terrified as they entered the cloud. Then from the cloud came a voice that said, "This is my Son, my Chosen; listen to him!" When the voice had spoken, Jesus was found alone. And they kept silent and in those days told no one any of the things they had seen.

- This scene invites me to "be there" and see and hear what is happening.
- In the presence of Jesus' glory how do I respond? Peter seems to ramble on with excitement. What about me?
- The Father's words are a remarkable affirmation. How do they touch me?

august 7–13

Something to think and pray about each day this week:

Do not be afraid

Fear is a huge obstacle in the lives of many people. It stops us going where we want to go. It stops us doing the right thing. It stops us from speaking out when something is wrong. Fear stops us reaching out to people, stops us trusting. It is a block to having free, open, loving relationships with others.

Jesus knew this, and liberating us from this fear was clearly a vital part of his mission. In the gospels, we hear him say "do not be afraid" no less than nineteen times.

Fear can be just as much an obstacle in prayer, in my relationship with God. I may be afraid of what I find if I look honestly at myself, or afraid of what I might let myself in for if I begin a conversation with the Lord that I am not in complete control of. But God, who knows me better than I know myself, loves me passionately despite all my faults. I have nothing to fear from opening myself to the Lord— I have only to reach out and accept his loving embrace.

The Presence of God
I pause for a moment
and reflect on God's life-giving presence
in every part of my body, in everything around me,
in the whole of my life.

Freedom
I ask for the grace to believe
in what I could be and do
if I only allowed God, my loving Creator,
to continue to create me, guide me and shape me.

Consciousness
In God's loving presence I unwind the past day,
starting from now and looking back, moment by moment.
I gather in all the goodness and light, in gratitude.
I attend to the shadows and what they say to me,
seeking healing, courage, forgiveness.

The Word
God speaks to each one of us individually. I need to listen
to what he is saying to me. (Please turn to your scripture on
the following pages. Inspiration points are there should you
need them. When you are ready, return here to continue.)

Conversation
How has God's Word moved me? Has it left me cold?
Has it consoled me or moved me to act in a new way?
I imagine Jesus standing or sitting beside me,
I turn and share my feelings with him.

Conclusion
Glory be to the Father, and to the Son, and to the Holy Spirit,
As it was in the beginning, is now and ever shall be,
World without end. Amen

Sunday 7th August, 19th Sunday of the Year
Matthew 14:22-33

Jesus made the disciples get into the boat and go on ahead to the other side, while he dismissed the crowds. And after he had dismissed the crowds, he went up the mountain by himself to pray. When evening came, he was there alone, but by this time the boat, battered by the waves, was far from the land, for the wind was against them. And early in the morning he came walking toward them on the sea. But when the disciples saw him walking on the sea, they were terrified, saying, "It is a ghost!" And they cried out in fear. But immediately Jesus spoke to them and said, "Take heart, it is I; do not be afraid." Peter answered him, "Lord, if it is you, command me to come to you on the water." He said, "Come." So Peter got out of the boat, started walking on the water, and came toward Jesus. But when he noticed the strong wind, he became frightened, and beginning to sink, he cried out, "Lord, save me!" Jesus immediately reached out his hand and caught him, saying to him, "You of little faith, why did you doubt?" When they got into the boat, the wind ceased. And those in the boat worshiped him, saying, "Truly you are the Son of God."

- Can I imagine myself in the boat going through all of this. I might even be Peter.
- What happens? What do I see and hear? What emotions do I have as the scene unfolds?
- Who is this Jesus?

Monday 8th August
Deuteronomy 10:14-20

Moses said to the people, "Although heaven and the heaven of heavens belong to the LORD your God, the earth with all that is in it, yet the LORD set his heart in love on your ancestors alone and chose you, their descendants after them, out of all the peoples, as it is today. Circumcise, then, the foreskin of your heart, and do not be stubborn any longer. For the LORD your God is God of gods and Lord of lords, the great God, mighty and awesome, who is not partial and takes no bribe, who executes justice for the orphan and the widow, and who loves the strangers, providing them food and clothing. You shall also love the stranger, for you were strangers in the land of Egypt. You shall fear the LORD your God; him alone you shall worship; to him you shall hold fast, and by his name you shall swear."

- Moses' words here invite me to remember exactly who we are, a people chosen by the Lord.
- Can I allow myself to feel the special-ness of being chosen?
- God has also chosen the poor and the outcast as my brothers and sisters. What does this mean for me?

Tuesday 9th August　　　　　　　　**Matthew 18:1-5, 10**

At that time the disciples came to Jesus and asked, "Who is the greatest in the kingdom of heaven?" He called a child, whom he put among them, and said, "Truly I tell you, unless you change and become like children, you will never enter the kingdom of heaven. Whoever becomes humble like this child is the greatest in the kingdom of heaven. Whoever welcomes one such child in my name welcomes me. Take care that you do not despise one of these little ones; for, I tell you, in heaven their angels continually see the face of my Father in heaven."

- What images come to my mind when I think of "greatness," in myself or in others.
- Am I challenged by Jesus' highlighting the virtues of children?
- Do I really want to be like a child?
- What is the Lord saying to me?

Wednesday 10th August, St Laurence   John 12:24-26

Jesus said "Very truly, I tell you, unless a grain of wheat falls into the earth and dies, it remains just a single grain; but if it dies, it bears much fruit. Those who love their life lose it, and those who hate their life in this world will keep it for eternal life. Whoever serves me must follow me, and where I am, there will my servant be also. Whoever serves me, the Father will honor."

- Is this business of the "grain of wheat" just a cliché for me?
- Can I think of any experience of suffering and loss that has borne fruit because of God's grace? How did it happen?
- Does the idea of "losing my life" simply frighten or confuse me? Can I talk about this to the Lord?

Thursday 11th August   Matthew 18:21-22

Then Peter came and said to him, "Lord, if another member of the church sins against me, how often should I forgive? As many as seven times?" Jesus said to him, "Not seven times, but, I tell you, seventy-seven times."

- Can I allow Jesus to address these words to me?
- Is there anybody in my life—now or in the past—whom I simply can't forgive?
- What does Jesus say to this situation? How would he like me to move forward?

Friday 12th August   Matthew 19:3-6

Some Pharisees came to Jesus, and to test him they asked, "Is it lawful for a man to divorce his wife for any cause?" He answered, "Have you not read that the one who made them at the beginning 'made them male and female,' and said, 'For this reason a man shall leave his father and mother and be joined to his wife, and the two shall become one flesh'? So they are no longer two, but one flesh. Therefore what God has joined together, let no one separate."

- Jesus invites us to remember how the union of man and woman in marriage is a part of God's plan.
- Can I discern the working out of this plan in marriages close to me?
- Do I experience pain due to a marriage which didn't work out? My own or someone else's. Can I allow the Lord to speak to me where I am?

Saturday 13th August   **Matthew 19:13-15**

Then little children were being brought to him in order that he might lay his hands on them and pray. The disciples spoke sternly to those who brought them; but Jesus said, "Let the little children come to me, and do not stop them; for it is to such as these that the kingdom of heaven belongs." And he laid his hands on them and went on his way.

- Why did the disciples speak sternly to the people bringing the children?
- What is it about Jesus that made him react to them as he did?
- What does this say to me?

Something to think and pray about each day this week:

The Narrow Way
What do we do when someone we love speaks hard words?
Feel wounded, misunderstood. Later we cool down and
recognize some merit.

What do I feel when Jesus the Lord speaks hard words? Can
I take it? Do I shrink from it? Hide from it? Over these few
days we hear Jesus speak very hard words.

The Presence of God

The world is charged with the grandeur of God (Gerard Manley Hopkins).
I dwell for a moment on the presence of God
around me, in every part of my body,
and deep within my being.

Freedom

"In these days, God taught me
as a schoolteacher teaches a pupil" (St Ignatius).
I remind myself that there are things God has to teach me yet,
and ask for the grace to hear them and let them change me.

Consciousness

I exist in a web of relationships—links to nature, people, God.
I trace out these links, giving thanks for the life that flows
through them.
Some links are twisted or broken: I may feel regret, anger,
disappointment.
I pray for the gift of acceptance and forgiveness.

The Word

I read the Word of God slowly, a few times over, and I listen
to what God is saying to me. (Please turn to your scripture on
the following pages. Inspirations points are there should you
need them. When you are ready, return here to continue.)

Conversation

What feelings are rising in me
as I pray and reflect on God's Word?
I imagine Jesus himself sitting or standing beside me,
and open my heart to him.

Conclusion

Glory be to the Father, and to the Son, and to the Holy Spirit,
As it was in the beginning, is now and ever shall be,
World without end. Amen

Sunday 14th August, 20th Sunday of the Year
Matthew 15:21-28

Jesus left that place and went away to the district of Tyre and Sidon. Just then a Canaanite woman from that region came out and started shouting, "Have mercy on me, Lord, Son of David; my daughter is tormented by a demon." But he did not answer her at all. And his disciples came and urged him, saying, "Send her away, for she keeps shouting after us." He answered, "I was sent only to the lost sheep of the house of Israel." But she came and knelt before him, saying, "Lord, help me." He answered, "It is not fair to take the children's food and throw it to the dogs." She said, "Yes, Lord, yet even the dogs eat the crumbs that fall from their masters' table." Then Jesus answered her, "Woman, great is your faith! Let it be done for you as you wish." And her daughter was healed instantly.

- What motivates this strong and tenacious woman? What deep desires and hopes keep her going in the face of rejection?
- God seems to be incapable of refusing this woman's determined faith.
- What does this say to me about my own life, about different forms of rejection and discouragement?

Monday 15th August, The Assumption
of the Blessed Virgin Mary
Luke 1:39-47

In those days Mary set out and went with haste to a Judean town in the hill country, where she entered the house of Zechariah and greeted Elizabeth. When Elizabeth heard Mary's greeting, the child leaped in her womb. And Elizabeth was filled with the Holy Spirit and exclaimed with a loud cry, "Blessed are you among women, and blessed is the fruit of your womb. And why has this happened to me, that the mother of my Lord comes to me? For as soon as I heard the sound of your greeting, the child in my womb leaped for joy. And blessed is she who believed that there would be a fulfillment of what was spoken to her by the Lord." And Mary said, "My soul magnifies the Lord, and my spirit rejoices in God my Savior."

- Here is a meeting between two extraordinary women, each of whom is expecting a baby. They both show a tremendous capacity to go beyond themselves.
- As I look at the scene what detail catches my eye? How does it move me?

Tuesday 16th August   Psalm 84:9,11-14

Let me hear what God the LORD will speak, for he will speak peace to his people, to his faithful, to those who turn to him in their hearts. Surely his salvation is at hand for those who fear him, that his glory may dwell in our land. Steadfast love and faithfulness will meet; righteousness and peace will kiss each other. Faithfulness will spring up from the ground, and righteousness will look down from the sky. The LORD will give what is good, and our land will yield its increase. Righteousness will go before him, and will make a path for his steps.

- God wants to shower blessings and give hope to his people.
- Is there any one of the words or images here that catches my attention?
- Can I just sit with that word and let its promise touch me?

Wednesday 17th August   Matthew 20:1-16

Jesus said to his disciples, "For the kingdom of heaven is like a landowner who went out early in the morning to hire laborers for his vineyard. After agreeing with the laborers for the usual daily wage, he sent them into his vineyard. When he went out about nine o'clock, he saw others standing idle in the marketplace; and he said to them, 'You also go into the vineyard, and I will pay you whatever is right.' So they went. When he went out again about noon and about three o'clock, he did the same. And about five o'clock he went out and found others standing around; and he said to them, 'Why are you standing here idle all day?' They said to him, 'Because no one has hired us.' He said to them, 'You also go into the vineyard.' When evening came, the owner of the vineyard said to his manager, 'Call the laborers and give them their pay, beginning with the last and then going to the first.' When those hired about five o'clock came, each of them received the usual daily wage. Now when the first came, they thought they would receive more; but each of them also received the usual daily wage. And when they received it, they grumbled against the landowner, saying, 'These last worked only one hour, and you have made them equal to us who have borne the burden of the day and the scorching heat.' But he replied to one of them, 'Friend, I am doing you no wrong; did you not agree with me for the usual daily wage? Take what belongs to you and go; I choose to give to this last the same as I give to you. Am I not allowed to do what I choose with what belongs to me? Or are you envious because I am generous?' So the last will be first, and the first will be last."

- Who do I identify with in this story?
- Does it leave me full of gratitude or feeling resentment?
- What is the Lord trying to tell me?

Thursday 18th August   Psalm 39:5, 7-10

Happy are those who make the LORD their trust, who do not turn to the proud, to those who go astray after false gods. Sacrifice and offering you do not desire, but you have given me an open ear. Burnt offering and sin offering you have not required. Then I said, "Here I am; in the scroll of the book it is written of me. I delight to do your will, O my God; your law is within my heart." I have told the glad news of deliverance in the great congregation; see, I have not restrained my lips, as you know, O LORD.

- This psalm is the song of the person who has gone beyond outward observance and has the Lord in their hearts.
- Can I make these words my own?

Friday 19th August   Matthew 22:34-40

When the Pharisees heard that he had silenced the Sadducees, they gathered together, and one of them, a lawyer, asked him a question to test him. "Teacher, which commandment in the law is the greatest?" He said to him, "'You shall love the Lord your God with all your heart, and with all your soul, and with all your mind.' This is the greatest and first commandment. And a second is like it: 'You shall love your neighbor as yourself.' On these two commandments hang all the law and the prophets."

- The very Word of God was there before them, wanting to give them his love, and some people were just interested in scoring points against him and against each other. It is just possible that this same Word of God is standing right in front of me in my daily life and I am missing him because I am caught up in some silly games of my own.
- I might want to gaze on this scene and look with compassion at the Sadducees and Pharisees. It might be a blessing if I can catch sight of myself among them.

Saturday 20th August　　　　　　　**Matthew 23:8-12**

Jesus addressed the people and his disciples, he said, "But you are not to be called rabbi, for you have one teacher, and you are all students. And call no one your father on earth, for you have one Father—the one in heaven. Nor are you to be called instructors, for you have one instructor, the Messiah. The greatest among you will be your servant. All who exalt themselves will be humbled, and all who humble themselves will be exalted."

- Jesus is reminding his disciples that they can be seduced by the outer trappings and titles and miss the inner reality of their lives.
- How does he challenge me? How am I seduced by things on the surface and deflected from the inner core?
- How does the Lord want to help me deepen my grasp on what is real?

Sacred Space

august 21–27

Something to think and pray about each day this week:

Hard words

How do I react when the scripture I am spending time with is full of stern words, when Jesus seems to be tough and uncompromising? What feelings does it spark off in me? Am I irritated? Angry? Ashamed? Discomforted? Am I tempted to dismiss the whole thing?

If I find it difficult to accept Jesus speaking in this way, it may be because of my image of him. I may have an image of Jesus as one who only says nice, gentle, affirming things to me. Or perhaps, for many years, I have thought of Jesus as someone who "gives out," "tells me off" and stops me doing what I really want to do, and just as I'm shaking this off, along comes one of these hard sayings and it all comes back.

If I have feelings like this, they should come into my prayer, not be ignored or excluded. Knowing that the Lord is passionately concerned for my good, I can share my feelings openly in "conversation" with him in my prayer, in an atmosphere of complete trust and unconditional love.

The Presence of God
As I sit here, God is present,
breathing life into me and into everything around me.
For a few moments, I sit silently,
and become aware of God's loving presence.

Freedom
If God were trying to tell me something, would I know?
If God were reassuring me or challenging me, would I notice?
I ask for the grace to be free of my own preoccupations
and open to what God may be saying to me.

Consciousness
How am I really feeling? Light-hearted? Heavy-hearted?
I may be very much at peace, happy to be here.
Equally, I may be frustrated, worried or angry.
I acknowledge how I really am. It is the real me that the
Lord loves.

The Word
I take my time to read the Word of God, slowly, a few times,
allowing myself to dwell on anything that strikes me. (Please
turn to your scripture on the following pages. Inspiration
points are there should you need them. When you are ready,
return here to continue.)

Conversation
What is stirring in me as I pray?
Am I consoled, troubled, left cold?
I imagine Jesus himself standing or sitting at my side,
and share my feelings with him.

Conclusion
Glory be to the Father, and to the Son, and to the Holy Spirit,
As it was in the beginning, is now and ever shall be,
World without end. Amen

Sunday 21st August, 21st Sunday of the Year
Matthew 16:13-20

Now when Jesus came into the district of Caesarea Philippi, he asked his disciples, "Who do people say that the Son of Man is?" And they said, "Some say John the Baptist, but others Elijah, and still others Jeremiah or one of the prophets." He said to them, "But who do you say that I am?" Simon Peter answered, "You are the Messiah, the Son of the living God." And Jesus answered him, "Blessed are you, Simon son of Jonah! For flesh and blood has not revealed this to you, but my Father in heaven. And I tell you, you are Peter, and on this rock I will build my church, and the gates of Hades will not prevail against it. I will give you the keys of the kingdom of heaven, and whatever you bind on earth will be bound in heaven, and whatever you loose on earth will be loosed in heaven." Then he sternly ordered the disciples not to tell anyone that he was the Messiah.

- Am I open to Jesus' question "Who do YOU say that I am"? How do I answer it?
- I listen to Jesus' confirmation of Peter's special call and mission in the church.
- Do I believe that Jesus has a unique role and place for me in his plans? Can I hear him speak to me?

Monday 22nd August · Matthew 23:13-15

Jesus said to the crowds and his disciples, "But woe to you, scribes and Pharisees, hypocrites! For you lock people out of the kingdom of heaven. For you do not go in yourselves, and when others are going in, you stop them. Woe to you, scribes and Pharisees, hypocrites! For you cross sea and land to make a single convert, and you make the new convert twice as much a child of hell as yourselves."

- Nothing stirs Jesus' wrath more thoroughly than a false religion that turns other people away from God.
- Is there anything of the hypocrisy of the Pharisees in my religiosity?
- Can I allow myself to be challenged?

Tuesday 23rd August   Matthew 23:23-26

Jesus said, "Woe to you, scribes and Pharisees, hypocrites! For you tithe mint, dill, and cummin, and have neglected the weightier matters of the law: justice and mercy and faith. It is these you ought to have practised without neglecting the others. You blind guides! You strain out a gnat but swallow a camel! "Woe to you, scribes and Pharisees, hypocrites! For you clean the outside of the cup and of the plate, but inside they are full of greed and self-indulgence."

- Jesus castigates the tendency to become "hung up" on small details or outward appearances. This kind of preoccupation seems to blind us to the things that really matter: justice, mercy and faith.
- Where in my life do I "strain out gnats"?
- How is God calling me to greater justice, mercy and faith?

Wednesday 24th August, St Bartholomew   John 1:45-51

Philip found Nathanael and said to him, "We have found him about whom Moses in the law and also the prophets wrote, Jesus son of Joseph from Nazareth." Nathanael said to him, "Can anything good come out of Nazareth?" Philip said to him, "Come and see." When Jesus saw Nathanael coming toward him, he said of him, "Here is truly an Israelite in whom there is no deceit!" Nathanael asked him, "Where did you get to know me?" Jesus answered, "I saw you under the fig tree before Philip called you." Nathanael replied, "Rabbi, you are the Son of God! You are the King of Israel!" Jesus answered, "Do you believe because I told you that I saw you under the fig tree? You will see greater things than these." And he said to him, "Very truly, I tell you, you will see heaven opened and the angels of God ascending and descending upon the Son of Man."

- Can I put myself in Nathanael's shoes?
- When I hear the great news is my reaction like his? How do I react?
- Do I hear the words "come and see" addressed to me?
- How do I respond?

Thursday 25th August   Matthew 24:42-46

Jesus said to his disciples, "Keep awake therefore, for you do not know on what day your Lord is coming. But understand this: if the owner of the house had known in what part of the night the thief was coming, he would have stayed awake and would not have let his house be broken into. Therefore you also must be ready, for the Son of Man is coming at an unexpected hour. "Who then is the faithful and wise slave, whom his master has put in charge of his household, to give the other slaves their allowance of food at the proper time? Blessed is that slave whom his master will find at work when he arrives."

- Do I expect that Jesus could arrive in my life at any moment? Or, have I slipped into an attitude that believes he's not interested?
- Do I need help to wake up and become more attentive, more expectant?

Friday 26th August   Matthew 25:1-13

Jesus said to his disciples, "Then the kingdom of heaven will be like this. Ten bridesmaids took their lamps and went to meet the bridegroom. Five of them were foolish, and five were wise. When the foolish took their lamps, they took no oil with them; but the wise took flasks of oil with their lamps. As the bridegroom was delayed, all of them became drowsy and slept. But at midnight there was a shout, 'Look! Here is the bridegroom! Come out to meet him.' Then all those bridesmaids got up and trimmed their lamps. The foolish said to the wise, 'Give us some of your oil, for our lamps are going out.' But the wise replied, 'No! there will not be enough for you and for us; you had better go to the dealers and buy some for yourselves.' And while they went to buy it, the bridegroom came, and those who were ready went with him into the wedding banquet; and the door was shut. Later the other bridesmaids came also, saying, 'Lord, lord, open to us.' But he replied, 'Truly I tell you, I do not know you.' Keep awake therefore, for you know neither the day nor the hour."

- This parable is about what happens when Christians grow casual and lose their sense of expectancy about the Lord's coming.
- When I look at my own life do I see the "oil" of the good works of love? Does my "lamp" run out at times?
- What help do I need from the Lord about this?

Saturday 27th August   Matthew 25:14-30

Jesus told his disciples this parable, "For it is as if a man, going on a journey, summoned his slaves and entrusted his property to them; to one he gave five talents, to another two, to another one, to each according to his ability. Then he went away. The one who had received the five talents went off at once and traded with them, and made five more talents. In the same way, the one who had the two talents made two more talents. But the one who had received the one talent went off and dug a hole in the ground and hid his master's money. After a long time the master of those slaves came and settled accounts with them. Then the one who had received the five talents came forward, bringing five more talents, saying, 'Master, you handed over to me five talents; see, I have made five more talents.' His master said to him, 'Well done, good and trustworthy slave; you have been trustworthy in a few things, I will put you in charge of many things; enter into the joy of your master.' And the one with the two talents also came forward, saying, 'Master, you handed over to me two talents; see, I have made two more talents.' His master said to him, 'Well done, good and trustworthy slave; you have been trustworthy in a few things, I will put you in charge of many things; enter into the joy of your master.' Then the one who had received the one talent also came forward, saying, 'Master, I knew that you were a harsh man, reaping where you did not sow, and gathering where you did not scatter seed; so I was afraid, and I went and hid your talent in the ground. Here you have what is yours.' But his master replied, 'You wicked and lazy slave! You knew, did you, that I reap where I did not sow, and gather where I did not scatter? Then you ought to have invested my money with the bankers, and on my return I would have received what was my own with interest. So take the talent from him, and give it to the one with the ten talents. For to all those who have, more will be given, and they will have an abundance; but from those who have nothing, even what they have will be taken away. As for this worthless slave, throw him into the outer darkness, where there will be weeping and gnashing of teeth.'"

august 2005 ————————————————

- How can I allow Jesus to challenge and support me in my own life through this parable?
- Do I acknowledge and appreciate my own gifts?
- Can I imagine the "Master" praising my efforts?
- Where do I see small-mindedness and fear of risk holding me back?
- What do I say to the Lord who desires only the best for me?

august 28 – september 3

Something to think and pray about each day this week:

Not what we were expecting
In the passages from Luke around this time, we encounter again and again the clash between our expectations of Jesus and what he is really like. The people expect a powerful Messiah who will come in glory and wipe out all opposition, thunderbolts flashing from his hands. They expect him to reward them for conforming to conventional "holiness," for being respectable and clever.

But what they get is very different. Jesus turns the tables on them. He is interested in the poor and weak, not just the powerful. He tells them to drop their big ideas about themselves and be like little children. He looks weak and vulnerable, even saying he expects to suffer. Not the "winner" they were expecting.

What do we expect Jesus to be like? Do we make him "in our own image"? Are we frightened of weakness or of being thought foolish? Or are we open to being challenged and surprised by him, realizing that, as St Paul puts it, "God's foolishness is wiser than human wisdom, and God's weakness is stronger than human strength"? (1 Corinthians 1:25)

The Presence of God
As I sit here with my book, God is here.
Around me, in my sensations, in my thoughts and deep
within me.
I pause for a moment, and become aware
of God's life-giving presence.

Freedom
I need to close out the noise, to rise above the noise;
The noise that interrupts, that separates,
The noise that isolates.
I need to listen to God again.

Consciousness
Knowing that God loves me unconditionally,
I can afford to be honest about how I am.
How has the last day been, and how do I feel now?
I share my feelings openly with the Lord.

The Word
God speaks to each one of us individually. I need to listen
to what he is saying to me. (Please turn to your scripture on
the following pages. Inspiration points are there should you
need them. When you are ready, return here to continue.)

Conversation
Do I notice myself reacting as I pray with the Word of God?
Do I feel challenged, comforted, angry?
Imagining Jesus sitting or standing by me,
I speak out my feelings, as one trusted friend to another.

Conclusion
Glory be to the Father, and to the Son, and to the Holy Spirit,
As it was in the beginning, is now and ever shall be,
World without end. Amen

290

Sunday 28th August, 22nd Sunday of the Year
Matthew 16:21-27

From that time on, Jesus began to show his disciples that he must go to Jerusalem and undergo great suffering at the hands of the elders and chief priests and scribes, and be killed, and on the third day be raised. And Peter took him aside and began to rebuke him, saying, "God forbid it, Lord! This must never happen to you." But he turned and said to Peter, "Get behind me, Satan! You are a stumbling block to me; for you are setting your mind not on divine things but on human things." Then Jesus told his disciples, "If any want to become my followers, let them deny themselves and take up their cross and follow me. For those who want to save their life will lose it, and those who lose their life for my sake will find it. For what will it profit them if they gain the whole world but forfeit their life? Or what will they give in return for their life? For the Son of Man is to come with his angels in the glory of his Father, and then he will repay everyone for what has been done."

- When Peter sets his mind "not on divine things but on human things," he loses contact with Jesus and his mission.
- In what times or areas of my life does this same thing happen to me?
- Do I really want to "find my life"?

Monday 29th August
Luke 4:16-21

When Jesus came to Nazareth, where he had been brought up, he went to the synagogue on the sabbath day, as was his custom. He stood up to read, and the scroll of the prophet Isaiah was given to him. He unrolled the scroll and found the place where it was written: "The Spirit of the Lord is upon me, because he has anointed me to bring good news to the poor. He has sent me to proclaim release to the captives and recovery of sight to the blind, to let the

oppressed go free, to proclaim the year of the Lord's favor."
And he rolled up the scroll, gave it back to the attendant,
and sat down. The eyes of all in the synagogue were fixed on
him. Then he began to say to them, "Today this scripture has
been fulfilled in your hearing."

- The "local boy" is speaking in public to his neighbours for the
  first time. How does he feel?
- He has a mission. How does this affect me?
- A beginning full of drama. Where will it go?

Tuesday 30th August   Luke 4:31-37

Jesus went down to Capernaum, a city in Galilee, and was
teaching them on the sabbath. They were astounded at his
teaching, because he spoke with authority. In the synagogue
there was a man who had the spirit of an unclean demon,
and he cried out with a loud voice, "Let us alone! What have
you to do with us, Jesus of Nazareth? Have you come to
destroy us? I know who you are, the Holy One of God." But
Jesus rebuked him, saying, "Be silent, and come out of him!"
When the demon had thrown him down before them, he
came out of him without having done him any harm. They
were all amazed and kept saying to one another, "What kind
of utterance is this? For with authority and power he
commands the unclean spirits, and out they come!" And a
report about him began to reach every place in the region.

- Before Jesus, evil is ultimately powerless.
- The bystanders—you and I—had no idea of his greatness.
- Who is this mysterious man?

Wednesday 31th August   Luke 4:38-39

After leaving the synagogue Jesus entered Simon's house.
Now Simon's mother-in-law was suffering from a high

fever, and they asked him about her. Then he stood over her and rebuked the fever, and it left her. Immediately she got up and began to serve them.

- Jesus comes into a home and brings healing.
- Her response is one of thanks.
- Who is this man? Who is he for me?

Thursday 1st September   Luke 5:4-11

When Jesus had finished speaking, he said to Simon, "Put out into the deep water and let down your nets for a catch." Simon answered, "Master, we have worked all night long but have caught nothing. Yet if you say so, I will let down the nets." When they had done this, they caught so many fish that their nets were beginning to break. So they signaled their partners in the other boat to come and help them. And they came and filled both boats, so that they began to sink. But when Simon Peter saw it, he fell down at Jesus' knees, saying, "Go away from me, Lord, for I am a sinful man!" For he and all who were with him were amazed at the catch of fish that they had taken; and so also were James and John, sons of Zebedee, who were partners with Simon. Then Jesus said to Simon, "Do not be afraid; from now on you will be catching people." When they had brought their boats to shore, they left everything and followed him.

- At Jesus' word, Peter goes out into deep water against his own instinct and experience.
- If I knew who he really was, would I fall on my knees?
- Peter heard the call in his boat. What about me?

Friday 2nd September   Luke 5:33-39

Then the Pharisees and the scribes said to Jesus, "John's disciples, like the disciples of the Pharisees, frequently fast and pray, but your disciples eat and drink. Jesus said to them, "You cannot make wedding guests fast while the bride-groom is with them, can you? The days will come when the bridegroom will be taken away from them, and then they will fast in those days." He also told them a parable: "No one tears a piece from a new garment and sews it on an old garment; otherwise the new will be torn, and the piece from the new will not match the old. And no one puts new wine into old wineskins; otherwise the new wine will burst the skins and will be spilled, and the skins will be destroyed. But new wine must be put into fresh wineskins. And no one after drinking old wine desires new wine, but says, 'The old is good.'"

- The "Pharisees" stood for an attitude that is negative and fearful.
- Is there a "Pharisee" in me?
- What does Jesus say to me?

Saturday 3rd September   Luke 6:1-5

One sabbath while Jesus was going through the grain-fields, his disciples plucked some heads of grain, rubbed them in their hands, and ate them. But some of the Pharisees said, "Why are you doing what is not lawful on the sabbath?" Jesus answered, "Have you not read what David did when he and his companions were hungry? He entered the house of God and took and ate the bread of the Presence, which it is not lawful for any but the priests to eat, and gave some to his companions?" Then he said to them, "The Son of Man is lord of the sabbath."

- The Pharisees needled Jesus with an unhelpful agenda.
- What needles me in my joyful following?
- See how Jesus handles contradiction.

september 4–10

Something to think and pray about each day this week:

The call of Jesus

This week we hear Jesus call a group of followers who would leave everything to follow him. He then sits down and presents his core vision for everyone to hear. In Luke it is the Sermon on the Plain. In this, as in everything we read this week, Jesus is pointing to a world that is totally different to what we expect. A new world is coming—it could break out right now if we let it—in which we will love as God loves. The initiative is God's but we are expected to play our part. If we really listen to them these words should either excite us or frustrate us—or both in turn. They shouldn't leave us unmoved.

The Presence of God
I pause for a moment, aware that God is here.
I think of how everything around me,
the air I breathe, my whole body,
is tingling with the presence of God.

Freedom
I will ask God's help,
to be free from my own preoccupations,
to be open to God in this time of prayer,
to come to love and serve him more.

Consciousness
In the presence of my loving Creator,
I look honestly at my feelings over the last day,
the highs, the lows and the level ground.
Can I see where the Lord has been present?

The Word
I read the Word of God slowly, a few times over, and I listen
to what God is saying to me. (Please turn to your scripture on
the following pages. Inspiration points are there should you
need them. When you are ready, return here to continue.)

Conversation
Remembering that I am still in God's presence,
I imagine Jesus himself standing or sitting beside me,
and say whatever is on my mind, whatever is in my heart,
speaking as one friend to another.

Conclusion
Glory be to the Father, and to the Son, and to the Holy Spirit,
As it was in the beginning, is now and ever shall be,
World without end. Amen

Sunday 4th September, 23rd Sunday of the Year
Matthew 18:15-20

Jesus said, "If another member of the church sins against you, go and point out the fault when the two of you are alone. If the member listens to you, you have regained that one. But if you are not listened to, take one or two others along with you, so that every word may be confirmed by the evidence of two or three witnesses. If the member refuses to listen to them, tell it to the church; and if the offender refuses to listen even to the church, let such a one be to you as a Gentile and a tax collector. Truly I tell you, whatever you bind on earth will be bound in heaven, and whatever you loose on earth will be loosed in heaven. Again, truly I tell you, if two of you agree on earth about anything you ask, it will be done for you by my Father in heaven. For where two or three are gathered in my name, I am there among them."

- Jesus' guarantee that he would be personally present whenever two or three are gathered in his name is truly extraordinary.
- Have I ever experienced this presence in a community of believers, great or small? Am I open to it?
- How does the challenge about confronting others lovingly sound to me?

Monday 5th September
Luke 6:6-11

On another sabbath Jesus entered the synagogue and taught, and there was a man there whose right hand was withered. The scribes and the Pharisees watched him to see whether he would cure on the sabbath, so that they might find an accusation against him. Even though he knew what they were thinking, he said to the man who had the withered hand, "Come and stand here." He got up and stood there. Then Jesus said to them, "I ask you, is it lawful to do good or to do harm on the sabbath, to save life or to destroy it?" After looking around at all of them, he said to him, "Stretch out your hand." He did so, and his hand was restored. But they were filled with fury and discussed with one another what they might do to Jesus.

- When I see Jesus in the synagogue surrounded by his listeners, the man with a withered hand, his friends and the scribes and Pharisees, where does my gaze rest?
- Jesus is risking a lot of trouble. I wonder why?

Tuesday 6th September   **Luke 6:12-19**

Now during those days Jesus went out to the mountain to pray; and he spent the night in prayer to God. And when day came, he called his disciples and chose twelve of them, whom he also named apostles: Simon, whom he named Peter, and his brother Andrew, and James, and John, and Philip, and Bartholomew, and Matthew, and Thomas, and James son of Alphaeus, and Simon, who was called the Zealot, and Judas son of James, and Judas Iscariot, who became a traitor.

- Naming the apostles only came after an all-night prayer vigil.
- Each one unique, a specific individual.
- Like the apostles, I too fit into Jesus' plan.

Wednesday 7th September   **Luke 6:20-23a**

Then Jesus looked up at his disciples and said: "Blessed are you who are poor, for yours is the kingdom of God. Blessed are you who are hungry now, for you will be filled. Blessed are you who weep now, for you will laugh. Blessed are you when people hate you, and when they exclude you, revile you, and defame you on account of the Son of Man. Rejoice in that day and leap for joy, for surely your reward is great in heaven."

- These words are not addressed at people who are sailing through life without a care. Jesus is speaking to those who know rejection and sorrow.
- His words seem to turn our understanding of "the good life" on its head.
- What is Jesus saying about the misery and pain of so many lives? What right does he have to speak like this?

Thursday 8th September, Birthday of the Blessed Virgin Mary   Matthew 1:18-23

Now the birth of Jesus the Messiah took place in this way. When his mother Mary had been engaged to Joseph, but before they lived together, she was found to be with child from the Holy Spirit. Her husband Joseph, being a righteous man and unwilling to expose her to public disgrace, planned to dismiss her quietly. But just when he had resolved to do this, an angel of the Lord appeared to him in a dream and said, "Joseph, son of David, do not be afraid to take Mary as your wife, for the child conceived in her is from the Holy Spirit. She will bear a son, and you are to name him Jesus, for he will save his people from their sins." All this took place to fulfill what had been spoken by the Lord through the prophet: "Look, the virgin shall conceive and bear a son, and they shall name him Emmanuel," which means, "God is with us."

- Ponder the mystery of Mary's motherhood.
- Mary's life is changed utterly, then Joseph's, and then …
- Emmanuel—God is with us.

Friday 9th September   Luke 6:39-42

He also told them a parable: "Can a blind person guide a blind person? Will not both fall into a pit? A disciple is not above the teacher, but everyone who is fully qualified will be like the teacher. Why do you see the speck in your neighbor's eye, but do not notice the log in your own eye? Or how can you say to your neighbor, 'Friend, let me take out the speck in your eye,' when you yourself do not see the log in your own eye? You hypocrite, first take the log out of your own eye, and then you will see clearly to take the speck out of your neighbor's eye.

• Jesus is very direct.

Saturday 10th September   Luke 6:47-49

Jesus said, "I will show you what someone is like who comes to me, hears my words, and acts on them. That one is like a man building a house, who dug deeply and laid the foundation on rock; when a flood arose, the river burst against that house but could not shake it, because it had been well built. But the one who hears and does not act is like a man who built a house on the ground without a foundation. When the river burst against it, immediately it fell, and great was the ruin of that house."

• Friendship with Jesus is not just a matter of words. It is about building.
• What foundations am I laying down?

september 11–17

Something to think and pray about each day this week:

The outsider and the sinner

If God can be said to be biased, then the prejudice is all in favour of the outsider. In St. Luke's Gospel that is highlighted again and again. When John the Baptist sent emissaries to Jesus to find out if he really was the one who was to come, he more or less said, "look around and what do you see? The blind see, the lame walk, the lepers are cleansed … the poor have good news preached to them." So, Jesus is biased in favour of the poor and the outsider.

We see Jesus respond to the wealthy Roman Centurion, who was seen by many as a heathen and an oppressor. Jesus delighted in his faith. Likewise, he favours the woman who was a known sinner over the Pharisee who kept the spirit of the law but showed no love.

Again and again we are reminded that God sees things differently to the way we see them. God perhaps judges me differently from the way I judge myself. In times of prayer I need to always open myself to the "God's eye view."

The Presence of God
For a few moments, I think of God's veiled presence in things:
in the elements, giving them existence;
in plants, giving them life; in animals, giving them sensation;
and finally, in me, giving me all this and more,
making me a temple, a dwelling-place of the Spirit.

Freedom
God is not foreign to my freedom.
Instead the Spirit breathes life into my most intimate desires,
gently nudging me towards all that is good.
I ask for the grace to let myself be enfolded by the Spirit.

Consciousness
Knowing that God loves me unconditionally,
I look honestly over the last day, its events and my feelings.
Do I have something to be grateful for? Then I give thanks.
Is there something I am sorry for? Then I ask forgiveness.

The Word
I take my time to read the Word of God, slowly, a few times,
allowing myself to dwell on anything that strikes me. (Please
turn to your scripture on the following pages. Inspiration
points are there should you need them. When you are ready,
return here to continue.)

Conversation
How has God's Word moved me? Has it left me cold?
Has it consoled me or moved me to act in a new way?
I imagine Jesus standing or sitting beside me,
I turn and share my feelings with him.

Conclusion
Glory be to the Father, and to the Son, and to the Holy Spirit,
As it was in the beginning, is now and ever shall be,
World without end. Amen

302

Sunday 11th September, 24th Sunday of the Year
Matthew 18:21-30

Then Peter came and said to him, "Lord, if another member of the church sins against me, how often should I forgive? As many as seven times?" Jesus said to him, "Not seven times, but, I tell you, seventy-seven times. For this reason the kingdom of heaven may be compared to a king who wished to settle accounts with his slaves. When he began the reckoning, one who owed him ten thousand talents was brought to him; and, as he could not pay, his lord ordered him to be sold, together with his wife and children and all his possessions, and payment to be made. So the slave fell on his knees before him, saying, 'Have patience with me, and I will pay you everything.' And out of pity for him, the lord of that slave released him and forgave him the debt. But that same slave, as he went out, came upon one of his fellow slaves who owed him a hundred denarii; and seizing him by the throat, he said, 'Pay what you owe.' Then his fellow slave fell down and pleaded with him, 'Have patience with me, and I will pay you.' But he refused; then he went and threw him into prison until he would pay the debt."

- Do I know what it is like to be forgiven or released from a great debt?
- What are my feelings towards the one who forgave me?
- Do I have a sense of God's continuing patience and forgiveness towards me?
- What next?

Monday 12th September
Luke 7:1-10

After Jesus had finished all his sayings in the hearing of the people, he entered Capernaum. A centurion there had a slave whom he valued highly, and who was ill and close to death. When he heard about Jesus, he sent some Jewish elders to him, asking him to come and heal his slave. When they came to Jesus, they appealed to him earnestly, saying, "He is worthy of having you do this for him, for he loves our people, and it is he who built our synagogue for us." And Jesus went with them, but when he was not far from the house, the centurion sent friends to say to him, "Lord, do not trouble yourself, for I am not worthy to have you come under my roof; therefore I did not presume to come to you. But only speak the word, and let my servant be healed. For I also am a man set under authority, with soldiers under me; and I say to one, 'Go,' and he goes, and to another, 'Come,' and he comes, and to my slave, 'Do this,' and the slave does it." When Jesus heard this he was amazed at him, and turning to the crowd that followed him, he said, "I tell you, not even in Israel have I found such faith." When those who had been sent returned to the house, they found the slave in good health.

- It would have been almost impossible for a Roman Centurion to put his faith, humbly, in an itinerant Jewish preacher. The culture and politics of supremacy would have ruled out contact, let alone this act of faith and homage.
- His act of faith, so unexpected and against the culture, was a gift. It made a huge impression on Jesus.
- Do I find myself, at times, weak in faith, discouraged by the atmosphere and culture around me? What about the gift that the centurion got? Am I open to receive it?

Tuesday 13th September   Luke 7:11-17

Soon afterwards Jesus went to a town called Nain, and his disciples and a large crowd went with him. As he approached the gate of the town, a man who had died was being carried out. He was his mother's only son, and she was a widow; and with her was a large crowd from the town. When the Lord saw her, he had compassion for her and said to her, "Do not weep." Then he came forward and touched the bier, and the bearers stood still. And he said, "Young man, I say to you, rise!" The dead man sat up and began to speak, and Jesus gave him to his mother. Fear seized all of them; and they glorified God, saying, "A great prophet has risen among us!" and "God has looked favorably on his people!" This word about him spread throughout Judea and all the surrounding country.

- Picture this scene. Nain was a walled town and Jesus and his followers were approaching the gate.
- What do they see? How does He react? What happens?
- How do I react to the scene? What do I want to say to Jesus?

Wednesday 14th September, Exaltation of the Holy Cross
John 3:14-17

Jesus said, "And just as Moses lifted up the serpent in the wilderness, so must the Son of Man be lifted up, that whoever believes in him may have eternal life. For God so loved the world that he gave his only Son, so that everyone who believes in him may not perish but may have eternal life. Indeed, God did not send the Son into the world to condemn the world, but in order that the world might be saved through him."

- Jesus says these words to Nicodemus, a Pharisee who came to him at night, searching for answers.
- His answer is not condemnation, but God's love and a promise of eternal life.
- What does all of this mean to me?

Thursday 15th September, Our Lady of Sorrows
Luke 2:33-35

And the child's father and mother were amazed at what was being said about him. Then Simeon blessed them and said to his mother Mary, "This child is destined for the falling and the rising of many in Israel, and to be a sign that will be opposed so that the inner thoughts of many will be revealed—and a sword will pierce your own soul too."

- Simeon recognised this apparently helpless child for who he really was. Can we?
- Jesus is "a sign that will be opposed." Are there parts of me that oppose Jesus?
- If I take a stand with Jesus, I too will have to face opposition.

Friday 16th September
Luke 8:1-3

Soon afterwards he went on through cities and villages, proclaiming and bringing the good news of the kingdom of God. The twelve were with him, as well as some women who had been cured of evil spirits and infirmities: Mary, called Magdalene, from whom seven demons had gone out, and Joanna, the wife of Herod's steward Chuza, and Susanna, and many others, who provided for them out of their resources.

- What Jesus has to say to us, and to me, is good news.
- Why do these people follow him? They know him. They have a relationship with him.
- They don't wait for total understanding before going with him.

Saturday 17th September, St Robert Bellarmine
Matthew 5:17-19

Jesus said, "Do not think that I have come to abolish the law or the prophets; I have come not to abolish but to fulfill. For truly I tell you, until heaven and earth pass away, not one letter, not one stroke of a letter, will pass from the law until all is accomplished. Therefore, whoever breaks one of the least of these commandments, and teaches others to do the same, will be called least in the kingdom of heaven; but whoever does them and teaches them will be called great in the kingdom of heaven."

- Strong words from Jesus about the law. He didn't come to make life softer but deeper.
- What is my own relationship with law and tradition? Am I naturally submissive or automatically rebellious?
- How is Jesus calling me to go deeper?

Sacred Space

september 18–24

Something to think and pray about each day this week:

Use what helps

Different ways of praying work for different people. There is no one way that we ought to pray—no obligation to stick to a particular method, technique or branch of spirituality. Rather, we should use what helps, and drop what doesn't help (once we've given it a fair trial!) as Saint Ignatius advises us:

> We ought to use things to the extent that they help us towards our end—to praise, reverence and serve God our Lord—and free ourselves from them to the extent that they hinder us from that end. (Spiritual Exercises no. 23)

This applies to *Sacred Space* as much as to anything else. If, after some time, I find that some of the steps work well for me, while other parts don't, I can spend more time on what works. If I find, after some time, that *Sacred Space* isn't helping me to pray at all, then I should drop it, at least for a while. The only important thing is that I do pray, and develop the living relationship with the Lord that he is offering me. My attitude to everything else—times, places and methods—should be one of complete freedom.

The Presence of God
I pause for a moment
and think of the love and the grace that God showers on me,
creating me in his image and likeness, making me his temple.

Freedom
Everything has the potential to draw forth from me a fuller
love and life.
Yet my desires are often fixed, caught, on illusions of fulfillment.
I ask that God, through my freedom, may orchestrate
my desires in a vibrant loving melody rich in harmony.

Consciousness
How do I find myself today?
Where am I with God? With others?
Do I have something to be grateful for? Then I give thanks.
Is there something I am sorry for? Then I ask forgiveness.

The Word
God speaks to each one of us individually. I need to listen
to what he is saying to me. (Please turn to your scripture on
the following pages. Inspiration points are there should you
need them. When you are ready, return here to continue.)

Conversation
What feelings are rising in me
as I pray and reflect on God's Word?
I imagine Jesus himself sitting or standing beside me,
and open my heart to him.

Conclusion
Glory be to the Father, and to the Son, and to the Holy Spirit,
As it was in the beginning, is now and ever shall be,
World without end. Amen

Sunday 18th September, 25th Sunday of the Year
Matthew 20:1-16a

And Jesus said, "For the kingdom of heaven is like a landowner who went out early in the morning to hire laborers for his vineyard. After agreeing with the laborers for the usual daily wage, he sent them into his vineyard. When he went out about nine o'clock, he saw others standing idle in the marketplace; and he said to them, 'You also go into the vineyard, and I will pay you whatever is right.' So they went. When he went out again about noon and about three o'clock, he did the same. And about five o'clock he went out and found others standing around; and he said to them, 'Why are you standing here idle all day?' They said to him, 'Because no one has hired us.' He said to them, 'You also go into the vineyard.' When evening came, the owner of the vineyard said to his manager, 'Call the laborers and give them their pay, beginning with the last and then going to the first.' When those hired about five o'clock came, each of them received the usual daily wage. Now when the first came, they thought they would receive more; but each of them also received the usual daily wage. And when they received it, they grumbled against the landowner, saying, 'These last worked only one hour, and you have made them equal to us who have borne the burden of the day and the scorching heat.' But he replied to one of them, 'Friend, I am doing you no wrong; did you not agree with me for the usual daily wage? Take what belongs to you and go; I choose to give to this last the same as I give to you. Am I not allowed to do what I choose with what belongs to me? Or are you envious because I am generous?' So the last will be first, and the first will be last."

- God's way of loving us "doesn't make sense." It isn't "fair."
- Can I learn from it?

311

Monday 19th September   Luke 8:16-18

Jesus said to his disciples, "No one after lighting a lamp hides it under a jar, or puts it under a bed, but puts it on a lampstand, so that those who enter may see the light. For nothing is hidden that will not be disclosed, nor is anything secret that will not become known and come to light. Then pay attention to how you listen; for to those who have, more will be given; and from those who do not have, even what they seem to have will be taken away."

- Are there some parts of my life that I want to keep hidden, out of the light?
- Listening means wanting to hear. Do I want to hear what God has to say to me?
- When we let our light shine—when we are ourselves—then God gives us all we need, and more.

Tuesday 20th September   Luke 8:19-21

Then Jesus' mother and his brothers came to him, but they could not reach him because of the crowd. And he was told, "Your mother and your brothers are standing outside, wanting to see you." But he said to them, "My mother and my brothers are those who hear the word of God and do it."

- It would be good to consider how close Jesus was to his mother and those closest to him.
- He wants to affirm, even at the risk of being blunt, that others are welcome in the same intimate relationship.
- Do I share in this closeness? What call do Jesus' words extend to me?

Wednesday 21st September, St Matthew

Matthew 9:9-13

As Jesus was walking along, he saw a man called Matthew sitting at the tax booth; and he said to him, "Follow me." And he got up and followed him. And as he sat at dinner in the house, many tax collectors and sinners came and were sitting with him and his disciples. When the Pharisees saw this, they said to his disciples, "Why does your teacher eat with tax collectors and sinners?" But when he heard this, he said, "Those who are well have no need of a physician, but those who are sick. Go and learn what this means, 'I desire mercy, not sacrifice.' For I have come to call not the righteous but sinners."

- Tax collectors were shunned and reviled, yet Jesus calls one of them, Matthew, to be his disciple.
- Notice Jesus' attitude to people and compare it to the Pharisees' attitude.
- Do I see myself as a sinner or a "righteous person"? What is my attitude towards other sinners and "righteous people"?

Thursday 22nd September

Luke 9:7-9

Now Herod the ruler heard about all that had taken place, and he was perplexed, because it was said by some that John had been raised from the dead, by some that Elijah had appeared, and by others that one of the ancient prophets had arisen. Herod said, "John I beheaded; but who is this about whom I hear such things?" And he tried to see him.

- Rumours are rife about this Jesus character, who he is and what he is about.
- Even Herod knows that the only way to find out the truth is to meet Jesus himself.

Friday 23rd September   **Luke 9:18-22**

O nce when Jesus was praying alone, with only the disciples near him, he asked them, "Who do the crowds say that I am?" They answered, "John the Baptist; but others, Elijah; and still others, that one of the ancient prophets has arisen." He said to them, "But who do you say that I am?" Peter answered, "The Messiah of God." He sternly ordered and commanded them not to tell anyone, saying, "The Son of Man must undergo great suffering, and be rejected by the elders, chief priests, and scribes, and be killed, and on the third day be raised."

- Lots of stories are circulating about Jesus.
- Everyone wants to have a way of pinning him down, a category to put him in.
- But what Jesus is interested in is "who am I to you?"

Saturday 24th September   **Luke 9:43-45**

A nd all were astounded at the greatness of God. While everyone was amazed at all that he was doing, he said to his disciples, "Let these words sink into your ears: The Son of Man is going to be betrayed into human hands." But they did not understand this saying; its meaning was concealed from them, so that they could not perceive it. And they were afraid to ask him about this saying.

- The people were expecting a powerful Messiah, a Saviour, a winner.
- Try letting those words "sink into your ears": "The Son of Man is going to betrayed into human hands."
- What does it feel like?

september 25 – october 1

Something to think and pray about each day this week:

The divine murmur

On one famous occasion the Prophet Elijah, when he felt he was all alone and threatened by enemies, called out to the Lord for help. He was told to go and stand on God's mountain where the Lord was going to pass by.

First there was a mighty hurricane that shattered the rocks. But the Lord was not in the hurricane. Then there was a great earthquake. But the Lord was not in the earthquake. Next, there was a fire. The Lord was not in the fire. Finally there was the murmur of a gentle breeze. The Lord spoke to Elijah in the soft whisper.

God doesn't bully or overpower us. Sometimes we may have to be quiet, listening carefully, to hear his voice, as it were, in a gentle murmur.

The Presence of God

I reflect for a moment on God's presence around me and in me.
Creator of the universe, the sun and the moon, the earth,
every molecule, every atom, everything that is:
God is in every beat of my heart. God is with me, now.

Freedom

There are very few people
who realize what God would make of them
if they abandoned themselves into his hands,
and let themselves be formed by his grace. (St Ignatius)
I ask for the grace to trust myself totally to God's love.

Consciousness

In God's loving presence I unwind the past day,
starting from now and looking back, moment by moment.
I gather in all the goodness and light, in gratitude.
I attend to the shadows and what they say to me,
seeking healing, courage, forgiveness.

The Word

I read the Word of God slowly, a few times over, and I listen
to what God is saying to me. (Please turn to your scripture on
the following pages. Inspiration points are there should you
need them. When you are ready, return here to continue.)

Conversation

What is stirring in me as I pray?
Am I consoled, troubled, left cold?
I imagine Jesus himself standing or sitting at my side,
and share my feelings with him.

Conclusion

Glory be to the Father, and to the Son, and to the Holy Spirit,
As it was in the beginning, is now and ever shall be,
World without end. Amen

Sunday 25th September, 26th Sunday of the Year
Matthew 21:28-32

Jesus said, "What do you think? A man had two sons; he went to the first and said, 'Son, go and work in the vineyard today.' He answered, 'I will not'; but later he changed his mind and went. The father went to the second and said the same; and he answered, 'I go, sir'; but he did not go. Which of the two did the will of his father?" They said, "The first." Jesus said to them, "Truly I tell you, the tax collectors and the prostitutes are going into the kingdom of God ahead of you. For John came to you in the way of righteousness and you did not believe him, but the tax collectors and the prostitutes believed him; and even after you saw it, you did not change your minds and believe him."

- Well, which am I?

Monday 26th September
Luke 9:46-48

An argument arose among the disciples as to which one of them was the greatest. But Jesus, aware of their inner thoughts, took a little child and put it by his side, and said to them, "Whoever welcomes this child in my name welcomes me, and whoever welcomes me welcomes the one who sent me; for the least among all of you is the greatest."

- Imagine the little child in this scene, the expression on the child's face. What is he or she like? Wide-eyed? Innocent? Trusting?
- I come with all my "baggage," my scepticism, competitiveness, self-regard. Can I put this aside and be like the little child?
- Jesus welcomes this child with open arms.

Tuesday 27th September, St Vincent de Paul

Matthew 9:35-38

Then Jesus went about all the cities and villages, teaching in their synagogues, and proclaiming the good news of the kingdom, and curing every disease and every sickness. When he saw the crowds, he had compassion for them, because they were harassed and helpless, like sheep without a shepherd. Then he said to his disciples, "The harvest is plentiful, but the laborers are few; therefore ask the Lord of the harvest to send out laborers into his harvest."

- Do I know any people who are "harassed and helpless, like sheep without a shepherd"? Can I hold them before my mind's eye for a moment?
- Can I now imagine Jesus looking at them? How does he see them?
- If I feel "harassed and helpless," how does he see me?
- Can I ask for the grace to look on the world around me with the compassionate eyes of Jesus?

Wednesday 28th September

Luke 9:57-62

As they were going along the road, someone said to him, "I will follow you wherever you go." And Jesus said to him, "Foxes have holes, and birds of the air have nests; but the Son of Man has nowhere to lay his head." To another he said, "Follow me." But he said, "Lord, first let me go and bury my father." But Jesus said to him, "Let the dead bury their own dead; but as for you, go and proclaim the kingdom of God." Another said, "I will follow you, Lord; but let me first say farewell to those at my home." Jesus said to him, "No one who puts a hand to the plow and looks back is fit for the kingdom of God."

- Here we see three apparently generous individuals who are ready to become followers. Jesus, in each case, seems to make things more difficult for them. What is my reaction to this? What is Jesus up to?

- If Jesus is calling his followers to give without the slightest reservation or hesitation, is he perhaps telling us something about himself? A disciple can only learn to love God unconditionally when they have first experienced that kind of love from God.
- Do I find myself hesitating or holding back in my following? How does this sit with the guarantee of God's unconditional love for me?

Thursday 29th September, Sts Michael, Gabriel and Raphael   John 1:47-51

When Jesus saw Nathanael coming toward him, he said of him, "Here is truly an Israelite in whom there is no deceit!" Nathanael asked him, "Where did you get to know me?" Jesus answered, "I saw you under the fig tree before Philip called you." Nathanael replied, "Rabbi, you are the Son of God! You are the King of Israel!" Jesus answered, "Do you believe because I told you that I saw you under the fig tree? You will see greater things than these." And he said to him, "Very truly, I tell you, you will see heaven opened and the angels of God ascending and descending upon the Son of Man."

- Can I put myself in Nathanael's shoes?
- When I hear the great news is my reaction like his? How do I react?
- Do I hear the words "come and see" addressed to me?
- How do I respond?

Friday 30th September   Luke 10:13-16

Jesus said to his disciples, "Woe to you, Chorazin! Woe to you, Bethsaida! For if the deeds of power done in you had been done in Tyre and Sidon, they would have repented long ago, sitting in sackcloth and ashes. But at the judgment it will be more tolerable for Tyre and Sidon than for you. And you, Capernaum, will you be exalted to heaven? No, you will be brought down to Hades. "Whoever listens to you listens to me, and whoever rejects you rejects me, and whoever rejects me rejects the one who sent me."

- How we respond really matters to God, it seems.
- Few things seem to annoy him as much as indifference.
- Have I witnessed "deeds of power" around me? What is my response?

Saturday 1st October, St Therese of the Child Jesus
Isaiah 66:10-13a

Rejoice with Jerusalem, and be glad for her, all you who love her; rejoice with her in joy, all you who mourn over her—that you may nurse and be satisfied from her consoling breast; that you may drink deeply with delight from her glorious bosom. For thus says the Lord: I will extend prosperity to her like a river, and the wealth of the nations like an overflowing stream; and you shall nurse and be carried on her arm, and dandled on her knees. As a mother comforts her child, so I will comfort you.

- This is God speaking to me now. Am I listening?
- God reveals aspects of "himself" here that are different to the usual ones.
- Can I relate to God as being "like a mother who comforts her child"?

october 2–8

Something to think and pray about each day this week:

Consolation and desolation

Some months ago, we introduced these two words which St Ignatius uses to describe two different feelings we may have when we are praying, and afterwards.

Consolation is happening when I feel drawn closer to God, to unselfishness and generosity. This might be accompanied by gratitude or peace or new hope, but equally it could be an experience of grief or regret, or sympathy for somebody's suffering. Consolation is the feeling when barriers between myself and God are being broken down, and this can be initially painful.

Desolation is the opposite of all this. It is happening when I feel withdrawn or alienated from God and turned in on myself, when I am determined to "put my faith in earthly things" or shut God out of some area of my life. Again, this is not always felt as sadness, but may be accompanied by a shallow, self-satisfied kind of happiness.

St Ignatius teaches us to take note of these feelings, since they can tell us about what is happening deep within us.

The Presence of God
I remind myself that, as I sit here now,
God is gazing on me with love and holding me in being.
I pause for a moment and think of this.

Freedom
I ask for the grace
to let go of my own concerns
and be open to what God is asking of me,
to let myself be guided and formed by my loving Creator.

Consciousness
I exist in a web of relationships—links to nature, people, God.
I trace out these links, giving thanks for the life that flows
through them.
Some links are twisted or broken: I may feel regret, anger,
disappointment.
I pray for the gift of acceptance and forgiveness.

The Word
I take my time to read the Word of God, slowly, a few times,
allowing myself to dwell on anything that strikes me. (Please
turn to your scripture on the following pages. Inspiration
points are there should you need them. When you are ready,
return here to continue.)

Conversation
Do I notice myself reacting as I pray with the Word of God?
Do I feel challenged, comforted, angry?
Imagining Jesus sitting or standing by me,
I speak out my feelings, as one trusted friend to another.

Conclusion
Glory be to the Father, and to the Son, and to the Holy Spirit,
As it was in the beginning, is now and ever shall be,
World without end. Amen

october 2005

Sunday 2nd October, 27th Sunday of the Year

Matthew 21:33-43

"Listen to another parable. There was a landowner who planted a vineyard, put a fence around it, dug a wine press in it, and built a watchtower. Then he leased it to tenants and went to another country. When the harvest time had come, he sent his slaves to the tenants to collect his produce. But the tenants seized his slaves and beat one, killed another, and stoned another. Again he sent other slaves, more than the first; and they treated them in the same way. Finally he sent his son to them, saying, 'They will respect my son.' But when the tenants saw the son, they said to themselves, 'This is the heir; come, let us kill him and get his inheritance." So they seized him, threw him out of the vineyard, and killed him.

Now when the owner of the vineyard comes, what will he do to those tenants?" They said to him, "He will put those wretches to a miserable death, and lease the vineyard to other tenants who will give him the produce at the harvest time." Jesus said to them, "Have you never read in the scriptures: 'The stone that the builders rejected has become the cornerstone; this was the Lord's doing, and it is amazing in our eyes'? Therefore I tell you, the kingdom of God will be taken away from you and given to a people that produces the fruits of the kingdom."

- Two very different attitudes are on display here. On the one hand there is the deeply gracious, patient generosity of the landowner. On the other we see the crass, blind selfishness of the tenants. Do I hear echoes of either attitude in myself or in others?
- This story, which centres on the murder of the "son and heir" is obviously very close to the heart of Jesus.
- Can I try and look him in the eye and hear the story from his own lips?

Monday 3rd October   Luke 10:30-37

Jesus replied, "A man was going down from Jerusalem to Jericho, and fell into the hands of robbers, who stripped him, beat him, and went away, leaving him half dead. Now by chance a priest was going down that road; and when he saw him, he passed by on the other side. So likewise a Levite, when he came to the place and saw him, passed by on the other side. But a Samaritan while traveling came near him; and when he saw him, he was moved with pity. He went to him and bandaged his wounds, having poured oil and wine on them. Then he put him on his own animal, brought him to an inn, and took care of him. The next day he took out two denarii, gave them to the innkeeper, and said, 'Take care of him; and when I come back, I will repay you whatever more you spend.' Which of these three, do you think, was a neighbor to the man who fell into the hands of the robbers?" He said, "The one who showed him mercy." Jesus said to him, "Go and do likewise."

- A man who was anxious to justify himself asked Jesus, "Who is my neighbor?" and Jesus replied with this story.
- Who is my neighbor? Jesus seems to suggest that it is the person whom I view with suspicion and don't like, or who views me with suspicion and doesn't like me.
- Do I have any neighbors in this challenging sense of the word? What is Jesus trying to say to me?

Tuesday 4th October, St Francis of Assisi
Matthew 11:28-30

Jesus said, "Come to me, all you that are weary and are carrying heavy burdens, and I will give you rest. Take my yoke upon you, and learn from me; for I am gentle and humble in heart, and you will find rest for your souls. For my yoke is easy, and my burden is light."

324

- I imagine Jesus saying these words to me, now.
- What burdens am I carrying? Can I share them with Jesus?

Wednesday 5th October   Luke 11:1-4

Jesus was praying in a certain place, and after he had finished, one of his disciples said to him, "Lord, teach us to pray, as John taught his disciples." He said to them, "When you pray, say: Father, hallowed be your name. Your kingdom come. Give us each day our daily bread. And forgive us our sins, for we ourselves forgive everyone indebted to us. And do not bring us to the time of trial."

- This is a prayer of complete reliance on, and trust in, God the Father.
- Take one sentence at a time, say it slowly, savouring the words and their meaning.
- Can I say the words of this prayer and mean them?

Thursday 6th October   Luke 11:9-13

Jesus said to the disciples, "So I say to you, Ask, and it will be given you; search, and you will find; knock, and the door will be opened for you. For everyone who asks receives, and everyone who searches finds, and for everyone who knocks, the door will be opened. Is there anyone among you who, if your child asks for a fish, will give a snake instead of a fish? Or if the child asks for an egg, will give a scorpion? If you then, who are evil, know how to give good gifts to your children, how much more will the heavenly Father give the Holy Spirit to those who ask him!"

- Am I thinking: "This isn't my experience. I don't get what I ask for"?
- God wants what is truly best for us all.

- Can I remember experiences of receiving what I asked for, and times when I didn't? What was it that I was asking for?

Friday 7th October   Joel 1:19-20

To you, O Lord, I cry. For fire has devoured the pastures of the wilderness, and flames have burned all the trees of the field. Even the wild animals cry to you because the watercourses are dried up, and fire has devoured the pastures of the wilderness.

- This seems to be a cry of desolation. Do I feel that way now, or can I remember a time when I did?
- The speaker—and even the animals—are turning to God in their time of need. Where do I look for help when I am in trouble?

Saturday 8th October   Luke 11:27-28

While Jesus was speaking, a woman in the crowd raised her voice and said to him, "Blessed is the womb that bore you and the breasts that nursed you!" But he said, "Blessed rather are those who hear the word of God and obey it!"

- What a blunt reply to the woman! Jesus doesn't mince his words here.
- Are words or actions more important to Jesus?
- What is my reply to his invitation to follow him?

october 9–15

Something to think and pray about each day this week:

Stick with it

After a few days the temptation arises to think, "This isn't going anywhere. Missing a few days won't make any difference." At that point it's important to persevere. Giving the time to these few steps regularly has a great value. When I stick with it for a while I begin to see it making a difference to my day in little ways.

The Presence of God

In the silence of my innermost being,
in the fragments of my yearned-for wholeness,
can I hear the whispers of God's presence?
Can I remember when I felt God's nearness?
When we walked together and I let myself be embraced by
God's love.

Freedom

A thick and shapeless tree-trunk would never believe
that it could become a statue, admired as a miracle of sculpture,
and would never submit itself to the chisel of the sculptor,
who sees by her genius what she can make of it. (St Ignatius)
I ask for the grace to let myself be shaped by my loving Creator.

Consciousness

How am I really feeling? Light-hearted? Heavy-hearted?
I may be very much at peace, happy to be here.
Equally, I may be frustrated, worried or angry.
I acknowledge how I really am. It is the real me that the Lord
loves.

The Word

God speaks to each one of us individually. I need to listen
to what he is saying to me. (Please turn to your scripture on
the following pages. Inspiration points are there should you
need them. When you are ready, return here to continue.)

Conversation

Remembering that I am still in God's presence,
I imagine Jesus himself standing or sitting beside me,
and say whatever is on my mind, whatever is in my heart,
speaking as one friend to another.

Conclusion

Glory be to the Father, and to the Son, and to the Holy Spirit,
As it was in the beginning, is now and ever shall be,
World without end. Amen

Sunday 9th October, 28th Sunday of the Year
Matthew 22:1-14

Once more Jesus spoke to them in parables, saying: "The kingdom of heaven may be compared to a king who gave a wedding banquet for his son. He sent his slaves to call those who had been invited to the wedding banquet, but they would not come. Again he sent other slaves, saying, 'Tell those who have been invited: Look, I have prepared my dinner, my oxen and my fat calves have been slaughtered, and everything is ready; come to the wedding banquet.' But they made light of it and went away, one to his farm, another to his business, while the rest seized his slaves, mistreated them, and killed them. The king was enraged. He sent his troops, destroyed those murderers, and burned their city. Then he said to his slaves, 'The wedding is ready, but those invited were not worthy. Go therefore into the main streets, and invite everyone you find to the wedding banquet.' Those slaves went out into the streets and gathered all whom they found, both good and bad; so the wedding hall was filled with guests. But when the king came in to see the guests, he noticed a man there who was not wearing a wedding robe, and he said to him, 'Friend, how did you get in here without a wedding robe?' And he was speechless. Then the king said to the attendants, 'Bind him hand and foot, and throw him into the outer darkness, where there will be weeping and gnashing of teeth.' For many are called, but few are chosen."

- An invitation is a free act of generosity. To receive a sincere invitation is always a privilege. To throw it back in someone's face is an awful thing to do.
- Do I feel myself to be privileged to be invited to share in the Banquet of Life? What is Jesus teaching me in this story about my own responses to God's invitation?

Monday 10th October   Luke 11:29-30

When the crowds were increasing, Jesus began to say, "This generation is an evil generation; it asks for a sign, but no sign will be given to it except the sign of Jonah. For just as Jonah became a sign to the people of Nineveh, so the Son of Man will be to this generation.

- Jonah was sent to warn the Ninevites of their imminent destruction, to tell them that the Lord was not happy with their attitude.
- The message Jesus gave to the people in his time was a mixture of love and challenge.
- What kind of signs am I looking for? Do I recognise the signs that are here already?

Tuesday 11th October   Luke 11:37-41

While Jesus was speaking, a Pharisee invited him to dine with him; so he went in and took his place at the table. The Pharisee was amazed to see that he did not first wash before dinner. Then the Lord said to him, "Now you Pharisees clean the outside of the cup and of the dish, but inside you are full of greed and wickedness. You fools! Did not the one who made the outside make the inside also? So give for alms those things that are within; and see, everything will be clean for you."

- The Pharisees are preoccupied with outward observance.
- Jesus' concern is the inner truth, not the outer appearance.
- Do I "give what is within" to God, or keep it to myself?

Wednesday 12th October   Luke 11:42-44

Jesus said, "Woe to you Pharisees! For you tithe mint and rue and herbs of all kinds, and neglect justice and the love of God; it is these you ought to have practised, without neglecting the others. Woe to you Pharisees! For you love to have the seat of honour in the synagogues and to be greeted with respect in the marketplaces. Woe to you! For you are like unmarked graves, and people walk over them without realizing it."

- This is not "gentle Jesus, meek and mild."
- The Pharisees take pride in following the law and being important. Am I overly concerned with status and respectability?
- How important to me are justice and the love of God?

Thursday 13th October   Luke 11:47-54

Jesus said: "Woe to you! For you build the tombs of the prophets whom your ancestors killed. So you are witnesses and approve of the deeds of your ancestors; for they killed them, and you build their tombs. Therefore also the Wisdom of God said, 'I will send them prophets and apostles, some of whom they will kill and persecute,' so that this generation may be charged with the blood of all the prophets shed since the foundation of the world, from the blood of Abel to the blood of Zechariah, who perished between the altar and the sanctuary. Yes, I tell you, it will be charged against this generation. Woe to you lawyers! For you have taken away the key of knowledge; you did not enter yourselves, and you hindered those who were entering." When he went outside, the scribes and the Pharisees began to be very hostile toward him and to cross-examine him about many things, lying in wait for him, to catch him in something he might say.

- Here Jesus is confronting people who, for reasons of vested interest, are resisting the challenge of the truth that Jesus brings.

- How does a righteous and angry Jesus make me feel? Do I want to run away? Do I start getting righteous myself?
- Can I get in touch with the parts of myself that resist the call and action of Jesus? I might humbly ask for help to change.

Friday 14th October   **Luke 12:1-7**

Meanwhile, when the crowd gathered by the thousands, so that they trampled on one another, Jesus began to speak first to his disciples, "Beware of the yeast of the Pharisees, that is, their hypocrisy. Nothing is covered up that will not be uncovered, and nothing secret that will not become known. Therefore whatever you have said in the dark will be heard in the light, and what you have whispered behind closed doors will be proclaimed from the housetops. "I tell you, my friends, do not fear those who kill the body, and after that can do nothing more. But I will warn you whom to fear: fear him who, after he has killed, has authority to cast into hell. Yes, I tell you, fear him! Are not five sparrows sold for two pennies? Yet not one of them is forgotten in God's sight. But even the hairs of your head are all counted. Do not be afraid; you are of more value than many sparrows."

- "Nothing secret that will not become known." Do I consider this prospect with calm and equanimity, or does it leave me in the grip of fear?
- Here, there is a challenge from Jesus to live in the truth no matter the cost. Can I face the challenge?
- If the challenge seems too great, can I hear the words "Do not be afraid; you are of more value than … ?"

Saturday 15th October, St Teresa of Avila   **John 15:4-5**

Jesus said to his apostles, "Abide in me as I abide in you. Just as the branch cannot bear fruit by itself unless it abides in the vine, neither can you unless you abide in me. I am the vine, you are the branches. Those who abide in me and I in them bear much fruit, because apart from me you can do nothing."

- Can I remember times when I have had this kind of connectedness with the Lord, this feeling of "abiding" in God?
- Can I remember when, without this rootedness, I have felt like a drifting boat?
- Which do I feel now? and what am I going to do about it?

Sacred Space

october 16–22

Something to think and pray about each day this week:

Wake up!!
In the scriptures this week we hear more than a hint of frustration in Jesus' voice. In one place he says, "You fool!" Elsewhere he tells us that he, "came to bring fire." The one who loves us unconditionally sounds angry and seems to be saying "You're not getting it. You're missing the point. Wake up!"

But, what's wrong? What are we not getting? What is Jesus so urgent about? It's as if we are wearing blinkers in the art gallery or ear plugs in the concert hall. There is something wonderful going on, and he seems to feel we are in danger of missing it.

When we hear Jesus raise his voice we might be tempted to skirt around it.

In my praying this week it would be good for me to ask humbly: "Show me Lord, what it is that I'm missing."

The Presence of God
God is with me, but more,
God is within me, giving me existence.
Let me dwell for a moment on God's life-giving presence
in my body, my mind, my heart
and in the whole of my life.

Freedom
I ask for the grace to believe
in what I could be and do
if I only allowed God, my loving Creator,
to continue to create me, guide me and shape me.

Consciousness
Knowing that God loves me unconditionally,
I can afford to be honest about how I am.
How has the last day been, and how do I feel now?
I share my feelings openly with the Lord.

The Word
I read the Word of God slowly, a few times over, and I listen
to what God is saying to me. (Please turn to your scripture on
the following pages. Inspiration points are there should you
need them. When you are ready, return here to continue.)

Conversation
How has God's Word moved me? Has it left me cold?
Has it consoled me or moved me to act in a new way?
I imagine Jesus standing or sitting beside me,
I turn and share my feelings with him.

Conclusion
Glory be to the Father, and to the Son, and to the Holy Spirit,
As it was in the beginning, is now and ever shall be,
World without end. Amen

Sunday 16th October, 29th Sunday of the Year
Matthew 22:15-21

Then the Pharisees went and plotted to entrap him in what he said. So they sent their disciples to him, along with the Herodians, saying, "Teacher, we know that you are sincere, and teach the way of God in accordance with truth, and show deference to no one; for you do not regard people with partiality. Tell us, then, what you think. Is it lawful to pay taxes to the emperor, or not?" But Jesus, aware of their malice, said, "Why are you putting me to the test, you hypocrites? Show me the coin used for the tax." And they brought him a denarius. Then he said to them, "Whose head is this, and whose title?" They answered, "The emperor's." Then he said to them, "Give therefore to the emperor the things that are the emperor's, and to God the things that are God's."

- Who is this Jesus and how has he inspired such devious, bitter opposition? What has he done against the Pharisees for them to treat him like this?
- Do I want to ask Jesus how he responds with justice and love to this kind of negativity?
- Do I have something to learn here?

Monday 17th October
Luke 12:13-21

Someone in the crowd said to Jesus, "Teacher, tell my brother to divide the family inheritance with me." But he said to him, "Friend, who set me to be a judge or arbitrator over you?" And he said to them, "Take care! Be on your guard against all kinds of greed; for one's life does not consist in the abundance of possessions." Then he told them a parable: "The land of a rich man produced abundantly. And he thought to himself, 'What should I do, for I have no place to store my crops?' Then he said, 'I will do this: I will pull down my barns and build larger ones, and there I will store all my grain and my goods. And I will say to my soul, 'Soul, you have ample goods laid up for many years; relax, eat, drink, be merry.' But God said to him, 'You fool! This very night your life is being demanded of you. And the things you have prepared, whose will they be?' So it is with those who store up treasures for themselves but are not rich toward God."

- Does this seem an outlandish parable? Can I imagine anyone—even me—allowing the beautiful things of life to come between me and God?
- Is there anything that I hoard?
- What does being "rich toward God" mean in my case?

Tuesday 18th October, St Luke Luke 10:1-7a

After this the Lord appointed seventy others and sent them on ahead of him in pairs to every town and place where he himself intended to go. He said to them, "The harvest is plentiful, but the labourers are few; therefore ask the Lord of the harvest to send out labourers into his harvest. Go on your way. See, I am sending you out like lambs into the midst of wolves. Carry no purse, no bag, no sandals; and greet no one on the road. Whatever house you enter, first say, 'Peace to this house!' And if anyone is there who shares in peace, your peace will rest on that person; but if not, it will return to you. Remain in the same house, eating and drinking whatever they provide, for the labourer deserves to be paid."

- This passage came up a few weeks ago, but it bears repetition. Reflecting on a passage a second time can be fruitful, whatever happened the first time.
- Jesus does not send them out alone, but in pairs. Do I see myself as part of a Christian "team" or as someone "going it on their own"?

338

- Someone sending you out on a journey today might tell you to take food, money—maybe even a gun—to avoid being vulnerable. But what does Jesus say about this?
- Have I asked Jesus where he wants me to go? What he wants me to do?

Wednesday 19th October　　　　　　　Luke 12:39-42

Jesus said, "But know this: if the owner of the house had known at what hour the thief was coming, he would not have let his house be broken into. You also must be ready, for the Son of Man is coming at an unexpected hour." Peter said, "Lord, are you telling this parable for us or for everyone?" And the Lord said, "Who then is the faithful and prudent manager whom his master will put in charge of his slaves, to give them their allowance of food at the proper time?"

- Peter asks if the parable is meant for them. It is easy to think that Jesus is addressing others, and not me.
- Jesus seems to be answering, "if the cap fits." If we are his followers then everything he says is for us.
- Are there things Jesus says I find difficult to accept or understand? Can I talk to him about this?

Thursday 20th October　　　　　　　Luke 12:49-53

Jesus said to the crowds, "I came to bring fire to the earth, and how I wish it were already kindled! I have a baptism with which to be baptized, and what stress I am under until it is completed! Do you think that I have come to bring peace to the earth? No, I tell you, but rather division! From now on five in one household will be divided, three against two and two against three; they will be divided: father against son and son against father, mother against daughter and daughter against mother, mother-in-law against her daughter-in-law and daughter-in-law against mother-in-law."

- The message of Jesus is meant to disturb us, to shake us out of complacency, to make our hearts burn within us.
- Christianity is not just about being nice. It means being angry at times, confronting injustice, making a stand.
- As a follower of Jesus, I can expect opposition. Am I ready for it?

Friday 21st October   Luke 12:54-56

Jesus said to the crowds, "When you see a cloud rising in the west, you immediately say, 'It is going to rain'; and so it happens. And when you see the south wind blowing, you say, 'There will be scorching heat'; and it happens. You hypocrites! You know how to interpret the appearance of earth and sky, but why do you not know how to interpret the present time?"

- When I look at the world around me, what do I see?
- What are the needs of the world today? What are the "signs of the times"?
- What am I going to do about this?

Saturday 22nd October   Luke 13:6-9

Then Jesus told this parable: "A man had a fig tree planted in his vineyard; and he came looking for fruit on it and found none. So he said to the gardener, 'See here! For three years I have come looking for fruit on this fig tree, and still I find none. Cut it down! Why should it be wasting the soil?' He replied, 'Sir, let it alone for one more year, until I dig around it and put manure on it. If it bears fruit next year, well and good; but if not, you can cut it down.'"

- This is a parable, so what is Jesus really talking about?
- Do I think I am wasting soil or bearing fruit, as far as God is concerned?
- If I want to change, God will always give me another chance. Am I going to take it?

Something to think and pray about each day this week:

Pray as you can
One of the biggest "dead-ends" in developing my spiritual life is to want to have someone else's spiritual life. If, for instance, I visit a convent one day or see a monastery on TV, I may find myself thinking, "I wish I could pray like them." But if I am a schoolteacher, or an accountant, or looking after my children all day, then that rhythm of prayer may just not be suited to me.

It seems obvious when you say it, but "pray as you can, not as you can't" is a maxim that is often overlooked, leading to some unrealistic expectations, and frustration.

Finding my own rhythm, a way of praying that suits me, may involve some experimentation with times and places and with different styles and approaches. I will need to persevere at times, and not give up on something too easily, but also be prepared to say, "this doesn't work for me." Finding a way of praying I can stick at is an important step in developing my relationship with God.

The Presence of God
To be present is to arrive as one is and open up to the other. At this instant, as I arrive here, God is present waiting for me. God always arrives before me, desiring to connect with me even more than my most intimate friend.
I take a moment and greet my loving God.

Freedom
"In these days, God taught me
as a schoolteacher teaches a pupil" (St Ignatius).
I remind myself that there are things God has to teach me yet, and ask for the grace to hear them and let them change me.

Consciousness
In the presence of my loving Creator,
I look honestly at my feelings over the last day,
the highs, the lows and the level ground.
Can I see where the Lord has been present?

The Word
I take my time to read the Word of God, slowly, a few times, allowing myself to dwell on anything that strikes me. (Please turn to your scripture on the following pages. Inspiration points are there should you need them. When you are ready, return here to continue.)

Conversation
What feelings are rising in me
as I pray and reflect on God's Word?
I imagine Jesus himself sitting or standing beside me, and open my heart to him.

Conclusion
Glory be to the Father, and to the Son, and to the Holy Spirit, As it was in the beginning, is now and ever shall be, World without end. Amen

october 2005

Sunday 23rd October, 30th Sunday of the Year
Matthew 22:34-40

When the Pharisees heard that he had silenced the Sadducees, they gathered together, and one of them, a lawyer, asked him a question to test him. "Teacher, which commandment in the law is the greatest?" He said to him, "'You shall love the Lord your God with all your heart, and with all your soul, and with all your mind.' This is the greatest and first commandment. And a second is like it: 'You shall love your neighbor as yourself.' On these two commandments hang all the law and the prophets."

- Everything of ultimate importance is contained in these few short words from the Son of God.
- Can hear them from his own lips and allow the words to sink deeply into my heart and soul?

Monday 24th October
Luke 13:10-13

Now Jesus was teaching in one of the synagogues on the sabbath. And just then there appeared a woman with a spirit that had crippled her for eighteen years. She was bent over and was quite unable to stand up straight. When Jesus saw her, he called her over and said, "Woman, you are set free from your ailment." When he laid his hands on her, immediately she stood up straight and began praising God.

- Spend some time imagining this scene. Picture the synagogue, the sights, sounds and smells.
- Imagine yourself as the woman, with the same ailment or one of your own, and let the scene unfold. What is it like?
- What do you feel like saying to Jesus at the end?

Tuesday 25th October   Luke 13:18-21

Jesus said, "What is the kingdom of God like? And to what should I compare it? It is like a mustard seed that someone took and sowed in the garden; it grew and became a tree, and the birds of the air made nests in its branches." And again he said, "To what should I compare the kingdom of God? It is like yeast that a woman took and mixed in with three measures of flour until all of it was leavened."

- What is the kingdom of God like? Jesus' description here doesn't sound like a place, nor an afterlife, but something that spreads and grows from humble beginnings into something big.
- Do I have a dream or a vision of what the kingdom of God is like?
- What traces do I see around me of the humble beginnings of the kingdom of God?

Wednesday 26th October   Luke 13:22-24, 30

Jesus went through one town and village after another, teaching as he made his way to Jerusalem. Someone asked him, "Lord, will only a few be saved?" He said to them, "Strive to enter through the narrow door; for many, I tell you, will try to enter and will not be able … Indeed, some are last who will be first, and some are first who will be last."

- Spend some time imagining the scene, with yourself as the one who asks the question of Jesus.
- What is Jesus like as he speaks the reply to you?
- How do his words sound to you? Surprising? Threatening? Liberating?

Thursday 27th October   Luke 13:31-35

At that very hour some Pharisees came and said to him, "Get away from here, for Herod wants to kill you." He said to them, "Go and tell that fox for me, 'Listen, I am casting out demons and performing cures today and tomorrow, and on the third day I finish my work. Yet today, tomorrow, and the next day I must be on my way, because it is impossible for a prophet to be killed outside of Jerusalem.' Jerusalem, Jerusalem, the city that kills the prophets and stones those who are sent to it! How often have I desired to gather your children together as a hen gathers her brood under her wings, and you were not willing! See, your house is left to you. And I tell you, you will not see me until the time comes when you say, 'Blessed is the one who comes in the name of the Lord.'"

- Jesus is under awful pressure. Herod, who was previously curious about him, now wants to kill him.
- Why does Jesus' fidelity to his divine mission stir up such hatred?
- How does Jesus' courage under pressure impress me?

Friday 28th October, Sts Simon and Jude
Ephesians 2:19-22

So then you are no longer strangers and aliens, but you are citizens with the saints and also members of the household of God, built upon the foundation of the apostles and prophets, with Christ Jesus himself as the cornerstone. In him the whole structure is joined together and grows into a holy temple in the Lord; in whom you also are built together spiritually into a dwelling place for God.

- These words directed to the Ephesians also have a meaning for us.
- We belong, we are part of God's household, and God dwells in us.
- Can I listen to this message, and take reassurance and strength from it?

Saturday 29th October   Luke 14:7-11

When Jesus noticed how the guests chose the places of honour, he told them a parable. "When you are invited by someone to a wedding banquet, do not sit down at the place of honour, in case someone more distinguished than you has been invited by your host; and the host who invited both of you may come and say to you, 'Give this person your place,' and then in disgrace you would start to take the lowest place. But when you are invited, go and sit down at the lowest place, so that when your host comes, he may say to you, 'Friend, move up higher'; then you will be honoured in the presence of all who sit at the table with you. For all who exalt themselves will be humbled, and those who humble themselves will be exalted."

- Has this ever happened to me? Where do I rank myself in relation to others?
- Do I always look for the place of honour, or on the other hand do I let people walk all over me?
- I imagine myself at the table with Jesus after everyone else has left, and talk to him about this.

october 30 – november 5

Something to think and pray about each day this week:

A question of attitude

Attitude seems to play a part in Chapter 14 of Luke's gospel. Jesus makes some stinging remarks about people who have the wrong attitude—guests invited to the king's banquet who make excuses or just don't bother to show up, and the people who are looking round for fireworks, for signs and wonders, when God's word is in front of their eyes. He has harsh words, too, for the Pharisees and their obsession with outward observance, and for the more "lukewarm" of his followers who are ashamed or embarrassed to talk of their allegiance to him.

If I just think back to a recent conversation I had with someone—one that went very well, or went very badly—and imagine how it would have been if my attitude at the start had been different (or perhaps if the other person's had), it is not too difficult to see the point: Attitude matters.

This is true of anything in life, and it is true of my relationship with God. If I go into prayer demanding that God comply with my wishes, expecting everything to be done on my terms, it is unlikely to be fruitful. It is not that God can't make allowances—God understands me, forgives my failings and loves me unconditionally—but prayer is about bending my will to God's, not the other way round.

The Presence of God
What is present to me is what has a hold on my becoming.
I reflect on the presence of God always there in love,
amidst the many things that have a hold on me.
I pause and pray that I may let God
affect my becoming in this precise moment.

Freedom
If God were trying to tell me something, would I know?
If God were reassuring me or challenging me, would I notice?
I ask for the grace to be free of my own preoccupations
and open to what God may be saying to me.

Consciousness
Knowing that God loves me unconditionally,
I look honestly over the last day, its events and my feelings.
Do I have something to be grateful for? Then I give thanks.
Is there something I am sorry for? Then I ask forgiveness.

The Word
God speaks to each one of us individually. I need to listen
to what he is saying to me. (Please turn to your scripture on
the following pages. Inspiration points are there should you
need them. When you are ready, return here to continue.)

Conversation
What is stirring in me as I pray?
Am I consoled, troubled, left cold?
I imagine Jesus himself standing or sitting at my side,
and share my feelings with him.

Conclusion
Glory be to the Father, and to the Son, and to the Holy Spirit,
As it was in the beginning, is now and ever shall be,
World without end. Amen

348

Sunday 30th October, 31th Sunday of the Year
Matthew 23:1-12

Then Jesus said to the crowds and to his disciples, "The scribes and the Pharisees sit on Moses' seat; therefore, do whatever they teach you and follow it; but do not do as they do, for they do not practice what they teach. They tie up heavy burdens, hard to bear, and lay them on the shoulders of others; but they themselves are unwilling to lift a finger to move them. They do all their deeds to be seen by others; for they make their phylacteries broad and their fringes long. They love to have the place of honor at banquets and the best seats in the synagogues, and to be greeted with respect in the marketplaces, and to have people call them rabbi. But you are not to be called rabbi, for you have one teacher, and you are all students. And call no one your father on earth, for you have one Father—the one in heaven. Nor are you to be called instructors, for you have one instructor, the Messiah. The greatest among you will be your servant. All who exalt themselves will be humbled, and all who humble themselves will be exalted."

- Can I take the time to imagine one of these Pharisees? What to they look like? Look at their clothes, their grooming, their bearing. How do they conduct themselves in relation to the people around them? In relation to them do I feel horrified, sympathetic, superior?
- I look into their eyes. Who do I see there? Can I recognize myself in the Pharisee—the Pharisee in me?
- What is Jesus saying to me?

Monday 31st October   Luke 14:12-14

Jesus said also to the one who had invited him, "When you give a luncheon or a dinner, do not invite your friends or your brothers or your relatives or rich neighbors, in case they may invite you in return, and you would be repaid. But when you give a banquet, invite the poor, the crippled, the lame, and the blind. And you will be blessed, because they cannot repay you, for you will be repaid at the resurrection of the righteous."

- Can I imagine my kitchen—or wherever I welcome my friends—with a group of "undesirables" instead of those friends?
- As I look around at my unattractive guests, how do I feel?
- What is Jesus talking about?

Tuesday 1st November, All Saints   Matthew 5:1-6

When Jesus saw the crowds, he went up the mountain; and after he sat down, his disciples came to him. Then he began to speak, and taught them, saying: "Blessed are the poor in spirit, for theirs is the kingdom of heaven. Blessed are those who mourn, for they will be comforted. Blessed are the meek, for they will inherit the earth. Blessed are those who hunger and thirst for righteousness, for they will be filled."

- Society's view of the poor and disadvantaged at this time was that they deserved their suffering and were far from holiness.
- Jesus turns all this upside-down. His vision of holiness is revolutionary.
- Whose side am I on?

Wednesday 2nd November, The Commemoration of All the Faithful Departed   Matthew 5:7-12

Jesus said to the crowds, "Blessed are the merciful, for they will receive mercy. Blessed are the pure in heart, for they will see God. Blessed are the peacemakers, for they will be called children of God. Blessed are those who are persecuted for righteousness' sake, for theirs is the kingdom of heaven. Blessed are you when people revile you and persecute you and utter all kinds of evil against you falsely on my account. Rejoice and be glad, for your reward is great in heaven, for in the same way they persecuted the prophets who were before you."

- If it were a criminal offence to be a Christian, would there be enough evidence to convict me?
- Do I do anything that would make people want to persecute me?
- Or is my priority to seek approval and respect?

Thursday 3rd November   Luke 15:1-7

Now all the tax collectors and sinners were coming near to listen to him. And the Pharisees and the scribes were grumbling and saying, "This fellow welcomes sinners and eats with them." So he told them this parable: "Which one of you, having a hundred sheep and losing one of them, does not leave the ninety-nine in the wilderness and go after the one that is lost until he finds it? When he has found it, he lays it on his shoulders and rejoices. And when he comes home, he calls together his friends and neighbors, saying to them, 'Rejoice with me, for I have found my sheep that was lost.' Just so, I tell you, there will be more joy in heaven over one sinner who repents than over ninety-nine righteous persons who need no repentance.

- Can I imagine the flock of ninety-nine in the wilderness and the shepherd heading off in search of the lost one? Then there's the image of him coming back with the stray across his shoulders.
- Jesus is putting these pictures before my mind in order to touch my heart.

- Can I let myself be moved by the compassion and mercy of God?

Friday 4th November, St Charles Borromeo
John 10:11-16

Jesus said to the Pharisees, "I am the good shepherd. The good shepherd lays down his life for the sheep. The hired hand, who is not the shepherd and does not own the sheep, sees the wolf coming and leaves the sheep and runs away—and the wolf snatches them and scatters them. The hired hand runs away because a hired hand does not care for the sheep. I am the good shepherd. I know my own and my own know me, just as the Father knows me and I know the Father. And I lay down my life for the sheep. I have other sheep that do not belong to this fold. I must bring them also, and they will listen to my voice. So there will be one flock, one shepherd."

- Not only does Jesus welcome everyone into his flock, but if I'm not there, he invites me in. Where am I?
- Jesus loves me and invites me to love him just like he knows and loves the Father. That is a serious depth of love.
- Do I hear Jesus' voice, or do I sometimes ignore it? If he comes searching, am I going to listen?

Saturday 5th November
Luke 16:9-15

Jesus said to his disciples, "And I tell you, make friends for yourselves by means of dishonest wealth so that when it is gone, they may welcome you into the eternal homes. "Whoever is faithful in a very little is faithful also in much; and whoever is dishonest in a very little is dishonest also in much. If then you have not been faithful with the dishonest wealth, who will entrust to you the true riches? And if you have not been faithful with what belongs to another, who will give you what is your own? No slave can serve two masters; for a slave will either hate the one and love the other, or be devoted to the one and despise the other. You cannot serve God and wealth." The Pharisees, who were lovers of money, heard all this, and they ridiculed him. So he said to them, "You are those who justify yourselves in the sight of others; but God knows your hearts; for what is prized by human beings is an abomination in the sight of God."

- The most telling word from Jesus to the Pharisees, here, is: "but God knows your hearts."
- When God looks at my heart from the point of view of honesty, fidelity or the love of "money" what does He see?
- Can I allow God to challenge me about these things—and still feel secure in His love? If I'm not sure about this—either the challenge or God's certain love—then I can talk to Jesus honestly about it.

Sacred Space

Something to think and pray about each day this week:

What if nothing happens?
There may be days when I spend my ten minutes or so in my sacred space and nothing happens. Nothing in the preparatory stages really touches me, nothing much has happened in the last day, the scripture doesn't move me, and I have nothing in particular to bring into conversation with the Lord.

This may even happen to me for days on end. It feels flat and empty, and I find myself reading through it a little bit faster every day, thinking it's a bit pointless.

But it isn't pointless. Everybody's prayer goes through stages like this, and it's important to remember then that spending time in God's presence has a value of its own, even if I don't see immediate results. Prayer is about my relationship with God, my close friendship with the Lord. Close friends spend time with each other, and persevere with each other through thick and thin. That's what any real, developing relationship is like.

The Presence of God
God is with me, but more, God is within me.
Let me dwell for a moment on God's life-giving presence
in my body, in my mind, in my heart,
as I sit here, right now.

Freedom
I need to close out the noise, to rise above the noise;
The noise that interrupts, that separates,
The noise that isolates.
I need to listen to God again.

Consciousness
How do I find myself today?
Where am I with God? With others?
Do I have something to be grateful for? Then I give thanks.
Is there something I am sorry for? Then I ask forgiveness.

The Word
I read the Word of God slowly, a few times over, and I listen
to what God is saying to me. (Please turn to your scripture on
the following pages. Inspiration points are there should you
need them. When you are ready, return here to continue.)

Conversation
Do I notice myself reacting as I pray with the Word of God?
Do I feel challenged, comforted, angry?
Imagining Jesus sitting or standing by me,
I speak out my feelings, as one trusted friend to another.

Conclusion
Glory be to the Father, and to the Son, and to the Holy Spirit,
As it was in the beginning, is now and ever shall be,
World without end. Amen

Sunday 6th November, 32nd Sunday of the Year
Matthew 25:1-13

"Then the kingdom of heaven will be like this. Ten bridesmaids took their lamps and went to meet the bridegroom. Five of them were foolish, and five were wise. When the foolish took their lamps, they took no oil with them; but the wise took flasks of oil with their lamps. As the bridegroom was delayed, all of them became drowsy and slept. But at midnight there was a shout, 'Look! Here is the bridegroom! Come out to meet him.' Then all those bridesmaids got up and trimmed their lamps. The foolish said to the wise, 'Give us some of your oil, for our lamps are going out.' But the wise replied, 'No! there will not be enough for you and for us; you had better go to the dealers and buy some for yourselves.' And while they went to buy it, the bridegroom came, and those who were ready went with him into the wedding banquet; and the door was shut. Later the other bridesmaids came also, saying, 'Lord, lord, open to us.' But he replied, 'Truly I tell you, I do not know you.' Keep awake therefore, for you know neither the day nor the hour."

- Do I have a sense of myself as waiting for something in life? What is it? Am I waiting for something to go wrong? somebody to offend me? somebody to be loving towards me? God to be gracious to me? What am I waiting for?
- Can I open up my heart and my deepest attitudes to the Lord? What do I need? Is it the gift of healing or encouragement? Do I need the grace of hope or perseverance? What do I want to ask the Lord for?

Monday 7th November
Luke 17:1-4

Jesus said to his disciples, "Occasions for stumbling are bound to come, but woe to anyone by whom they come!

It would be better for you if a millstone were hung around your neck and you were thrown into the sea than for you to cause one of these little ones to stumble. Be on your guard! If another disciple sins, you must rebuke the offender, and if there is repentance, you must forgive. And if the same person sins against you seven times a day, and turns back to you seven times and says, 'I repent,' you must forgive."

- There is a real awareness of community and people in what Jesus is saying here. His followers need to look out for one another.
- Love is the key to this concern for others, and regard for their wellbeing. Am I as tuned in to the needs of my fellow Christians as Jesus seems to be advising? Or do I like to do things independently?
- As for the call to forgiveness, is my heart open to this challenge? Can I respond positively?

Tuesday 8th November   **Wisdom 3:2-5a**

But the souls of the righteous are in the hand of God, and no torment will ever touch them. In the eyes of the foolish they seemed to have died, and their departure was thought to be a disaster, and their going from us to be their destruction; but they are at peace. For though in the sight of others they were punished, their hope is full of immortality. Having been disciplined a little, they will receive great good.

- Do I hear these words full of promise: "hope full of immortality"?
- Can I let the vision of hope speak to the parts of me that are limited and uncertain?
- Do I still find myself worried about my own picture and the picture of those I love?
- What do I think the Lord wants for me?

Wednesday 9th November, Dedication of the
Lateran Basilica   John 2:13-16

The Passover of the Jews was near, and Jesus went up to Jerusalem. In the temple he found people selling cattle, sheep, and doves, and the money changers seated at their tables. Making a whip of cords, he drove all of them out of the temple, both the sheep and the cattle. He also poured out the coins of the money changers and overturned their tables. He told those who were selling the doves, "Take these things out of here! Stop making my Father's house a marketplace!"

- Try to imagine the scene, the place, the sounds, the smells …
- Where and who are you? What does it look like, and feel like?
- How do you feel towards this angry Jesus? Can you talk to him about it?

Thursday 10th November   Luke 17:20-21

Once Jesus was asked by the Pharisees when the kingdom of God was coming, and he answered, "The kingdom of God is not coming with things that can be observed; nor will they say, 'Look, here it is!' or 'There it is!' For, in fact, the kingdom of God is among you."

- How do I imagine the Kingdom of God?
- Can I recognise it around me?
- What signs of the Kingdom have I noticed in the last few days?

Friday 11th November   Luke 17:26, 31-33

Jesus said to the disciples, "Just as it was in the days of Noah, so too it will be in the days of the Son of Man … On that day, anyone on the housetop who has belongings in the house must not come down to take them away; and likewise anyone in the field must not turn back. Remember

Lot's wife. Those who try to make their life secure will lose it, but those who lose their life will keep it."

- Lot's wife's only concern was for her home and security (see Genesis 19).
- What do I really put my faith in? My property? My position? My relationship with God?
- Do I let my responsibilities make me "unavailable" to respond to God's call?

Saturday 12th November   **Luke 18:2-7**

Jesus said to his disciples, "In a certain city there was a judge who neither feared God nor had respect for people. In that city there was a widow who kept coming to him and saying, 'Grant me justice against my opponent.' For a while he refused; but later he said to himself, 'Though I have no fear of God and no respect for anyone, yet because this widow keeps bothering me, I will grant her justice, so that she may not wear me out by continually coming.'" And the Lord said, "Listen to what the unjust judge says. And will not God grant justice to his chosen ones who cry to him day and night? Will he delay long in helping them?"

- Do I bother to ask God for the things that I need, or do I think it is a waste of time?
- The widow only wanted the judge to "grant her justice." Do I ask God for more than is just?
- What is the grace I most want to ask God for right now?

november 13–19

Something to think and pray about each day this week:

Jesus present now

The scriptures on some of these days give us the opportunity to contemplate a variety of scenes from the life of Jesus. That can be a very special opportunity to be present to the mystery of God.

The events of Jesus' life, his words and actions, are not dead and gone. Our revisiting them in our imagination is not a purely speculative thing. Since Jesus rose from the dead and returned to the Father, his whole life is present in the eternal Now of God. This means that I, in contemplation, can be present as he reaches out to cure the blind beggar at the gates of Jericho or when he calls Zacchaeus down from the sycamore tree. Through my praying, those words and actions of Jesus can be as real for me, now, as for them, then.

Can I let myself be open to see and hear and be challenged by the life of Jesus and, in that way, be open to the mystery of God?

The Presence of God

As I sit here, the beating of my heart,
the ebb and flow of my breathing, the movements of my mind
are all signs of God's ongoing creation of me.
I pause for a moment, and become aware
of this presence of God within me.

Freedom

I will ask God's help,
to be free from my own preoccupations,
to be open to God in this time of prayer,
to come to love and serve him more.

Consciousness

In God's loving presence I unwind the past day,
starting from now and looking back, moment by moment.
I gather in all the goodness and light, in gratitude.
I attend to the shadows and what they say to me,
seeking healing, courage, forgiveness.

The Word

I take my time to read the Word of God, slowly, a few times,
allowing myself to dwell on anything that strikes me. (Please
turn to your scripture on the following pages. Inspiration
points are there should you need them. When you are ready,
return here to continue.)

Conversation

Remembering that I am still in God's presence,
I imagine Jesus himself standing or sitting beside me,
and say whatever is on my mind, whatever is in my heart,
speaking as one friend to another.

Conclusion

Glory be to the Father, and to the Son, and to the Holy Spirit,
As it was in the beginning, is now and ever shall be,
World without end. Amen

Sunday 13th November, 33rd Sunday of the Year
Matthew 25:14-22

"For it is as if a man, going on a journey, summoned his slaves and entrusted his property to them; to one he gave five talents, to another two, to another one, to each according to his ability. Then he went away. The one who had received the five talents went off at once and traded with them, and made five more talents. In the same way, the one who had the two talents made two more talents. But the one who had received the one talent went off and dug a hole in the ground and hid his master's money. After a long time the master of those slaves came and settled accounts with them. Then the one who had received the five talents came forward, bringing five more talents, saying, 'Master, you handed over to me five talents; see, I have made five more talents.' His master said to him, 'Well done, good and trustworthy slave; you have been trustworthy in a few things, I will put you in charge of many things; enter into the joy of your master.' And the one with the two talents also came forward … "

- How do I react to this talk of different "talents"? Does it make me happy or, perhaps, uncomfortable? Am I encouraged or resentful when I think of my own talents or other people's?
- Understanding "talents" as widely as possible, what "talents" is the Lord giving me right now in my life? (People to love, things to be patient about, things I can do …)
- Do I need special help in order to "trade with" my talents? I can talk to the Lord about this.

Monday 14th November
Luke 18:35-43

As Jesus approached Jericho, a blind man was sitting by the roadside begging. When he heard a crowd going by, he asked what was happening. They told him, "Jesus of

Nazareth is passing by." Then he shouted, "Jesus, Son of David, have mercy on me!" Those who were in front sternly ordered him to be quiet; but he shouted even more loudly, "Son of David, have mercy on me!" Jesus stood still and ordered the man to be brought to him; and when he came near, he asked him, "What do you want me to do for you?" He said, "Lord, let me see again." Jesus said to him, "Receive your sight; your faith has saved you." Immediately he regained his sight and followed him, glorifying God; and all the people, when they saw it, praised God.

- Spend some time imagining this scene—the sights and sounds and smells—and replaying it in your mind.
- Put yourself in the scene, maybe as the blind man. What does it feel like?
- What do you really want to say when Jesus asks you: "What do you want me to do for you"?

Tuesday 15th November   Luke 19:1-6

Jesus was passing through Jericho, and a man was there named Zacchaeus; he was a chief tax collector and was rich. He was trying to see who Jesus was, but on account of the crowd he could not, because he was short in stature. So he ran ahead and climbed a sycamore tree to see him, because he was going to pass that way. When Jesus came to the place, he looked up and said to him, "Zacchaeus, hurry and come down; for I must stay at your house today." So he hurried down and was happy to welcome him.

- Zacchaeus, despite his limitations, was anxious to see who Jesus was.
- Jesus responds with enthusiasm to Zacchaeus' openness, even though tax collectors were shunned by Jewish society, and it wasn't "the done thing."

- Can I overcome blocks in approaching Jesus, knowing that, like Zacchaeus, Jesus will respond and my house will be visited?

Wednesday 16th November   Psalm 16:1, 5-6, 8, 15

Hear a just cause, O LORD; attend to my cry; give ear to my prayer from lips free of deceit. My steps have held fast to your paths; my feet have not slipped. I call upon you, for you will answer me, O God; incline your ear to me, hear my words. Guard me as the apple of your eye; hide me in the shadow of your wings, As for me, I shall behold your face in righteousness; when I awake I shall be satisfied, beholding your likeness.

- As I make these words my own, how do they sit with me?
- Am I confident in my own righteousness?
- Do I feel I am the apple of God's eye? Do I feel safe in the shadow of his wings?

Thursday 17th November, St Elizabeth of Hungary
Luke 6:31-35

Jesus said to the disciples, "Do to others as you would have them do to you. If you love those who love you, what credit is that to you? For even sinners love those who love them. If you do good to those who do good to you, what credit is that to you? For even sinners do the same. If you lend to those from whom you hope to receive, what credit is that to you? Even sinners lend to sinners, to receive as much again. But love your enemies, do good, and lend, expecting nothing in return. Your reward will be great, and you will be children of the Most High; for he is kind to the ungrateful and the wicked."

- How generously have I responded in the last few days to things that were asked of me?

- Are there people in my life that I find difficult to love? Can I ask God for the grace to love them?
- One way to ask for this grace is the following prayer, which you might already know: "Dearest Jesus, teach me to be generous. Teach me to love as you deserve: to give and not to count the cost, to fight and not to heed the wounds, to toil and not to seek for rest, to labour and to look for no reward, save that of knowing that I do your holy will. Amen."

Friday 18th November   Luke 19:45-48

Then Jesus entered the temple and began to drive out those who were selling things there; and he said, "It is written, 'My house shall be a house of prayer'; but you have made it a den of robbers." Every day he was teaching in the temple. The chief priests, the scribes, and the leaders of the people kept looking for a way to kill him; but they did not find anything they could do, for all the people were spellbound by what they heard.

- Something about Jesus made some people spellbound and others want to kill him.
- Try to imagine the scene: what is it about Jesus that gives rise to these reactions?
- We will encounter those same reactions, if Jesus is real in our lives. He isn't just an historical figure.

Saturday 19th November   Luke 20:37-38

Jesus said to the Sadducees, "The fact that the dead are raised Moses himself showed, in the story about the bush, where he speaks of the Lord as the God of Abraham, the God of Isaac, and the God of Jacob. Now he is God not of the dead, but of the living; for to him all of them are alive."

366

- The Sadducees didn't believe in the resurrection of the dead. Jesus comes back at them with a counter argument: Abraham, Isaac and Jacob must be living because God is their God and is the God of the living.
- The story of Moses and the burning bush is in chapter 3 of Exodus. God tells Moses he has observed the sufferings of his people and heard their cry.
- God is passionately concerned for every one of us, and wants each one of us to live life to the full. St Irenaeus tells us "the glory of God is a person fully alive." Do I want to be fully alive?

Sacred Space

Something to think and pray about each day this week:

What about the others?

At the end of each day's prayer, we can remind ourselves that we are not alone when we are praying in our sacred space.

Responses on the feedback page of the *Sacred Space* website give us a feel for the kind of people who are praying with us, where they are in the world, and how much it means to them to join the rest of us in prayer. It is no different when we use this book to lead us in prayer.

Without getting carried away about being a "virtual Christian community" or a "Cyber Church," perhaps we can reflect on the simple fact that we—thousands of us—really are united in prayer across national, continental and denominational boundaries. It's not an insignificant thing.

Everyone needs support in prayer, and it will be a great support to the others to know that we are thinking about them and praying for them.

The Presence of God
I pause for a moment
and reflect on God's life-giving presence
in every part of my body, in everything around me,
in the whole of my life.

Freedom
God is not foreign to my freedom.
Instead the Spirit breathes life into my most intimate desires,
gently nudging me towards all that is good.
I ask for the grace to let myself be enfolded by the Spirit.

Consciousness
I exist in a web of relationships—links to nature, people, God.
I trace out these links, giving thanks for the life that flows
through them.
Some links are twisted or broken: I may feel regret, anger,
disappointment.
I pray for the gift of acceptance and forgiveness.

The Word
God speaks to each one of us individually. I need to listen
to what he is saying to me. (Please turn to your scripture on
the following pages. Inspiration points are there should you
need them. When you are ready, return here to continue.)

Conversation
How has God's Word moved me? Has it left me cold?
Has it consoled me or moved me to act in a new way?
I imagine Jesus standing or sitting beside me,
I turn and share my feelings with him.

Conclusion
Glory be to the Father, and to the Son, and to the Holy Spirit,
As it was in the beginning, is now and ever shall be,
World without end. Amen

Sunday 20th November, Christ the King
Matthew 25:31-46

"When the Son of Man comes in his glory, and all the angels with him, then he will sit on the throne of his glory. All the nations will be gathered before him, and he will separate people one from another as a shepherd separates the sheep from the goats, and he will put the sheep at his right hand and the goats at the left. Then the king will say to those at his right hand, 'Come, you that are blessed by my Father, inherit the kingdom prepared for you from the foundation of the world; for I was hungry and you gave me food, I was thirsty and you gave me something to drink, I was a stranger and you welcomed me, I was naked and you gave me clothing, I was sick and you took care of me, I was in prison and you visited me.' Then the righteous will answer him, 'Lord, when was it that we saw you hungry and gave you food, or thirsty and gave you something to drink? And when was it that we saw you a stranger and welcomed you, or naked and gave you clothing? And when was it that we saw you sick or in prison and visited you?' And the king will answer them, 'Truly I tell you, just as you did it to one of the least of these who are members of my family, you did it to me.' Then he will say to those at his left hand, 'You that are accursed, depart from me into the eternal fire prepared for the devil and his angels; for I was hungry and you gave me no food, I was thirsty and you gave me nothing to drink, I was a stranger and you did not welcome me, naked and you did not give me clothing, sick and in prison and you did not visit me.' Then they also will answer, 'Lord, when was it that we saw you hungry or thirsty or a stranger or naked or sick or in prison, and did not take care of you?' Then he will answer them, 'Truly I tell you, just as you did not do it to one of the least of these, you did not do it to me.' And these will go away into eternal punishment, but the righteous into eternal life."

- Am I prepared to be shocked again? Why is Jesus talking about people who are sick and hungry, naked and in prison?
- Can I make a mental picture of someone that I know—even a little bit—who is in prison or sick or hungry? When I picture them can I see Jesus in them?
- Being honest, is it easy for me to see Jesus in poor people? When I am confronted with real poverty am I threatened, moved to compassion, disgusted … ?
- What is Jesus calling me to here?

Monday 21st November   Luke 21:1-4

Jesus looked up and saw rich people putting their gifts into the treasury; he also saw a poor widow put in two small copper coins. He said, "Truly I tell you, this poor widow has put in more than all of them; for all of them have contributed out of their abundance, but she out of her poverty has put in all she had to live on."

- Some people become enslaved to their wealth and possessions, and the richer they get, the more their lives are darkened by fear of losing it.
- Others, whether rich or poor, are free, and give like the widow. Freedom—not abject poverty—is what Jesus is advocating.
- True generosity is giving what you can't easily do without, not giving what is spare. In my relationship with God and with others, do I give like the widow, or like the rich who ostentatiously offload what they don't need?

Tuesday 22nd November   Luke 21:5-11

When some were speaking about the temple, how it was adorned with beautiful stones and gifts dedicated to God, Jesus said, "As for these things that you see, the days will come when not one stone will be left upon another; all will be thrown down." They asked him, "Teacher, when will this be, and what will be the sign that this is about to take place?" And he said, "Beware that you are not led astray; for many will come in my name and say, 'I am he!' and, 'The time is near!' Do not go after them. "When you hear of wars and insurrections, do not be terrified; for these things must take place first, but the end will not follow immediately." Then he said to them, "Nation will rise against nation, and kingdom against kingdom; there will be great earthquakes, and in various places famines and plagues; and there will be dreadful portents and great signs from heaven."

- The temple was not just the centre of their civilisation: it was the place where God lived among them. Jesus told them that it was all going to fall apart!
- Is there any way in which my "secure centre"—either personal or national—threatens to collapse? (The fall of the Twin Towers is a powerful symbol for many of us.)
- The key words from Jesus in all of this are, "Do not be terrified." Can I allow Jesus, the Consoler, to speak to me, wherever I am?

Wednesday 23rd November, St Columban   Luke 9:57-62
As they were going along the road, someone said to him, "I will follow you wherever you go." And Jesus said to him, "Foxes have holes, and birds of the air have nests; but the Son of Man has nowhere to lay his head." To another he said, "Follow me." But he said, "Lord, first let me go and bury my father." But Jesus said to him, "Let the dead bury their own dead; but as for you, go and proclaim the kingdom of God." Another said, "I will follow you, Lord; but let me first say farewell to those at my home." Jesus said to him, "No one who puts a hand to the plough and looks back is fit for the kingdom of God."

- Tough words here from Jesus. Following him is no world cruise.
- It is easy to settle down into the comfort of my life and forget the cost of discipleship. The decision to follow Jesus has to be made and re-made.
- Sacrifice is not a fashionable word today, but Jesus doesn't apologise for the fact that it is an essential part of the life of a disciple.

Thursday 24th November   Luke 21:25-28

Jesus said to the disciples, "There will be signs in the sun, the moon, and the stars, and on the earth distress among nations confused by the roaring of the sea and the waves. People will faint from fear and foreboding of what is coming upon the world, for the powers of the heavens will be shaken. Then they will see 'the Son of Man coming in a cloud' with power and great glory. Now when these things begin to take place, stand up and raise your heads, because your redemption is drawing near."

- The foreboding and panic that Jesus talks about was around then, and again today.
- Can I stand with my head held high, or am I weighed down by worry, or cowed by fear?

Friday 25th November   Luke 21:29-31

Then Jesus told them a parable: "Look at the fig tree and all the trees; as soon as they sprout leaves you can see for yourselves and know that summer is already near. So also, when you see these things taking place, you know that the kingdom of God is near."

- What, for me, would be "signs of the kingdom"?
- Do I see any of these around me?

- What am I doing to advance the kingdom of God?

Saturday 26th November   Luke 21:34-36

Jesus said to the disciples, "Be on guard so that your hearts are not weighed down with dissipation and drunkenness and the worries of this life, and that day catch you unexpectedly, like a trap. For it will come upon all who live on the face of the whole earth. Be alert at all times, praying that you may have the strength to escape all these things that will take place, and to stand before the Son of Man."

- Amid the worries of my daily life, "eternal truths" can seem irrelevant or unreal.
- But Jesus reminds me here not to be weighed down and completely preoccupied by the immediate, concrete, here-and-now part of reality.
- A good question to focus my mind on this is: "What do I want to be remembered for when I die?"